# CONSCIENTIOUS OBJECTORS

# CONSCIENTIOUS OBJECTORS IN THE CIVIL WAR

*By*

Edward Needles Wright

A Perpetua Book ∞

A. S. Barnes & Company, Inc.

New York

*"It should be the aim of a wise man neither to mock, nor to bewail, nor to denounce men's actions but to understand them."*—SPINOZA

# Contents

# Introduction

ANY study which attempts to understand and to interpret the operation of the human conscience cannot be undertaken lightly. In war time the individual conscience may be largely influenced by the social conscience, but at all times conscientious scruples or convictions are governed by spiritual rather than by temporal forces. An individual, who objects to war on grounds of conscience, may do so because of obedience to a Divine law rather than to a human law. "To him, . . . no man overcomes his enemy until he has made him his friend, and as that will never happen by killing that enemy, therefore he prefers, but without retaliation, to return good for evil, although 'the despised and rejected of men'."[1]

The person who first made use of the term *conscientious objector* is unknown, although General Jan Smuts is credited by at least one author with being its originator.[2] There is no indication that the expression was used during the Civil War in America even though *conscientious objection* appears frequently in the records of the period.[3] Objectors to military service on conscientious or religious grounds were merely referred to as *non-resistants, non-combatants, those scrupulous against bearing arms,* and by similar titles. In the chapters which follow, the term *conscientious objector* is limited to persons of certain religious sects whose tenets or articles of faith opposed participation in all wars or warlike measures and to persons who, although unaffiliated with any religious denomina-

---

[1] Parry, C. Egerton. *The Psychology of Conscientious Objection,* p. 54.

[2] Case, Clarence Marsh. *Non-Violent Coercion,* pp. 3–4.

[3] *Official Records of the Union and Confederate Armies* (referred to hereinafter as *Official Records*), series 3, III, p. 64; *Congressional Globe,* XLIV, pt. 1, p. 206; and *Harper's Weekly,* VI, p. 579.

tion, were opposed to all wars on moral or other intellectual grounds. The term does not include those persons who opposed the military measures of the North and of the South for political, or other reasons. Religious objectors are to be distinguished particularly from *Copperheads*, with whom they are sometimes confused. According to one Quaker author, "A Copperhead was the name applied to the numerous persons who were more pleased at hearing of Confederate than of Union victories."[4] Conscientious objectors likewise differed from the *Peace Democrats* of the North and the general class of *slackers* of both the North and the South. The confusion in the minds of some people of these various groups at one time called forth the following statement by a meeting of the Society of Friends:

> Although our religious Society is known as the unfeigned advocate of peace, it is cause of embarrassment to us at this time, that unscrupulous men, assuming the name of peace makers, are doing all they can to further the objects of those who seek to destroy our general Government, and to rivet the chains of slavery in this land. And while we find it our duty to refrain from all connection with war, both in spirit and in practice, we cannot do or say anything calculated, even remotely, to identify our members with these men.[5]

This investigation of conscientious objectors in the Civil War has been undertaken with a five-fold purpose in mind; first, to discover what types of individuals and which religious denominations were actually opposed to the war on conscientious grounds; second, to find out what efforts were made on behalf of objectors and what changes took

---

[4] Atkinson, Wilmer. *An Autobiography*, p. 93.
[5] Extract from an essay addressed "To the Meeting for Sufferings of London Yearly Meeting" in the minutes of the Meeting for Sufferings of New York (Orthodox) Yearly Meeting, 9 mo. 2, 1863, p. 186.

place in their political status; third, to learn the attitude of the civil and military authorities towards them; fourth, to ascertain their numbers; and, finally, to compare the problem of conscientious objection in the Civil War with the same problem as it existed for the United States in the World War. It is only indirectly a story of the sufferings of objectors. In the chapters which deal with the attitude of the civil and military authorities some individual experiences of conscientious objectors are related, but chiefly for illustrative purposes. The suffering of individuals for conscience' sake during the Civil War has already been related in considerable detail by other authors.[6] Many of the cases cited in this book, however, appear for the first time in printed form.

The study is limited to the North and the South during the actual war period, 1861 to 1865 inclusive, although it has been necessary to trace back the growth of non-resistant sentiment in various Christian sects prior to the outbreak of hostilities. Furthermore, only such denominations or persons who are opposed on principle to *all* wars are included. In the Civil War the scruples of conscience of these people led them to oppose various forms of military service, and, in some cases, the payment of military taxes, requisitions, commutation charges, and bounty fees. Sometimes their objection to military service also involved such civil matters as oath-taking and voting. However, as these latter forms of opposition seem less important than the opposition to the bearing of arms less attention has been paid to them in making this study.

---

[6] Pringle, Cyrus G. *The Record of a Quaker Conscience;* Foster, Ethan. *The Conscript Quakers; An Account of the Sufferings of Friends of North Carolina Yearly Meeting;* Cartland, Fernando G. *Southern Heroes;* Jones, Rufus M. *The Later Periods of Quakerism;* Hirst, Margaret E. *The Quakers in Peace and War;* Smith, C. Henry. *The Mennonites of America;* Sanger, Samuel F. and Hays, Daniel. *The Olive Branch of Peace and Good Will to Men;* and Zigler, David H. *A History of the Brethren in Virginia.*

Objectors in the North are treated separately from those in the South, chiefly because their backgrounds, and later, their experiences in the war, were dissimilar. In most instances conscientious objectors in the Confederacy were strongly opposed both to slavery and to secession. All of the members of the Society of Friends, for example, who lived in the South had freed their slaves prior to the outbreak of the war, whereas many others had migrated to the West, largely because of their opposition to the institution of slavery.[7] Furthermore many Friends voted for Lincoln for President and against secession in the years 1860 and 1861. It was stated by John Jolliffe to the author that his father, Joseph N. Jolliffe, was the only person in Frederick County, Virginia, who voted for Abraham Lincoln in 1860. Joseph Jolliffe was afterward a conscientious objector.[8] During the war Southern objectors were generally subjected to greater trials than were those in the North partly because of the shortage of fighting men in the Confederacy. On the other hand, their numbers were smaller and more concentrated and their actions were more united.

Finally, this study deals chiefly with the Society of Friends in the North and the South for the following reasons: first, because the Society was the largest of the so-called noncombatant religious denominations and contained the greatest number of persons opposed to the war on conscientious grounds; second, because Friends were more active in supporting their testimony against war, and were therefore best known to the authorities; third, because they kept more systematic records of the war period than did the other denominations; and, finally,

---

[7] *A Brief Statement of the Rise and Progress of the Testimony of the Religious Society of Friends against Slavery, and the Slave Trade* (1843); Weeks, Stephen B. *Southern Quakers and Slavery;* and Jones, Rufus M. *The Later Periods of Quakerism,* II, chap. 15.

[8] See also Cartland, Fernando G. *Southern Heroes,* pp. 340–341.

because they were the only organized body of objectors who claimed unconditional exemption from military service on grounds of conscience.[9] Extensive use has been made of Friends' manuscript material, and, in many instances, the reports of committees and the minutes of Friends' meetings have been quoted in full, not only because of their authenticity but also because of their unique wording.

A study of this nature can be made only with the encouragement, coöperation, and assistance of other persons. The author feels that he was peculiarly fortunate in receiving aid wherever he called for it, whether it was from a living conscientious objector, a church authority, a librarian, or an interested friend. Without such assistance the study would have been impossible; with such assistance the study became both a stimulating and interesting one. To those who made this book possible, therefore, the author feels deeply grateful.

[9] See the chapters which follow for evidence. See also Shannon, Fred Albert. *The Organization and Administration of the Union Army*, II, pp. 248–249; Smith, C. Henry. *The Mennonites of America*, Introduction; Krehbiel, H. P. *The History of the General Conference of the Mennonites of North America*, p. 364; and letters to the author from L. J. Heatwole, Dale Enterprise, Va., Nov. 5, 1928 and John Horsch, Scottdale, Pa., Aug. 6, 1928.

# Chapter I

# The Noncombatant Religious Sects of the Civil War

AT THE outbreak of hostilities between the North and the South in 1861 there were certain religious sect in the United States whose doctrines and practice were opposed to war and whose members were restrained by conscience from taking any part in military service. Most of these bodies were relatively small in numbers but their opposition to military demands of all sorts was so persistent that the authorities were forced to listen to them, and, in some cases, to accede to their requests. These sects were the Society of Friends (Quakers), the Mennonite Church, the Church of the German Baptist Brethren (Dunkers), the United Society of Believers in Christ's Second Appearing (Shakers), the Community of True Inspiration (Amana Society), the Schwenkfelder Church, Christ's Brethren (Christadelphians), and the Rogerines. In addition to these mention might be made of certain Catholic orders, such as the Benedictines and Order of the Holy Cross, and of certain communal groups, such as the Hopedale Community in Massachusetts. Likewise, in a law relating to noncombatants, passed by the Confederate Congress in 1862, reference is made to Nazarenes.[1] No other mention is made of them, however, in any of the records of the period. It is known that Josef Bela, who was acquainted with the founders of the Nazarene Communities of Hungary, came to America in 1850, "where he was very active and had great success,"[2] but as the Church of

[1] *Official Records*, series 4, II, p. 161.
[2] *Nazarenes in Jugoslavia* (pamphlet), p. 5.

the Nazarene did not come into existence in this country until the twentieth century[3] the term Nazarene may have referred to the *Mystics* of Ephrata, Pennsylvania, and Moravian missionaries, "who for many years travelled through the South where they were known as 'recluses' and occasionally were located in solitary places separate from the society of the world, and of course were averse to the turmoils of strife and war."[4] It is at least certain that there was no denomination with the name of Nazarene at the time of this study.

First in importance, both in point of size and influence, was the Religious Society of Friends, frequently called Quakers. This Society was founded by George Fox, an English Dissenter of the seventeenth century. It was never Fox's intention to found a distinct religious sect, but the organization and beliefs peculiar to the Society of Friends were natural outgrowths of his inspiration and teachings.[5] Quakerism became deeply rooted in Great Britain and on the continent of Europe and was given some organization during Fox's lifetime (1624–1690),[6] but, as in the case of many other Protestant denominations, it found a more congenial atmosphere in the free soil of America.

The first Quakers to reach America were two women, named Mary Fisher and Ann Austin, who landed at Boston in July, 1656.[7] They were soon followed by others, men and women alike, who settled in the various colonies

[3] Fleming, E. J., General Secretary, Church of the Nazarene, in a letter to the author from Kansas City, Mo., Nov. 8, 1928.

[4] Heatwole, Rev. L. J., in a letter to the author from Dale Enterprise, Va., Nov. 16, 1928.

[5] Harvey, T. Edmund. *The Rise of the Quakers*, p. 143.

[6] Sewel, William. *The History of the Rise, Increase, and Progress of the Christian People called Quakers*; Braithwaite, William C. *The Beginnings of Quakerism*; and Barclay, Robert. *The Inner Life of the Religious Societies of the Commonwealth*, p. 251.

[7] Jones, Rufus M. *The Quakers in the American Colonies*, pp. 3–4.

from Massachusetts in the north to the Carolinas in the south.[8]   However, Pennsylvania, and, to a less extent, Delaware and the Jerseys, became the principal seat of Quaker influence in America, due chiefly to the fact that the founder of the former colony, William Penn, was himself a member of the Society of Friends. Friends emigrated to the province rapidly, not only because of persecutions in England, but also because of Penn's encouragement.[9] The Quakers maintained their control of the goverment of Pennsylvania for about seventy-four years[10] during which period their peace testimonies were often severely tried because of conflict with the neighboring French and Indians. The number of Friends in the various colonies continued to increase during the eighteenth century until by the year 1760 it is estimated that there were 50,000 or more.[11]

During the early part of the nineteenth century Friends in America were divided into various *branches*, largely because of theological differences.   The Orthodox and Hicksite division occured in 1827–28, caused chiefly by the teachings and influence of Elias Hicks.   The Wilburite separation began in 1845 when a distinct group of about five hundred Friends was formed in New England.   This second schism arose because of theological differences between Joseph John Gurney, a well-known English Friend of the day, and John Wilbur, a minister from New England, and their respective followers.   It continued to disrupt the Society until the present century.   Other minor divisions took place within the Hicksite and Orthodox

---

[8] A good account of the development of Quakerism in the North is to be found in Jones, Rufus M. *The Quakers in the American Colonies* and *The Later Periods of Quakerism*, and in the South, in Weeks, Stephen B. *Southern Quakers and Slavery*.

[9] Jones, Rufus M. *The Quakers in the American Colonies*, p. 420.

[10] Sharpless, Isaac. *Two Centuries of Pennsylvania History*, p. 145.

[11] Thomas, Allen C. *A History of the Friends in America*, p. 103.

branches which led to the establishment of several groups of Congregational Friends, an anti-slavery group in Indiana, a group known as Primitive Friends, and a special meeting in Philadelphia.[12] Throughout these various divisions, however, the pyramidal organization of the Society into local or preparative, monthly, quarterly, and yearly meetings was maintained.

At the time of the Civil War Friends were scattered widely throughout the North and South with yearly meetings of the Orthodox branch in New England, New York, Philadelphia, Baltimore, Ohio, Indiana, Western (Indiana), Iowa (organized in 1863), and North Carolina; of the Hicksite branch in New York City, Genessee (New York), Philadelphia, Baltimore, Ohio, and Indiana; and of the Wilburite branch in New England, Ohio, Western (Indiana), and Iowa.[13] There is no certainty, however, as to the number of Friends in America before the first comprehensive religious census in 1890.[14] In that year there were a total of 107,208, of whom 80,655 were claimed by the Orthodox branch, 21,992 by the Hicksite branch, 4,329 by the Wilburite branch, and 232 by the Primitive branch.[15]

Friends, as a religious Society, have always borne a testimony against war.[16] "It is no accident that this now historically famous peace testimony came to be an inherent and indissoluble part of the Quaker way of life. It

[12] *Ibid.*, chap. 5; Grubb, Edward. *Separations, their Causes and Effects;* and Jones, Rufus M. *The Later Periods of Quakerism*, I and II.

[13] Thomas, Allen C. *op. cit.*, pp. 166, 194, and 255. Also Friends' Central Bureau, Philadelphia.

[14] In 1860 religious statistics were gathered by United States marshals and their agents. Three items only were given in the census of 1860; namely, churches, church accommodations, and the value of church property. See *Statistics of the United States in 1860* (U. S. Census, 1860), p. xiv.

[15] U. S. Census, 1890.

[16] See *The Position of the Society of Friends in Regard to War*, Bulletin 77 of the American Friends' Service Committee, Philadelphia.

never was 'adopted.' It was hardly discussed or reasoned about. Like everything else that was fundamental in primitive Quakerism, this testimony seemed to the first Friends to be a 'revelation' to them."[17]  The famous speech of George Fox, " . . . that I lived in the virtue of that life and power that took away the occasion of all wars"[18] has proved an inspiration for many of his followers.[19] Fox many times repeated his disbelief in war as a means of accomplishing any good result.[20]  In writing to Oliver Cromwell at one time, he said:

'I denied the wearing or drawing of a carnal sword, or any other outward weapon, against him or any man: and that I was sent of God to stand a witness against all violence, and against the works of darkness; and to turn people from darkness to light; and to bring them from the causes of war and fighting, to the peaceable gospel, and from being evil-doers, which the magistrates' swords should be a terror to.'[21]

Not only have Friends been opposed to war and military measures, but also to the swearing of oaths. Again George Fox led the way. He said that in 1661, when the oaths of allegiance and supremacy were tendered Friends, many of them were imprisoned and præmuniried, because of their refusal to swear. They published, therefore, a statement of *The grounds and reasons why they refused to swear* and Fox himself issued the following lines, to be given to the magistrates: " 'The world saith, "Kiss the book"; but the book saith, "Kiss the Son, lest he be angry." And the Son saith, "Swear not at all," but keep to Yea and Nay in all

[17] *Report of Commission I* of *Report of American Commissions of the Conference of All Friends*, pp. 2-3.

[18] *Journal of George Fox*, I, pp. 68-69.

[19] For a description of the attitude of early Friends on the subjects of war and of military service, see Braithwaite, William C. *The Beginnings of Quakerism.*

[20] *Journal of George Fox*, I, pp. 72, 448, 450, 494; II, p. 298.

[21] *Ibid.*, I, p. 209.

your communications; for whatsoever is more than this cometh of evil . . .' "[22]

When the English Quakers emigrated in large numbers to the Colonies in the seventeenth and eighteenth centuries they carried with them their scruples against fighting and military requirements. It was partly because of these scruples that William Penn found it so difficult to govern his colony: Friends would not perform duties which involved military declarations and offices,[23] nor would they coöperate with other colonies in military measures against the French and the Indians.

During the American Revolution individual Friends were not united in their peace testimony, although the Society as a body, in its meetings and its writings, steadfastly opposed the war. Many who tried to hold aloof from the struggle suffered severely, especially a group of Philadelphia Quakers who were exiled temporarily to Virginia.[24] Also in a single Quarterly Meeting in Pennsylvania it is estimated that over $68,000 was levied in military fines between the years 1778 and 1786.[25] On the other hand, those who participated in some form of military service were expelled from their meetings.[26] Some of the younger Friends even left the main body of the Society voluntar-

---

[22] *Ibid.*, I, p. 521.

[23] Jones, Rufus M. *The Quakers in the American Colonies*, p. 424.

[24] *Exiles in Virginia;* Sharpless, Isaac. *Two Centuries of Pennsylvania History*, p. 216; Weeks, Stephen B. *Southern Quakers and Slavery*, pp. 189–194; and Thomas, Allen C. *A History of the Friends in America*, p. 117.

[25] Sharpless, Isaac. *A History of Quaker Government in Pennsylvania*, II, p. 177.

[26] *Report of Commission I*, p. 13, and Jones, Rufus M. *The Later Periods of Quakerism*, II, p. 715. Jones makes the statement, on the authority of Isaac Sharpless, that by actual count of cases in the minutes of Monthly Meetings it appears that there were at least four hundred members of the Philadelphia (Orthodox) Yearly Meeting who were *disowned* for taking some part in the Revolution (1776–1783). See also Bulletin of the Chester County, (Pa.) Historical Society, 1902–03, pp. 15–26 for numbers disowned.

ily, and in Philadelphia organized an independent Society, called the Free Quakers.[27]

In the early days of the nineteenth century there were, on the one hand, many cases of disownment for military practices and, on the other hand, of suffering for refusal to coöperate with the military authorities. The following instances are typical.

Isaac Lamborn was disowned for 'attending a mustary [mustering] parade' and several other offenses.[28]

John Peck Dukehart, having violated our testimony against war, by joining a Military Company, and having been dealt with, in order to convince him of his error, without the desired effect, we hereby disown him, from membership with us.[29]

It is comforting to observe that our testimony against war appears to have been better observed beside the loss of property taken from our members by distraint, three of our young men have suffered imprisonment for different periods rather than submit to military requisitions and we advise Friends to continue care in maintaining our testimony against war.[30]

The Committee for Suffering report one Friend has had property taken from him to the value of $30.25 in a military demand amounting to $8.00: that four others had property taken from them to the amount of $40.50, for a later demand of $16.00, and one Friend was imprisoned part of a day on similar account.[31]

---

[27] Wetherill, Charles. *History of the Religious Society of Friends called by some The Free Quakers, in the City of Philadelphia,* and Jones, Rufus M. *The Later Periods of Quakerism,* II, p. 715.

[28] Min. of Center Monthly Meeting (Center County, Pa.), 3 mo. 4, 1807.

[29] Min. of Baltimore Monthly Meeting for Western District, 3 mo. 4, 1847.

[30] Min. of New York (Hicksite) Yearly Meeting, 1845.

[31] Min. of New York (Hicksite) Monthly Meeting, 4 mo. 1, 1846. See also archives of the Society of Friends at 3rd and Arch Streets, Philadelphia, under *Sufferings.*

In the records of another Quaker meeting opposition to the payment of military requisitions is mentioned in each of the following years—1780, 1788, 1789, 1790, 1792, 1793, 1805, 1807, 1808, 1847, 1848, and 1861—showing that the problem was a fairly constant one.[32]

Throughout the nineteenth century Friends were subjected to the various militia laws of the states and territories in which they resided.[33] As they were known to the national government and to the authorities in most of the states to be strictly opposed to wars on religious grounds provision was frequently made for them, exempting them by name. Too often, however, the exempting provisions were drawn up by persons who did not understand the ground on which Friends objected to military service, and consequently the provisions were frequently unsatisfactory or inadequate.[34]

In 1810 a typical memorial was sent by the Friends of Indiana to William Henry Harrison, Governor of Indian Territory, and to the Legislative Council and House of Representatives. The memorial began with the words:

Few if any of the present members of Government, we presume, are altogether unacquainted with the conscientious scruples of Friends against bearing arms, or acting in any manner as military men, ever since they became a Religious Society.

The memorial went on to state that heavy fines had frequently been imposed on Friends for non-attendance at musters or that seizures had been made in lieu of fines. A change in the military laws was therefore requested to

---

[32] *General and Important Extracts from the Minutes of the Baltimore* (Hicksite) *Yearly Meeting*, pp. 616–620.
[33] *Report of Commission I*, p. 31.
[34] Jones, Rufus M. *The Later Periods of Quakerism*, II, pp. 718–719.

correct these grievances. Such a change was actually made.[35]

Friends did not suffer greatly because of their religious scruples during the War of 1812.[36] It was at this time, however, that the Clerk of the Virginia Yearly Meeting[37] prepared a memorial for the Legislature of Virginia concerning the militia law then in existence. He said:

> In this enlightened age and country, and before this Legislature, your Memorialists conceive it unnecessary to urge the unalienable rights of conscience, or to adduce any arguments to shew that the relations between man and his Creator, neither can, nor ought to be prescribed or controuled by any human authority. It is unnecessary, because the proposition is self evident, and especially because it is one of the fundamental principles, upon which the civil and political institutions of this country are established ... the *state itself*, by its convention which ratified the federal constitution, expressly declared, that 'the liberty of conscience cannot be cancelled, abridged, restrained, or modified by any authority of the United States.' ... They therefore respectfully petition, that the laws imposing military requisitions and penalties for non-compliance, may be considered as they respect your petitioners, and such relief afforded as to the wisdom of the legislature shall seem just and necessary.[38]

In a letter accompanying this memorial, the Clerk, Benjamin Bates, further explains the position of the Society

---

[35] Min. of Whitewater Monthly Meeting, 8 mo., 1810 and 1811. See also *Report of Commission I*, p. 32.

[36] Weeks, Stephen B. *op. cit.*, pp. 195–197; Jones, Rufus M. *The Later Periods of Quakerism*, II, p. 721; and *Report of Commission I*, p. 33.

[37] The Virginia Yearly Meeting was discontinued prior to the time of the Civil War, most of its members being transferred to the Baltimore Yearly Meeting.

[38] *Memorial of the Religious Society of Friends to the Legislature of Virginia on the Militia Laws*. (Reprint from *Georgetown Federal Republican*, May 31, 1813.) See also *Niles' Weekly Register*, XI, no. 14, pp. 211–212.

of Friends in regard to conscientious scruples against war.
He says:

> This society *maintain*, with the *framers* of our constitu-
> tion, and in conformity *with the repeatedly declared sense* of
> the American people, that government has no right to
> bring the *laws of God* and man into *competition*, . . . .

At the close of the War of 1812 the executive committee
(known among Friends as the *Meeting for Sufferings* or
*Representative Committee*) of the Baltimore Yearly Meeting
adopted a message to its members, worded as follows:

> 'Friends are united in a renewed sense of the preciousness
> of our religious Testimony against War . . . whatever may
> be our share of sufferings, our sincerity cannot be better
> manifested than by a conduct upon our part correspondent
> with the meekness and gentleness of Christ.  We feel an
> earnest desire that Friends, when called upon for military
> requisitions, may carefully guard against any conduct
> either at variance with our peaceful profession, or tending
> to lessen their sufferings by any indirect payment of fines or
> other military demands.'[39]

Friends in America also opposed vigorously the Mexican
War,[40] took part in the founding of the American Peace
Society (1828), and in the inauguration of international
peace congresses.[41]  From all of these facts it would seem
as though Friends were particularly well fitted to meet the
stress of the Civil War, and to act unitedly in behalf of
peace.  However, Friends had long borne a testimony, not
only against war, but also against slavery. The Civil War
found many Quakers in the North, therefore, faced with
a serious dilemma—a desire to aid in the abolition of the

---

[39] Quoted in *Report of Commission I*, p. 34, and Jones, Rufus M. *The Later
Periods of Quakerism*, II, p. 722.  See also Weeks, Stephen B. *Southern Quakers
and Slavery*, pp. 194–197.

[40] *Friends' Review*, I, pp. 281 and 343.

[41] *Report of Commission I*, pp. 34–36.

institution of slavery, but a conscientious conviction that war was the wrong way to do it.

Next to the Quakers in numbers and influence at the time of this study were the Mennonites and Dunkers of America. The communicants of the Mennonite Church trace their origin directly to Menno Simons, a learned man who became a Protestant during the first part of the sixteenth century, and indirectly to the Anabaptists or to the Waldenses of an even earlier period.[42] Simons was born in the town of Witmarsum in West Friesland either in the year 1492 or 1496 (authorities are not agreed on the date) and before his death, which occurred in 1559, his influence had spread throughout the Anabaptist communites of the Netherlands and Germany.[43] The followers of Simons on the continent of Europe underwent severe religious hardships before they emigrated to America. They were persecuted for their beliefs by both Catholic and Reformed Churches, chiefly in the Netherlands, Switzerland, the Palatinate, and northern Germany.[44] It is not surprising, therefore, that William Penn was able to interest a great many of them in his new colony in America when he preached among them in the lower Rhine country.[45]

It is claimed that as early as 1640 families of Mennonites came to America and settled in New Jersey and New York.[46] Also about twenty-five Dutch Mennonites, led by Cornelisz Plockhoy, settled on Delaware Bay about the year 1662.[47] The first large body of Mennonites, however, came to America in 1683 and settled in and around Germantown, Pennsylvania. Their early history in the

---

[42] Smith, C. Henry. *The Mennonites of America*, p. 17; Cassel, Daniel K. *History of the Mennonites*, p. 9.

[43] Smith, C. Henry, *op. cit.*, p. 64.

[44] *Ibid.* pp. 65–80.

[45] Hartzler, J. S. and Kauffman, Daniel. *Mennonite Church History*, p. 96.

[46] Lyon, William H. *A Study of the Christian Sects*, p. 85.

[47] Hartzler and Kauffman, *op. cit.*, p. 125.

Colony is closely connected with that of the Quakers, with whom they held so many religious views in common. At the beginning of the eighteenth century the immigration of Mennonites began on a larger scale and new settlements were formed at Skippack in Montgomery County (1702) and at Pequea in what is now Lancaster County, Pennsylvania (1710). More than a century passed before any more permanent settlers arrived from Europe,[48] but in the meantime the first Pennsylvania settlers had spread into the neighboring counties of Berks, Lehigh, Union, Mifflin, Somerset, and Lawrence. Later the Amish branch of the Mennonite Church sent settlers to portions of Pennsylvania, Ohio, New York, Illinois, Indiana, and Iowa. Many of those who originally settled in Pennsylvania followed the Cumberland and Shenandoah Valleys into Maryland and Virginia. In fact land was purchased in these regions as early as 1729.[49] By the middle of the nineteenth century churches had been established in Pennsylvania, Virginia, New York, Ohio, Indiana, Illinois, Michigan, Iowa, and Canada although the majority of Mennonites were still located in the southern counties of Pennsylvania.[50] It is estimated that there were some 128,000 Mennonites in the United States and Canada by 1860.[51]

Although the Mennonites are divided into many branches, known by the titles of Mennonite, Bruederhoef, Amish, Old Amish, Apostolic, Reformed, General Conference, Church of God in Christ, Old (Wisler), Brueder-Gemeinde,

[48] *Ibid.*, pp. 129–130.

[49] Smith, C. Henry, *op. cit.*, p. 199, and Hartzler and Kauffman, *op. cit.*, pp. 139–145.

[50] Carroll, H. K. in *The Religious Forces of the United States*, p. 220, states that out of a total of 41,541 communicants in 1890, 15,330, or about 37% were located in Pennsylvania. See also Krehbiel, H. P. *The History of the General Conference of the Mennonites of North America*, pp. 12–13.

[51] Krehbiel, H. P. *op. cit.*, p. 55.

Defenseless, and Brethren in Christ,[52] they all support the same faith and hold approximately the same views in regard to war and non-resistance.[53]   Beginning with Menno Simons himself there are numerous evidences of the pacific nature of the Mennonite faith.[54]   In one of his written treatises entitled, *A Fundamental Doctrine, From the Word of the Lord, Concerning the New Birth*, he says of truly Christian people:

> They are the children of peace, who have beaten their swords into ploughshares, and their spears into pruning hooks, and know of no war; . . .[55]

The Mennonite Articles of Faith, known as the Dort Confession of 1632, are specific on the question of defense. Article XIV says:

> 'As regards revenge or defense, in whom men resist their enemies with the sword, we believe and confess that the Lord Jesus Christ forbade His disciples, His followers, all revenge and defense, and commanded them, besides, not to render evil for evil, nor railing for railing, but to sheath their swords, or in the words of the prophet, "to beat them into ploughshares" . . .'[56]

During the American Revolution the Mennonites in general took no part in the contest, not because of their lack of interest, but because military opposition to government was opposed to their religious principles.[57]   In general

---

[52] Carroll, H. K., *op. cit.*, p. 212, and Smith, C. Henry, *op. cit.*, pp. 291–314.

[53] Wick, Barthinius L. *The Amish Mennonites*, p. 13; Cassell, Daniel K. *op. cit.*, p. 42; and Smith, C. Henry, *op. cit.*, p. 314.

[54] Horsch, John. *The Principle of Nonresistance as held by the Mennonite Church.* This is an historical survey based on primary sources.

[55] Simons, Menno. *A Foundation and Plain Instruction of the Saving Doctrine of Our Lord Jesus Christ* (Translation), p. 261.

[56] Horsch, John. *op. cit.*, pp. 31–32; Cassel, Daniel K. *op. cit.*, p. 36; and Wick, Barthinius L. *op. cit.*, p. 58.

[57] Smith, C. Henry. *op. cit.*, p. 253.

their scruples were recognized by the authorities although services of a non-military nature were required of them and some were imprisoned temporarily for refusing to serve in the army.    In Pennsylvania the Assembly on June 30, 1775, remembering that " 'many of the good People of this Province are conscientiously scrupulous of bearing arms . . . recommended to the associators for the defence of their country and others, that they bear a tenderly and brotherly Regard toward this class of their Fellow subjects and Countrymen.' "[58]   However, to such conscientious objectors the Assembly suggested, that " 'they cheerfully assist in proportion to their abilities such associators as cannot spend their time and substance in the Public Service without great injury to themselves.' "[59]   In Maryland, both the Constitutional Convention of 1776 and the local Committee of Observation exempted Mennonites from military service, "but required them to furnish transportation for the county troops and contribute to the support of the families of the men in the army."[60]   At this same period some of the Mennonite faith were opposed not only to military service, but to the payment of military fines and war taxes and to the taking of oaths.   That such military fines were imposed and collected can be seen in the records of the time.[61]   It is difficult to judge how prevalent was this opposition to the payment of military exactions, but a well-known Mennonite, Christian Funk, writing of the conditions at this time said, " 'The majority of the ministers in the western part of Montgomery county [Pennsylvania] were opposed to the

---

[58] *Votes of Assembly*. I, p. 594, quoted in *Ibid*, p. 368.

[59] For a good account of the attitude of the Mennonites during the American Revolution, see Martin, E. K. *The Mennonites*, pp. 14–15.

[60] Smith, C. Henry. *op. cit.*, pp. 198–199.

[61] *Pa. Archives*, Sec. Ser., VI, p. 433, quoted in Smith, C. Henry, *op. cit.*, p. 254.

payment of a new war tax of three pounds, and ten shillings which had been levied in 1777.' "[62]

There is no evidence of change in the general attitude of Mennonites in America during the first half of the nineteenth century. The War of 1812 and the Mexican War were not of sufficient duration to test the non-resistant principles of the' Mennonites; but it is clear that their peace principles were not allowed to slumber.[63]

The Church of the German Baptist Brethren was one of the many sects of German dissenters which was established in Pennsylvania during the colonial era and in other parts of America at a later period. The members of this denomination refer to themselves merely as *Brethren*, but to others they are known as *Dunkers, Dunkards, or Tunkers*.[64] The name Dunker is derived from the old German verb, *tunken*, which means *to dip*.[65] These people are to be distinguished from other German dissenters, such as the Mennonites, the Labadists, Rosicrucians, Neugeborenen or Stillen im Lande, Schwenkfelders, and the Unitas Fratrum, all of whom arrived in Pennsylvania at various times between the years 1683 and 1734, and who are classified under the general heading of German Seventh Day Baptists.[66]

As is the case with the other sectarians, the Dunkers were the descendents of the early Pietists of the Continent of Europe. The Dunker Church was organized in 1708

[62] Funk, Christian. *Mirror for all Mankind*, quoted in Smith, C. Henry. *op. cit.*, p. 255.

[63] For an account of Mennonites in Europe and elsewhere, especially a discussion of their peace principles, see Hartzler and Kauffman, *op. cit.*, pp. 105–112.

[64] Sachse, Julius Friedrich. *The German Sectarians of Pennsylvania*, I, p. 86, and Brumbaugh, Martin G. *A History of the German Baptist Brethren in Europe and America*, pp. xiv and 335.

[65] Gillin, John Lewis. *The Dunkers; a Sociological Interpretation*, Preface.

[66] Sachse, Julius Friedrich. *The German Pietists of Provincial Pennsylvania*, pp. 1–10, or *Seventh Day Baptists in Europe and America*, II, pp. 938–945.

at a place called Schwartzenau in the Grand Duchy of Hesse-Darmstadt[67] to give expression to the ideals which had been forming in the mind of a man named Alexander Mack. "While the Dunker church has always refused to acknowledge any man as its founder, yet it looks back to Alexander Mack as the one who had the most to do with its formation. He was the natural leader of the original band, and during his life-time [1679-1735] was the most influential person among them both in Europe and, later, in America."[68] One of Mack's ideals, or doctrines, was that of non-resistance, or more particularly refusal to bear arms in defense of one's country. Later this doctrine was extended to include refusal to protect one's self against violence. Another of the doctrines was the refusal to take a civil oath. These and other principles to which the early Dunkers clung led to their emigration from their settlements at Schwartzenau and Crefeld (or Creyfelt) in Germany, especially after the friendly protection of the Counts of Wittgenstein had been withdrawn.[69]

Their first settlement in America was at Germantown, Pennsylvania, in 1719. This was composed of about twenty persons belonging to the Crefeld congregation. The first settlers soon divided into two factions, one group remaining in the vicinity of Germantown under the leadership of Peter Becker and Alexander Mack, and the other settling at Conestoga (or Cocalico) and later at Ephrata, in Lancaster County, under the leadership of Conrad Beissel. Some of the Dunkers, in common with others of the German sects, early migrated from Pennsylvania to Maryland and Virginia by way of the Cumberland and Shenandoah Valleys. In the early forties of the eighteenth

---

[67] *Seventh Day Baptists in Europe and America,* II, p. 976, and Brumbaugh, Martin G. *op. cit.,* p. 29.

[68] Gillin, John Lewis, *op. cit.,* pp. 55–56, and Brumbaugh, Martin G. *op. cit.,* p. 71.

[69] Gillin, John Lewis, *op. cit.,* p. 80.

century Johannes Funk, a Dunker from Pennsylvania, purchased 320 acres of land on the Shenandoah River near the present town of Strasburg.[70] In 1745 Alexander Mack, the Younger, and several others left Pennsylvania and settled in what are now the counties of Montgomery and Pulaski, Virginia. Here they were joined by other Brethren, although "many, attracted by the fertile bottoms of the Shenandoah and its tributaries, remained or eventually settled in the upper valley, where their descendents still live in the Dunker faith."[71] Prior to the time of the American Revolution many Dunkers had also established themselves west of the Susquehanna River, in the present county of Franklin, Pennsylvania, and in what was then commonly called the Conecocheague Valley.[72] By 1770 there were approximately fifteen congregations of Dunkers in Pennsylvania with a total membership of 623 and one church in New Jersey with 46 members. Beissel's congregation at Ephrata had, at the same time, 135 members. By 1790 there were also seven churches in Maryland and ten in the more southern states. By the time of the Civil War the Brethren had settled in the northern states of Pennsylvania, New Jersey, Maryland, Ohio, Indiana, Illinois, Iowa, Missouri, and California, and in the southern states of Virginia, the Carolinas, Tennessee, and Kentucky. They were also divided into four distinct branches, known as the Conservatives, Progressives, Old Order, and Seventh Day. Their exact numbers at the time of the Civil War are unknown.[73]

---

[70] Sachse, Julius Friedrich. *The German Sectarians of Pennsylvania*, II, p. 334, and Sanger, Samuel F. and Hays, Daniel. *The Olive Branch of Peace and Good Will to Men*, p. 33.

[71] Sachse, Julius Friedrich. *The German Sectarians of Pennsylvania*, II, p. 337.

[72] *Ibid.*, p. 457.

[73] Gillin, John Lewis, *op. cit.*, pp. 144–148 and 200.

At various times the Dunkers have expressed in words and maintained in deeds their abhorrence of war and their liberty of conscience. For example, the Confession of Faith, which was the accepted fundamental doctrine of both the Germantown and Ephrata branches, and which was originally published in Germany in 1702, contained the following statement:

> 'As to the Government,—I believe it to be the order of God in the kingdom of nature, to which I must in all civil things submit . . . , but I do not permit the exercise of power in the things claimed under this power, which are against God's word and my conscience: or the liberty of Christ. For it is said "we ought to obey God rather than man." '[74]

The Christopher Sowers,[75] father and son, who were prominent in the Church of the Brethren in America during the eighteenth century both voiced their objection to war on many occasions.[76] Among the writings of the first Christopher Sower were articles on such topics as *War and Peace*, *On War*, *A Protest against War*, and *The Use of Fire Arms*, and in his *Almanac* for 1778 he wrote:

> Earth's pregnant fields lie waste, untouched by
> Who erst, full-peaceful turned the soil;
> The unwilling sword he grasps and dashes in the fight;
> What tears will flow from this turmoil![77]

In 1777 the requirement of the Legislature of Pennsylvania that every citizen should take the oath of allegiance to the State of Pennsylvania worked considerable hardship on the Dunkers, as they were opposed not only to

---

[74] Sachse, Julius Friedrich. *The German Sectarians of Pennsylvania*, II, p. 82 (English translation).

[75] Spelled sometimes *Sauer* or *Saur*. See Brumbaugh, Martin G., *op. cit.*, p. 341.

[76] *Ibid.*, pp. 376, 413–419, and 433.

[77] *Ibid.*, pp. 413–414.

all war, but also to oaths. It was during the excitement caused by the invasion of Maryland by the British in 1814 that the annual conference of the Brethren of 1815 met and passed the following resolution:

> 2nd, It has been discussed by us concerning the war matter, and it is agreed by all the brethren that if a brother or brother's sons who consider themselves according to the teaching of the brethren 'defenseless' and prove themselves to be such and wish to obey the teachings of the Brethren— when these shall be hard oppressed with the payment of fines they shall be assisted by the brethren according to the teaching of the apostle—let one bear the burden of another, thus you will fulfill the law of Jesus Christ.[78]

No further reference to war is made in the minutes of the annual meetings until the year 1845 and again in 1864, when the non-resistant principles of the Brethren were reaffirmed.[79]

It seems evident, therefore, that the Dunkers conscientiously opposed war throughout their history. As one writer expresses it:

> The Church of the Brethren never sanctioned, never encouraged, never participated in war. Peace as a fundamental principle was and always has been honored by the members. Every war that has swept the country was steadfastly opposed by the church. The Revolutionary War was a severe test. Many of the members were anxious to see the new government prosper and succeed. But they could not, they did not fight. We have seen how Elder Sower was persecuted and robbed for conscience' sake.[80]

And again:

> *Peace*, as a doctrine of the church, is fundamental. The Brethren do not go to war, and have steadfastly, and amid

---

[78] *Ibid.*, p. 492.

[79] *Ibid.*, p. 492, and Sanger and Hays, *op. cit.*, p. 29.

[80] Brumbaugh, Martin G., *op. cit.*, pp. 537–538.

great persecution, refused to take up arms. There is no peace society in America that more steadfastly and consistently honors the teachings of Jesus on this point than the Brethren.[81]

The religious sect, known variously as the United Society of Believers in Christ's Second Appearing, the Millennial Church, or the Shaker Church, was likewise opposed to military service or exactions when the Civil War broke out. This sect, which is communistic in its organization, originated in England during the middle of the eighteenth century. When first organized it practiced no forms and adopted no creeds, but was "led and guided entirely by the operations of the Spirit of God."[82] The Society was guided primarily by the life and inspirations of Ann Lee, who was born in Manchester, England, in 1736.

In 1774 she and others of her followers emigrated to America where they settled in the vicinity of New York City.[83] From this point the Shakers spread to Watervliet and New Lebanon in the same state. By 1793 other communities had been organized at Hancock, Harvard, Shirley, and Tyringham in Massachusetts; at Canterbury and Enfield in New Hampshire; at Enfield, Connecticut; at Alfred and New Gloucester, Maine; and at Groveland, New York.[84] In the years following 1793 Shakerism made progress less rapidly. However, settlements were made at South Union and Pleasant Hill, Kentucky, and at Busro, Union Village, White Water, and Watervliet, Ohio. From a sect of nine persons in 1780

---

[81] *Ibid.*, p. 558.

[82] Evans, F. W. *Compendium of the Origin, History, Principles, Rules and Regulations, Government and Doctrines of the United Society of Believers in Christ's Second Appearing*, pp. 20–21.

[83] Robinson, Charles Edson. *A Concise History of the United Society of Believers called Shakers*, pp. 13–19.

[84] *Ibid.*, pp. 42–57.

the Millennial Church grew until it contained a membership of approximately five thousand in 1839. There is no definite record of the number of Shakers at the time of the Civil War, but when the first comprehensive census of religious bodies was taken in 1890, their numbers had decreased to seventeen hundred and twenty-eight.[85]

Under one of their early leaders, Father Joseph Meacham, the doctrines of the Society in 1808 were collected and published for the first time in a work entitled *Christ's Second Appearing*. In explaining Shaker faith and practices it is difficult to separate the civil and religious features, so closely are they related. It is doubtful if the communistic basis of their communities would be possible without their religious beliefs. The foundation of their non-resistant principles is found in the third of their so-called cardinal virtues, which is "Humanity and kindness to both friend and foe."[86]

Their aversion to the participation in military affairs was recognized long before the time of the Civil War. In fact, when General William Henry Harrison was Governor of the Indian Territory in 1811 the Shakers disregarded his summons to join the militia. During the War of 1812, when they appealed to General Harrison for exemption from military service, their request was granted and they were assigned to duty in various hospitals. Later, in 1821, when Harrison became a member of the Ohio Legislature he presented a petition for the relief of Shakers in that State from military duty, suggesting that three day's work on the highways be required instead. This exemption was allowed in the bill which the Legislature adopted.[87]

The Community of True Inspiration, known more com-

---

[85] Carroll, H. K. *The Religious Forces of the United States*, p. 113.
[86] Robinson, Charles Edson. *op. cit.*, p. 32.
[87] *Ibid.*, pp. 74–76.

monly as the Amana Society, was another one of the peace sects in America at the time of the Civil War. "As a religious movement the Community of True Inspiration traces its origin to the German Mystics and Pietists of the sixteenth and seventeenth centuries. Its rise was one of the many protests against the dogmatism and formality that had grown up in the Lutheran Church. As a distinct religious sect the Community dates from the year 1714 with the writings and teachings of Eberhard Ludwig Gruber and Johann Friedrich Rock, who are regarded as its real founders."[88]

Although the Community does not have a creed, in the orthodox use of the word, there are three documents which form the basis of Community faith. These documents, which underlie the Society's opposition to war, are known as *Der Glauben*, the Twenty-four Rules of True Godliness, and the Twenty-one Rules for the Examination of our Daily Lives.[89]

In 1842 the first settlement of these Inspirationists in America was begun by the purchase of the Seneca Indian Reservation, a tract of five thousand acres, in Erie County, New York. The settlement, composed of several villages, was called Ebenezer and the Community itself was formally organized under the name of the Ebenezer Society in 1843. The Society was organized from its inception along communistic lines.[90]

By 1854 the Community had decided to emigrate to the west, partly because of the encroachments of the growing city of Buffalo and partly because such a movement was believed to be the will of God. A committee of four chose

---

[88] Shambaugh, Bertha M. H. *Amana, The Community of True Inspiration*, p. 21. See also Perkins, William R. and Wick, Barthinius L. *History of the Amana Society, or Community of True Inspiration*, and Noe, Charles F. *A Brief History of the Amana Society (1714-1900)*.

[89] Shambaugh, Bertha M. H. *op. cit.*, p. 265.

[90] *Ibid.*, pp. 59-61.

the present site of Amana, in Iowa County, Iowa, as best suited to their needs. The foundation and organization of the Amana Society in its new site is best described in the following Preamble to the Constitution and By-laws of the Community, which were adopted in December, 1859.[91]

> Whereas the Community of True Inspiration hath in the year 1843, and the following years emigrated from Germany into the United States of America, for the sake of enjoying the noble civil and religious liberty of this country, and hath settled at Eben-Ezer, in the County of Erie and State of New York, on the Buffalo Creek Indian Reservation, where they have since existed, under the protection of God, in peace and prosperity; and whereas the said Community in the year 1854, according to the known will of God, resolved unanimously to sell the Eben-Ezer lands, and to undertake a new settlement in the western country, and hath consequently in the year 1855 and the years following, purchased a tract of land in the State of Iowa, and paid for the same out of the funds of the Community; and whereas since a beginning hath been made of this new settlement, with the purpose to continue and accomplish such resettlement by degrees, as the times and circumstances will permit.
>
> Now therefore, we the undersigned members of the Community of True Inspiration, feeling thankful for the grace and beneficence of God, to be privileged under the liberal laws of this state to an incorporation as a religious Society, do hereby associate ourselves anew under the corporate name of
>
> 'The Amana Society,'
>
> in the Town of Amana, and have adopted and do hereby adopt the following Constitution and By-Laws.

The new lands in Iowa were occupied rapidly. The villages of West Amana and South Amana were settled

---

[91] Perkins and Wick. *op. cit.*, pp. 82–83, Appendix A (Authorized translation from the German text).

in 1856; High Amana in 1857; East Amana in 1860; Homestead in 1861; and Middle Amana in 1862. By that time "the sale of the Ebenezer land was . . . almost completed, and the last of the remaining members came to Iowa on December 13th, 1864."[92]

The Schwenkfelders were followers of Casper Schwenkfeld, a religious reformer of the sixteenth century. In 1734 they migrated in a body from Saxony to Pennsylvania, where they hoped to avoid the persecutions to which they had been subject in Germany. The Schwenkfelders in America early showed their opposition to the bearing of arms. One of their leaders, Christopher Schultz, wrote that:

'In the year 1755, many war rumors arose in this and other provinces, and towards the end of the year unfriendly Indians made frequent attacks, people were killed and houses were laid desolate. It became necessary to place a heavy guard along the exposed frontier, and residents were at times called upon to come to the rescue in resisting the enemy. Our people willingly helped to bear their respective shares of the burdens that fell to the various townships without personally taking up arms against the enemy, a substitute being placed by them as their term of service came.'[93]

During the American Revolution the Society issued the following declaration, to emphasize their attitude towards military service and to strengthen their members in refusing such service:[94]

'A Candid Declaration of Some So-called Schwenkfelders Concerning Present Militia Affairs, May 1, 1777. We who are known by the name Schwenkfelders hereby

---

[92] Noe, Charles F. *op. cit.*, pp. 20–21.
[93] Kriebel, Howard Wiegner. *The Schwenkfelders in Pennsylvania, A Historical Sketch*, p. 141.
[94] *Ibid.*, pp. 152–153.

confess and declare that for conscience' sake it is impossible for us to take up arms and kill our fellowmen; we also believe that so far as knowledge of us goes this fact is well known concerning us.

We have hitherto been allowed by our lawmakers to enjoy this liberty of conscience.

We have felt assured of the same freedom of conscience for the future by virtue of the public resolution of Congress and our Assembly.

We will with our fellow citizens gladly and willingly bear our due share of the common civil taxes and burdens excepting the bearing of arms and weapons.

We can not in consequence of this take part in the existing militia arrangements, though we would not withdraw ourselves from any other demands of the government.

———

Whereas, at present through contempt of the manifested divine goodness and through other sins, heavy burdens, extensive disturbances by war and divers military regulations are brought forth and continued.

Whereas, we on the first of this month made a candid declaration concerning present military arrangements to the effect that we can not on account of conscience take part in said military affairs and

Whereas, it seems indeed probable that military service will be exacted from many of our people and that on refusal to render such service heavy fines will be imposed.

*Therefore*, the undersigned who adhere to the apostolic doctrines of the sainted Casper Schwenkfeld and who seek to maintain the same by public services and by instruction of the young have mutually agreed, and herewith united themselves to this end that they will mutually with each other bear such fines as may be imposed on account of refusal for conscience' sake to render military service in case deadly weapons are carried and used. Those on whom such burdens may fall will render a strict account to the mana-

gers of the Charity Fund in order that steps may be taken
to a proper adjustment.

                              Coschehoppe, May 2, 1777.'

During the ninteenth century the Schwenkfelders maintained their opposition to military services. At a Church
conference in 1828 the members took into consideration
the attendance of their young people at military parades.
It was decided to expel them from the Church if they
persisted in this practice.[95]

At no time were the Schwenkfelders a numerous sect.
In 1875 their numbers were placed at 800 and the number
of families at 300.[96]

The Christadelphians, or Christ's Brethren, were the
followers of John Thomas, an English Protestant of the
last century. Thomas was born in London in 1805 but
came to the United States in 1844 where he began his
religious writings and teachings. He organized a number of
societies in the United States, Canada, and Great Britain,
but "no name was adopted for the societies until the break-
ing out of the Civil War, when the members applied to
the Government to be relieved from military duty in
consequence of religious and conscientious scruples."[97]

Even though the Christadelphians were a comparatively
new religious group, their ideas regarding war were well
established by the middle of the century. Their leader,
John Thomas, sought to strengthen their religous faith
along peaceful lines and to secure their exemption from
military service.[98] Members of this sect were to be found

---

[95] *Ibid.*, p. 160.

[96] Barclay, Robert. *The Inner Life of the Religious Societies of the Commonwealth*, p. 243. See also Beard, Charles. *The Reformation of the Sixteenth Century
in its Relation to Modern Thought and Knowledge*, p. 212.

[97] *Christadelphians. Census of Religious Bodies, 1926* (Department of
Commerce; Bureau of the Census), p. 8. See also Carroll, H. K. *op. cit.*, p. 89.

[98] Aue, Gustav F., in a letter to the author from Rutherford, N.J., Nov. 7,
1928, says that Thomas sent a certificate to certain of his followers in Illinois

in both the North and South, in such widely scattered states as Virginia, Mississippi, Massachusetts, and Illinois.[99]

The Rogerenes were a very small group of people who settled mostly in the Connecticut towns of New London, Groton, and Ledyard. They were the followers of John Rogers (1648–1721), a prominent non-conformist of Colonial Connecticut. By the middle of the nineteenth century they had begun to scatter or to be merged with other religious groups around them.[100]

It is not strange that Rogerenes have frequently been confused with Quakers because many of their religious beliefs and practices are the same and two of their settlements in Connecticut are still referred to as Quaker Hill and Quakertown. On such questions as baptism, the celebration of the Lord's Supper, and the observance of the Sabbath they differ considerably in their opinions but in their early opposition to slavery and war they were in accord with Friends.

It is possible that the Rogerenes refused on grounds of conscience from the very first to pay military fines, but no record of such refusal has come to light.[101] However, an interesting petition to his "Fellow Countrymen," prepared by Alexander Rogers in 1810, leaves no doubt as to his conscientious scruples in regard to paying military fines, and there is considerable evidence that other Rogerenes were willing to suffer during and after the Civil War rather than violate their conscientious convictions regarding the

"wherein he set forth their faith and conscientious objections to participation in warfare under the present order of things in the world, the Christadelphians being related to Christ and His Kingdom and not to the nations or the governments in the world today."

[99] Walker, C. C. *Christ and War, a Lecture by the Editor of the Christadelphian,* p. 28, and Carroll, H. K. *op. cit.,* p. 90. In 1890 their total membership was 1277.

[100] Bolles, John Rogers and Williams, Anna B. *The Rogerenes,* p. 301.

[101] *Ibid.,* p. 304, footnote.

sinfulness of bearing arms.[102] Rogers' petition began with the following quaint introduction:

Whereas I am once more called to suffer for conscience's sake, in defense of the gospel of Christ; on account of my son, who is under age, in that it is against my conscience to send him into the train-band. For which cause, I have sustained the loss of my only cow that gave milk for my family; through the hands of William Stewart, who came and took her from me and the same day sold her at the post. Which circumstance, together with the infirmity of old age, has prevented my making my usual defence at such occasion. I have therefore thought proper and now do (for myself and in behalf of all my brethren that shall stand manfully with me in defense of the gospel of Christ) publish the following as a petition to my countrymen for my rights and privileges; and especially to those that have or shall have any hand in causing me to suffer.

and the petition itself continued:

Fellow Countrymen, this case between you and me I shall now lay open before your eyes, seeing it is pending before the judgment seat of the same Lord. Our Lord and Master hath commanded us not to hate our enemies, like them of old time under the law of Moses. But hath, under the clear gospel dispensation, commanded us, saying: 'I say unto you love your enemies, do good to them that hate you and pray for them that despitefully use you and persecute you, and if any man shall sue you at the law and take away your coat, forbid him not to take your cloak also.' 'If thine enemy hunger, feed him, if he thirst, give him drink.' And again: 'I say unto you that ye resist not evil.'

For these, and many other like commands of our Saviour, Christ, I have refused to bear arms against any man in defense of my rights and privileges of this world. For which cause, you have now taken me by the throat, saying: 'Go

---

[102] *Ibid.*, p. 315.

break the laws of your Lord and Master.' And because I have refused to obey man rather than God, you have taken away the principal part of the support of my family and commanded it to be sold at the post.[103]

The Unitas Fratrum, or Moravian Church, had been in former times a peace sect, but by 1861 its opposition to war had largely disappeared. As late as 1792 the United States Congress granted Moravians the rights to abstain from taking oaths and from bearing arms, but with the passage of years both of these rights were voluntarily renounced.· In the South their opposition to bearing arms had so far declined that a military company was organized in Salem, N. C., on July 4, 1831, the officers of which were Moravians.[104]

In the Civil War members of the Church fought in the armies of both the North and South.[105] In the South especially the younger generation of Moravians apparently had no conscientious scruples against fighting, for in June, 1861, three companies left Forsyth County, N. C. for the front, "the first two containing a number of Salem Moravians, the third composed of men from the neighborhood, including some from Bethabara and Bethania."[106]

The militant attitude of the Moravian Church in the

---

[103] *Ibid.*, Appendix. An original printed copy of this petition is extant at Quakertown.

[104] Clewell, John Henry. *History of Wachovia in North Carolina*, p. 235.

[105] *Ibid.*, pp. 246–249 contain lists of Moravians who fought for the Confederacy during the Civil War. Bishop J. Taylor Hamilton, in a letter to the author, from Bethlehem, Pa., Sept. 3, 1928, states that, "During the Civil War the Moravian Church took no special position in contrast to that of the majority of citizens with regard to bearing arms—as its members had done in the middle of the eighteenth century. Both North and South its members were to be found in the ranks of the combatants. I believe that the change in sentiment began to make itself felt during the War of Independence, among the younger men of that day."

[106] Fries, Adelaide L. and Pfohl, J. Kenneth. *The Moravian Church, Yesterday and Today*, p. 76.

North is shown by the fact that its Synod, which met at Bethlehem, Pennsylvania, June 3, 1864, adopted as part of its resolutions on the state of the country, the following:

> That this Synod considers an earnest support of the Constitution and Laws, which, in God's providence, have come down to us from our forefathers, as well as an earnest support of the General and State Governments under them— a religious duty; and that we, of this Synod, hereby express our willingness to render the constituted authorities of our land all the aid in our power to subdue unrighteous rebellion, and to extend the righteous authority of the Government over every portion of our country.[107]

However, there is some evidence that individual Moravians in the North were opposed to the war on religious grounds because Representative Henry C. Deming, Chairman of the House Committee on Military Affairs, in explaining to Congress the difficulty experienced by his committee in providing for those conscientiously scrupulous against bearing arms, said, "The Committee found that in addition to those before them by petition there was a vast crowd ready to rush in for exemption if the door was once opened, and the principle once admitted that conscientious scruples is a ground of exemption. There are the Dunkers, the Shakers, *and the Moravians*,[108] all holding principles in common with the Quakers."[109]

A brief survey of other religious sects shows, for the most part, that they entered heartily into the spirit of the conflict, North and South.[110] For example, the Baptist Convention of New York in 1862 declared that " '. . . considering the interests to be preserved and transmitted to

---

[107] McPherson, Edward. *The Political History of the United States of America during the Great Rebellion*, p. 483, and Nicolay, John G. and Hay, John. *Abraham Lincoln—A History*, VI, p. 319.

[108] Italics mine.

[109] *Congressional Globe*, XLIV, Pt. 1, p. 575.

[110] Nicolay, John G. and Hay, John. *op. cit.*, VI, chap. 15.

future generations we cannot regard the sacrifice of treasure and of life too much for the object to be secured.' " The American Baptist Missionary Union, in the same year, adopted with unanimity resolutions characterizing " 'the war now waged by the National Government to put down the unprovoked and wicked rebellion that has risen against us, . . . as a most righteous and holy one, sanctioned alike by God and all right-thinking men.' "

In 1864 Albert Barnes, at a meeting of the American Board of Foreign Missions in Worcester, Massachusetts, introduced resolutions which were adopted unanimously with great enthusiasm, " 'the audience rising to their feet and singing the national anthem,' " expressing the hearty sympathy of the Board in the efforts of the Government to suppress the rebellion, and gratefully acknowledging " 'the divine interposition in the success which has attended the arms of the nation as an indication that we shall again be one people united under one glorious Constitution, united in our efforts to spread the Gospel around the world.'"

State conferences of the Congregational Church also passed similar resolutions from time to time. For example, the Conference of Massachusetts in 1864 stated that, " 'there can be no effectual reestablishment of the national authority by any negotiation which confesses the inability of the Government to subdue the rebellion by force of arms and proposes terms of peace to rebels still flying the flag of defiance.' "

The German Reformed Synod passed yearly resolutions of encouragement and support in every state where the church had an organization; the Lutheran General Synod, which met at York in 1864, proclaimed " 'the righteousness of the war which is waged by the Government of the United States for the maintenance of the national life and the duty of every Christian to support it by the whole weight of his influence, his prayers, and his efforts.' "

In 1862 the General Assembly of the Presbyterian Church of the United States at Columbus, Ohio, issued a paper claiming that " 'This whole treason, rebellion, anarchy, fraud, and violence, is utterly contrary to the dictates of natural religion and morality, and is plainly condemned by the revealed will of God. It is the clear and solemn duty of the National Government to preserve, at whatever cost, the National Union and Constitution, to maintain the laws in their supremacy, to crush force by force, and to restore the reign of public order and peace to the entire nation by whatever lawful means that are necessary thereunto. . . .' " Two hundred and six ministers and ruling elders voted for this declaration; twenty voted against it. "The General Assembly of the United Presbyterian Church had passed equally strong and uncompromising resolutions." Likewise the Reformed Presbyterian Church and the New School Presbyterians protested their loyalty to the actions of Lincoln and of the National Government.

"No church was more ready or powerful in its support of the Government than the wide-spread Methodist Episcopal Church. . . . The western armies especially were filled with the young and vigorous fighting men of that connection." According to Lincoln (in an address to a committee of the General Conference of 1864) "' . . . the Methodist Church sends more soldiers to the field, more nurses to the hospitals, and more prayers to heaven than any other.' "

The Catholic Church also spoke through its leaders in favor of the Union and of the necessity for appealing to arms. As an example, Archbishop Purcell, of Cincinnati, took occasion to say that, " 'It is time . . . that all . . . should rally around the . . . powers which the Apostle commands us to obey, and thus, presenting an undivided front to the enemy, reestablish the Union, without which there can be no panacea, present or prospective, for the ills we suffer.' "

The statements and resolutions of the churches in the North can be paralleled by similar statements of Churches in the South; in fact, "the cause of the rebellion was adopted and carried on by the Churches in the South, if not with more zeal and determination, at least with greater vehemence at the beginning than was shown by the religious organizations of the North."[111]

Most members of the above denominations who were opposed on grounds of conscience to participation in the conflict either sought to ally themselves with the more widely known of the peace sects or else avoided actual military service by the purchase of substitutes or the payment of the commutation fee. In fact some of the conscientious objectors who suffered most were those who joined the Quakers or one of the other peace denominations, after the war commenced.[112]

---

[111] *Ibid.*, pp. 315–325, 331 et seq. See also McPherson, Edward. *op. cit.*, Appendix, pp. 461–521.

[112] Letter from Thomas W. Johnson to John B. Crenshaw, Iredell County, N.C., April 23, 1863, and letters from Joseph Newlin to John B. Crenshaw, New Market, N.C., May 29, 1863 and July 20, 1863, in North Carolina Yearly Meeting Collection. See also Cartland, Fernando G. *Southern Heroes*, pp. 150–152 for the case of a Methodist conscientious objector and *Quaker Biographies*, Series 2, II, pp. 177–181.

# Chapter II

## Struggle in the North for Political Recognition

BY THE middle of the nineteenth century the attitude of the noncombatant sects was recognized by most of the legislators in the North and provisions for their conscientious scruples against bearing arms had been inserted in many of the state constitutions and laws. These provisions, for the most part, exempted conscientious objectors from active participation in the militia and from the necessity of oath-taking. The fact that equivalents for personal service in the militia were often required shows, however, that the authorities misunderstood the religious basis for the objection to such service. Those states whose constitutions provided for exemption from service in the militia upon the payment of some equivalent were Indiana, Iowa, Illinois, Kansas, Kentucky, and Pennsylvania.[1] The provision in the Indiana Constitution of 1851 is typical. Article XII, Section 6, says, "No person conscientiously opposed to bearing arms shall be compelled to do milita duty; but such person shall pay an equivalent for exemption; the amount to be prescribed by law."[2] The constitutions of other states, such as Michigan, Minnesota, New York, Ohio, and Vermont placed the question of militia in the hands of the Legislature,[3] or provided for exemption "upon such conditions as shall be prescribed by law."[4] The constitutions of

---

[1] Thorpe, Francis Newton. *The Federal and State Constitutions, etc.*, II, pp. 1089, 1132, 1004, 1190; III, p. 1307; V, p. 3111.

[2] *Ibid.*, II, p. 1089.

[3] *Ibid.*, IV, pp. 1966, 2017; V, pp. 2671, 2927; VI, p. 3768.

[4] *Ibid.*, IV, p. 1966. Michigan State Const. of 1850 (Art. XVII, sec. 1).

Connecticut, Massachusetts, Missouri, New Hampshire, New Jersey, Rhode Island, and Wisconsin were silent on the question of exemptions[5] but all allowed affirmations instead of swearing for those who were conscientiously opposed to the taking of oaths. Maryland's Constitution of 1864 allowed exemptions from militia service but her earlier constitutions had merely provided that "Quakers, Menonists, Tunkers, or Nicolites, or New Quakers, and who shall be conscientiously scrupulous of taking an oath on any occasion" might make affirmation instead.[6] Delaware, in her Constitutions of 1776, 1792, and 1831 merely guaranteed "the rights, privileges, immunities, and estates of religious societies and corporate bodies."[7] The only Northern State to grant exemption to certain sects without conditions was Maine. Her Constitution of 1819 (Article VII, Section 5) stated that, "Persons of the denominations of Quakers and Shakers, . . . may be exempted from military duty, but no other person of the age of eighteen and under the age of forty-five years, . . . shall be so exempted, unless he shall pay an equivalent to be fixed by law."[8] These constitutional and statutory provisions were superseded by the national conscription acts, passed by Congress during the war, but they were important as marking the privileges accorded religious objectors up to that time and they were referred to frequently when the enrollment and conscription acts were under discussion.[9]

As early as January, 1861, those who were opposed to forceful means of settling the controversies between North and South began inquiring of themselves what their atti-

---

    [5] *Ibid.*, I, p. 546; III, p. 1909; IV, pp. 2161, 2488; V, p. 2600; VI, p. 3231; VII, pp. 4094–4095.
    [6] *Ibid.*, III, pp. 1702, 1739–1740, 1773–1774.
    [7] *Ibid.*, I, pp. 579, 596.
    [8] *Ibid.*, III, p. 1660.
    [9] *Cong. Globe*, XLIII, Pt. 2, p. 994.

tude should be.[10] One conscientious member of the Society of Friends questioned the advisability of Friends voting, even for those opposed to slavery, because their official duties might involve war, in which case Friends would be unable to follow the persons they had voted for.  As he expressed it:

> The President we have aided to elect, in the fulfillment of his official duty, calls upon us, through his subordinate, to do our share of military service. We unhesitatingly object, and proceed, forthwith, to state the grounds of the objection—that we are Christians, therefore cannot fight; . . .  Our demanding officer is struck with surprise, and inquires where our christianity and conscientious scruples were at the time we voted for the President, whose official duties, in part, we knew to be of a military character, and were now only in proper progress of fulfillment; and further urging that they who place a man in office, pledge themselves to the observance of all such requisitions upon them as the duties of that office in its execution may require. And again, if this conscientious testimony against war be founded upon a Christian principle, a permanent basis, why its variableness? sometimes binding, at others not; on some occasions made paramount, on others subordinate. Is there not some reason to fear that those who, without scruple, submit to military burdens themselves, may conclude (judging from our present practice), that Friends' testimony against war must be grounded upon a principle possessed of remarkable elasticity?  Can we escape the conviction, that willingly to countenance war, even indirectly, is to be in some degree responsible for its evils.[11]

Quite a different attitude of mind is shown in a reply to the above query a few weeks later by a Virginian. He said:

---

[10] Min. of the Meeting for Sufferings of New York (Orthodox) Yearly Meeting, 1 mo. 24, 1861, pp. 138-139.

[11] "D. I." (anon.) in *Friends' Intelligencer*, XVII, no. 45, p. 708.

We cannot pay any tax without the risk of its being converted to war purposes. Are all to be passive under the law?
If we all become Friends are all laws to cease? I think not,
but the laws will be modified according to justice and the
golden rule. Were the last thoroughly now in practice,
war need not be one of the obligations of the President.

The writer goes on to question what would happen if all
Friends in Virginia refrained from voting on the question
of secession which was to be submitted to the voters in
that State on the fourth of March, 1861.[12]

Neither of the above views, however, are as typical of
the Society's attitude as the following extract from the
Epistle of the Yearly Meeting of Philadelphia (Orthodox)
to its members.[13]

Friends have ever believed civil government to be a
Divine ordinance, and that active or passive obedience to
the laws is an incumbent duty. While holding these views,
we wish also to encourage and to strengthen our members
faithfully and firmly to uphold the plain Scripture testimony against all wars and fightings, whatever it may cost
them, and to be on their guard how they strike hands with
those whose spirit and actions are in direct opposition to
it; or advocate a policy which, if carried out, may end in
strife, and possibly in bloodshed. Consistency is not only an
invaluable ornament of the Christian life, but it cogently
recommends it to others; and we are enjoined by inspired
authority so to walk, that others, 'beholding our good
works, may glorify God in the day of visitation.'

Consistency, however desirable, was not easy to maintain, so that this problem of the proper attitude for conscientious objectors to assume was one which was never

---

[12] "G.A.N." (anon.) in *Friends' Intelligencer*, XVII, no. 49, pp. 772–773.
[13] Min. of the Meeting for Sufferings of Philadelphia (Orthodox), Yearly
Meeting, 4 mo. 12, 1861, p. 158. See also Min. of the Meeting for Sufferings of
New York (Orthodox) Yearly Meeting, 4 mo. 23, 1861, pp. 140–142.

satisfactorily solved throughout the war. There were too many varying degrees of conscience among those opposed to military service and too many different interpretations placed on the obligations of conscience.

As the threatened storm approached Friends realized only too well the difficulties ahead of them in supporting their testimony against war. One Friend wrote:

> ... It would seem that the 'irripressible conflict' is close upon us—that the wrath of Heaven is about to be poured out upon this guilty nation. ... I am afraid when we examine ourselves closely according to the christian rule that there are not many who have borne an entire testimony against this great iniquity. ... It would be a comfortable reflection if we knew that all friends were safely north of the slave lines—I very much wish I was, but now see no prospect as property will not sell.[14]

When hostilities actually began Friends, as a body, were quick to express their disapproval and regret. Furthermore, they cautioned their members to abstain from taking part in the conflict; and to be guarded in both word and action. These admonitions were constantly repeated throughout the entire war period. A minute of the Philadelphia (Orthodox) Yearly Meeting of Friends which convened on April 15, 1861, said:

> In view of the serious commotions now agitating the community, and the threatening of civil war, which must necessarily produce great distress, and subject Friends to many trials of faith and obedience to the law of righteousness, the Meeting for Sufferings was desired to keep upon the watch, and to seek for wisdom and strength to stand forth in the support of our christian testimonies, and to strengthen the hands of our members in whatever trials may be permitted to come upon them.[15]

---

[14] Letter from William J. Schofield to Aaron H. Griffith from Sandy Spring, Md., Feb. 26, 1861, among mss. of Baltimore (Orthodox) Yearly Meeting.

[15] *The Friend*, XXXIV, no. 34, p. 271.

Special committees were appointed by the various Meetings for Sufferings of the Society of Friends to draft "epistles of counsel and caution" to members of the Society.[16] These were chiefly long exhortations against taking sides politically or otherwise in the strife. Suggestions of a practical nature, however, were also offered. One address recommended " . . . in regard to taxes, it has been the practice of our Society to pay them honestly to the government when legally assessed upon us as upon other citizens, unless they be assessed for specific purposes to which we cannot conscientiously contribute such as are stated in our discipline."[17] Reviews of Friends' testimony against war were also published in their own periodicals, giving each new interpretation by the Society as a question arose. Friends were recommended to adhere strictly to these testimonies.[18]

Throughout the summer and fall of 1861 Friends and other noncombatants watched anxiously the progress of the conflict, hoping for an early termination of hostilities, but growing more and more depressed as the warlike preparations continued. Although the Society officially maintained its attitude of aloofness during this first year of the conflict individual members volunteered in the service, or aided the military establishment in more indirect ways.[19]

[16] Min. of the Meetings for Sufferings of Western Yearly Meeting (5 mo. 2, 1861), pp. 27–33; of Indiana Yearly Meeting (5 mo. 30, 1861); of Baltimore (Hicksite) Yearly Meeting (9 mo. 8, 1861); and of Philadelphia (Orthodox) Yearly Meeting (12 mo. 20, 1861).

[17] Min. of the Meeting for Sufferings of Indiana Yearly Meeting (5 mo .30, 1861), p. 285.

[18] *The Friend*, XXXIV, no. 35, p. 278, and *Friends' Intelligencer*, XVIII, pp. 131 et seq., 147, 355 et seq., and 562.

[19] Minutes of the various Yearly Meetings of the Society of Friends, 1861. See also *Atlantic Monthly*, VII, (June, 1861), p. 746; Shannon, Fred Albert. *The Organization and Administration of the Union Army*, II, p. 254; Jones, Rufus M. *The Later Periods of Quakerism*, II, p. 729; and Chapter VI of this study.

It was a time when Friends as well as others found it difficult to follow their ordinary modes of thought and action. Many attempts were made by Friends to reconcile their abhorrence of war with their genuine interest in the progress of the conflict. Such an attempt was made by John Greenleaf Whittier in his circular letter addressed "To Members of the Society of Friends," containing suggestions as to ways in which the philanthropy of the sect might properly find expression. In this circular, which was dated Amesbury, June 18, 1861, he said, among other things:

> 'We have no right to ask or expect an exemption from the chastisement which the Divine Providence is inflicting upon the nation. Steadily and faithfully maintaining our testimony against war, we owe it to the cause of truth, to show that exalted heroism and generous self-sacrifice are not incompatible with our pacific principles . . . '[20]

The editors of Quaker periodicals found it particularly difficult to decide how much news of the war should be included in their columns. The editor of one paper explained this difficulty in the following words:

> Some Friends having communicated to us their doubts of the propriety of spreading before the readers of 'The Friend' information of any of the military events transpiring, as our readers are aware, we concluded to discontinue— at least for a time—that portion of our 'Summary of Events.' Since doing so, we have had transmitted to us abundant complaint of the omission. Friends, of equal religious standing with those who suggested the discontinuance, say it is information of transactions affecting the welfare, not only of the country at large, but of every citizen within it, which should be given in the least objec-

---

[20] Pickard, Samuel Thomas. *Life and Letters of John Greenleaf Whittier*, II, pp. 440–441.

tionable manner, and they earnestly request the resumption of our former condensed statement.[21]

News of the war was thereafter given considerable space in *The Friend* and in *The Friends' Review* but *The Friends' Intelligencer* completely ignored the conflict in many of its numbers.

Prior to the time of the first draft of soldiers the most important question of a military nature which agitated Friends was that of war taxes and bounty fees. On this question there was much disagreement. In December, 1861, a Quaker, named Joshua Maule, wrote almost bitterly of the lax attitude taken by some of the meetings of Friends.

> If the Society of Friends was in a healthy condition, there would, I have no doubt, be some action taken in the yearly meeting, in giving counsel and encouragement to strengthen the hands of Friends faithfully to maintain a Christian testimony against war and all warlike measures, including the present levying of a tax for the support of the war. The latter subject was brought before the meeting, but the spirit which prevails, and has ruled for years past, turned judgment away backward, and the honest-hearted, who had hoped for counsel and advice from the Church, were discouraged through the position taken by the leaders of the meeting, who endeavored to make it appear that our testimony did not require us to decline paying the tax now demanded. They referred to the writings of early Friends on the subject of taxes, intimating that their testimony was not against such a tax as the present; but they did not produce the proof of such an assertion, neither could they.[22]

Maule proceeded by telling how he refused to pay to the County Treasurer the $8\frac{1}{2}\%$ of the tax for 1861 "which was

---

[21] *The Friend*, XXXV, no. 17, p. 136.
[22] Maule, Joshua. *Transactions and Changes in the Society of Friends, and Incidents in the Life and Experiences of Joshua Maule*, pp. 220–221.

the part expressly named in the tax-list as for the war at that time." An attempt was made to collect the tax by borrowing from Maule an amount sufficient to pay it, but he would not stand for this. Therefore, several pieces of goods were taken in payment, much against the desire of the Collector.[23] Maule explained how other Friends paid half the tax and then decided it was wrong to pay the balance: later, however, they paid the balance without reserve. "They had consulted Friends' writings, etc, and come to the conclusion that as this was a mixed tax, and as Friends had always paid taxes, part of which had gone to support a military establishment, it was better to pay this tax, and make no trouble about it."[24] When the question came up before Maule's quarterly meeting those who had the management of affairs in the meeting favored paying the tax. As the Clerk expressed it, " 'We can pay the tax, but we cannot fight!' " Maule, naturally disagreed with this opinion. He stated further that "This subject of taxes occupied much time in our monthly meetings," and that a letter was addressed to him urging him not to cause dissention in the Society by bringing up the subject of taxes.[25]

An address to the members of the Baltimore (Hicksite) Yearly Meeting by the Meeting for Sufferings of that body, under date of September 8, 1861, was somewhat indefinite on the subject of war taxes. It said:

The true position of Friends in the civil community is, to be quiet, peaceable citizens, under whatever government is established over them, cheerfully obeying all laws with which they can conscientiously comply; and as they are found to do this, greater respect will be paid to their scruples for non-compliance with those laws which they

[23] *Ibid.*, p. 221.
[24] *Ibid.*, pp. 233–234.
[25] *Ibid.*, pp. 234–235, 243, and 256–261.

cannot obey, and against which the grounds of their testimony can be made more obviously manifest.[26]

A similar attitude was taken by a special committee
of the Western Yearly Meeting of Friends, which said:

> Our obligations to government may be shown after the
> example of our Savior; and we feel that we escape con-
> demnation when the Magistrate and not the tax payer
> assumes the responsibility of its specific appropriations;
> such has been the settled practice of our Society, to pay all
> duties and taxes, that are not exclusively for War pur-
> poses.[27]

The New England Yearly Meeting, however, was more
specific in recommending its members to pay all taxes. It
said:

> The payment of taxes levied upon us, for the increase of
> public revenue has at this time claimed our consideration;
> and we would encourage Friends cheerfully to comply with
> the requisitions of our discipline, in regard to being punctual
> in the payment of every tribute which they can justly do,
> without attempting to make any impracticable distinc-
> tions respecting such taxes as may be imposed upon them
> for the support of our Government.[28]

On the subject of military fines and bounty fees, however, Friends were more in agreement. The address to the
members of the Baltimore Yearly Meeting was positive on
this point. It said:

> We are all united in the belief, that as we are opposed
> to war, in all its aspects and consequences, and cannot
> perform military services of any kind, we therefore cannot

---

[26] Min. of the Meeting for Sufferings of Baltimore (Hicksite) Yearly Meeting,
9 mo. 8, 1861, p. 85, and *Friends' Intelligencer*, XVIII, no. 33, p. 515.

[27] Min. of the Meeting for Sufferings of Western Yearly Meeting, 9 mo. 19,
1861, p. 40.

[28] Min. of the Meeting for Sufferings of New England Yearly Meeting, 8 mo.
20, 1862, p. 274.

consistently or conscientiously, pay any *fines* imposed as a punishment 'for non-performance of these services,' or any thing connected therewith.[29]

By the end of 1861 Friends were aware of the possibility of a military draft, but it was still hoped that volunteering would fill the ranks of the Northern Army. In October, 1861, *The Friend* stated: "The government has satisfactory assurances that there will be as many volunteers tendered as will be needed, without resorting to drafting, and has, therefore, refused to sanction the latter process for filling the ranks of the army."[30] Even as late as April, 1862, this same periodical took an optimistic view by referring to an order of the War Department which closed all recruiting stations in the various states because of the excess of troops in the field.[31]

Any optimism, however, which people may have had was dispelled by the Federal Militia Act of July 17, 1862. This act provided for the mustering in of the militia between the ages of 18 and 45 when called upon by the President. The enrollment was to be under state control unless the already existing state laws were deficient or improperly executed, in which case the President was impowered to make all necessary rules and regulations for carrying out the provisions of the act.[32] On August 4th the President issued a call for 300,000 men for nine months' service, and five days later General Order #99 was issued by the Adjutant General's Office regulating the enrollment and draft of these men.[33]

---

[29] Min. of the Meeting for Sufferings of Baltimore (Hicksite) Yearly Meeting, p. 84. Also *Friends' Intelligencer*, XVIII, no. 33, pp. 515-516, and *The Friend*, XXXVI, no. 2, p. 13.

[30] *The Friend*, XXXV, no. 5, p. 40.

[31] *Ibid.*, p. 256.

[32] *U. S. Statutes at Large*, (37 Cong. Sess. II, chap. 201), XII, pp. 597-600.

[33] *Official Records*, Series 3, II, pp. 333-335.

On the whole it does not appear that those conscientious about bearing arms were immediately alarmed by this mobilization of the nation's military forces. As late as August 27, 1862, the Meeting for Sufferings of the Indiana Yearly Meeting of Friends made the following reassuring minute:

> This Meeting having been called together in consequence of a communication received by one of its members from Friends in Iowa, relative to the probable situation of Members of our Society in that State, under the operation of the late order of the President of the United States for a draft of the militia; has taken the matter under solid and deliberate consideration, and came to the united judgment that the present is not a proper time for this meeting to appear before our rulers on behalf of the Society on this deeply interesting subject.[34]

In the East the Meeting for Sufferings of the Philadelphia (Orthodox) Yearly Meeting, which met August 25th, "in consequence of a recent order of the Government of the United States directing the enrollment of all the male Citizens between the ages of 18 and 45 years preparatory to a draft for service in the Army: in consequence of which many of the members of our Society will be likely to be brought into difficulty and trial, and may require the advice and assistance of Friends," appointed a committee of twenty-five "to give such advice and assistance to our young Friends as they may be favored to do, encouraging and strengthening them in the faithful support of our Christian testimony against war, . . ."[35]

*The Friend* merely mentioned without comment the Militia Act of July 17th, the President's call for 300,000 men,

---

[34] Min. of the Meeting for Sufferings of Indiana Yearly Meeting, 8 mo. 27, 1862, pp. 308–309.

[35] Min. of the Meeting for Sufferings of Philadelphia (Orthodox) Yearly Meeting 8 mo. 25, 1862, p. 181.

and the regulations provided for in General Orders #99.[36] An editorial in *The Friends' Intelligencer* explained how Friends in New York were exempt by special legislative enactment and how in Pennsylvania they were partly protected by Article 6 of the State Constitution. The editorial continued, however, in an optimistic tone, " . . . It has seemed to us that before the time comes to which the commencement of the draft has been postponed in Pennsylvania, it will probably be abandoned."[37]

Neither the Militia Act of July 17th nor the General Order of August 9th was specific, however, in the matter of exemptions, so that those who were conscientiously opposed to serving in the militia soon sought to have the question clarified. As the General Order provided for the exemption of "all persons exempted by the laws of the respective States from military duty, on sufficient evidence, . . . " it was natural that noncombatant bodies should first approach the state authorities in an effort to have the state laws interpreted. For example, the Mennonites, Amana Inspirationists, German Baptists and Quakers of Iowa petitioned the Governor and the General Assembly, which met in extra session in September, 1862, for relief from military service.[38] Governor Kirkwood, in his message to the Senate and House, on September 3rd, supported the petition in the following words:

> There are in this State some religious bodies who entertain peculiar views upon the subject of bearing arms, and whose religious opinions conscientiously entertained, preclude their so doing. Their members are among our most quiet, orderly, industrious and peaceful citizens, and their sympathies are wholly with the Government in this

---

[36] *The Friend*, XXXV, pp. 376, 392, 400.

[37] *Friends' Intelligencer*, XIX, no. 26, pp. 408–409.

[38] Jones, Louis T. *The Quakers of Iowa*, p. 333, and Cook, Darius B. *The Quaker Divide* p. 208.

struggle now going on for its preservation, yet they cannot conscientiously bear arms in its support. It appears to me it would be unjust and wholly useless to force such men into the army as soldiers, and yet it would not be just to the Government or to other citizens that they should be wholly relieved from the burdens that others have to bear. I suggest, therefore, that these persons who cannot conscientiously render military duty, be exempted therefrom in case of draft, upon the payment of a fixed sum of money to be paid to the State.[39]

A bill for the relief of conscientious objectors was later introduced in the Iowa House during the extra session, but it was defeated after a great deal of discussion.[40] Instead another bill was passed, allowing for exemption in case of a draft, upon the payment of $300. or the furnishing of a substitute.[41]

In another instance representatives of the Society of Friends appealed to Governor Morton, of Indiana, for an interpretation of the Militia Act as it applied to them.[42] In turn he appealed to Secretary of War Stanton, in the following communication, under date of September 24, 1862.

Hon. E. M. Stanton:
The constitution of the State of Indiana contains the following provision:
'No person conscientiously opposed to bearing arms shall be compelled to do military duty, but such person shall pay an equivalent for exemption, the amount to be prescribed by law.'
Our Legislature has omitted to fix any equivalent for such exemption. This omission can be supplied by you under sec-

---

[39] Shambaugh, Benjamin F. *Messages and Proclamations of the Governors of Iowa*, II, pp. 316–317.
[40] *Iowa House Journal, 1862*, Extra Session pp. 41, 42, 43, 44, 67, and 70.
[41] Cook, Darius B. *op. cit.*, p. 208.
[42] Foulke, William Dudley. *Life of Oliver P. Morton*, I, p. 199.

tion 1 of the act of July 17, 1862. Will you please fix the amount and advise me of it as early as possible?

O. P. Morton[43]

Secretary Stanton turned the matter over to C. P. Buckingham, Assistant Adjutant-General, who wrote to Governor Morton on September 26th, asking his opinion as to "a fair commutation to be paid by persons conscientiously opposed to bearing arms."[44] In reply, Morton suggested a sum "not less than $200. per man."[45] Subsequently this sum was decided upon as the correct amount to charge.[46]

Governor John A. Andrew, of Massachusetts, also wrote to Brig. General Buckingham on August 7th asking for clarification of the exemption provisions. "Are there not large classes of persons in other military and in civil employments," he said, "and Quakers, and the like, who should be exempt from duty?"[47]

Governor David Tod, of Ohio, wrote to Stanton on October 5th, saying, "Without any well-defined authority therefor, I have exempted all State and county officers, also members of religious denominations whose creed forbids taking up arms, upon payment of $200. each; all of which I ask you to approve. I purpose using the money thus obtained in hiring substitutes and in caring for the sick and wounded, through Quartermaster-General Wright."[48] He later (October 10, 1862) sent Stanton a copy of his order relating to non-resistants, which he asked the Secretary to approve. The order was as follows:

Upon satisfactory evidence that a drafted man belongs to a church the creed of which forbids self-defense or the

---

[43] *Official Records*, Series 3, II, p. 587.

[44] *Ibid.*, p. 588.

[45] *Ibid.*, p. 589.

[46] Ibid., p. 590.

[47] *Ibid.*, p. 319.

[48] *Ibid.*, p. 650.

use of arms, you will discharge him upon the payment to you of the sum of $200 . . . . .[49]

In New York, General Orders #79, issued by the Adjutant-General's Office at Albany, October 14, 1862, exempted in Article XI, section 5, "persons being of the people called Shakers or Quakers."[50]

In Maryland the laws exempting from military duty those who were conscientiously scrupulous against bearing arms were evidently interpreted quite liberally. A mere petition to William H. Dallam, a commissioner to superintend the drafting in that State, signed by twenty-seven members of the Society of Friends asking that their names be stricken from the militia roll, "proved effectual in releasing them from military service required by the Government."[51]

The Meeting for Sufferings of Baltimore Yearly Meeting of Friends stated, on the 18th of October:

> Since the last meeting there has been a requisition on the State of Maryland for its proportion of three hundred thousand men for the United States Army: several members of this Meeting examined our State laws, and had interviews with the Governor, and the Commissioners of Enrollment from which they felt assured that Friends would be undisturbed in their conscientious scruples against War, and that a special call of this Meeting on the subject would be unnecessary. The draft has recently taken place, and Friends have been exempted. . . .[52]

In Pennsylvania Friends were actively engaged in behalf of those opposed to bearing arms, even prior to the

[49] *Ibid.*, p. 662.
[50] *Ibid.*, p. 669.
[51] *Friends' Intelligencer*, XIX, no. 39, p. 616.
[52] Min. of the Meeting for Sufferings of Baltimore (Orthodox) Yearly Meeting, 10 mo. 18, 1862, quoted in *Bulletin of Friends' Historical Society*, IV, no. 1, p. 13.

passage of the Militia Act.[53]   The State Constitution provided, however, for their exemption upon the payment of an equivalent, which prior to the war had usually taken the form of a levy upon goods.[54]   This same form of exemption was continued under the Act of July, 1862.

In New York special Yearly Meeting committees were appointed "to keep themselves advised of any laws that may be proposed in Congress, and in the Legislatures of New York and New Jersey affecting any of our christian testimonies or be likely to bring any of our members into suffering . . . "[55] These groups visited Albany, had interviews with many members of the Legislature, and discussed the question of exemption for conscience' sake with the Committees on Military Affairs. Apparently these Friends were treated with great courtesy and their sentiments thoroughly examined. However, a new law was passed (or rather, the previous law was revised) exempting those scrupulous against bearing arms only upon the payment of $300. or the furnishing of a substitute.[56]

In New England Friends were also active politically. In February, 1862, a committee of thirteen members was chosen by the Yearly Meeting "to take such care as may be necessary, in order for a continuance of the exemption of Friends from military requisitions."[57] This committee reported that the legislature of Maine favored an extension of the privileges already accorded the Society of Friends,[58] but that the State of Rhode Island had suddenly repealed

---

[53] *Elkinton, Diary of Joseph S.*, p. 34.

[54] *Friends' Intelligencer*, XIX, no. 26, pp. 408–409.

[55] Min. of the Meeting for Sufferings of New York (Hicksite) Yearly Meeting, 10 mo. 7, 1861.  See also Min. of the Meeting for Sufferings of New York (Orthodox) Yearly Meeting, 12 mo. 5, 1861.

[56] Min. of the Meeting for Sufferings of New York (Orthodox) Yearly Meeting, 5 mo. 29, 1863, pp. 176–177.

[57] Min. of the Meeting for Sufferings of New England Yearly Meeting, 2 mo. 5, 1862, p. 270.

[58] *Ibid.*, 6 mo. 14, 1862, p. 272.

an act which exempted Friends and others from military requirements.[59] This latter action resulted in a memorial to the Legislature, which concluded in the following words:

> They would further represent, that the military law enacted at the last session of the General Assembly, will necessarily subject them and others who are conscientious against bearing arms, to much suffering, as they cannot consistently pay a fine in lieu of performing military service—and they therefore earnestly petition you to enact a law which shall relieve from military requirements all who shall give evidence satisfactory to such tribunal as in your wisdom you may appoint, that they are sincerely conscientious against bearing arms . . . .[60]

Similar action was taken in Massachusetts after that State passed a law repealing Friends' privileges and requiring them to enroll for military service the same as others.[61] The Committee was unsuccessful in its attempt to have this law altered, but later the status of Friends was at least clarified by the following communication which they obtained from the Federal War Department.

> War Department
> Washington City, D.C.
> September 20, 1862.

His Excellency
John A. Andrew
Governor of Massachusetts.

Sir—In reply to yours transmitting the letter of Stephen A. Chase & others concerning the exemption of Quakers from draft for military duty, I am directed to say that they cannot be exempted from draft by this department, but anyone that is drafted may subscribe, & take the enclosed oath or affirmation, and transmit it to this depart-

[59] *Ibid.*, 11 mo. 11, 1862, p. 275.
[60] *Ibid.*, 2 mo. 4, 1863, p. 277.
[61] *Ibid.*, 6 mo. 13, 1863, p. 283.

ment with proper testimony, as to the standing of the
party, and an order will be made relieving him from military
duty.

Very respectfully

Your obedient servant

C. P. Buckingham

Brig. Gen. G. d. a. G.[62]

Before the end of the year 1862 Friends and other non-
combatants realized the seriousness of the military situation, and braced themselves for the struggle ahead. The
Indiana Yearly Meeting, held at Waynesville, Ohio, from
September 29 to October 2, 1862, reaffirmed its position
against all wars and fighting. " . . . We desire to advise
all our members," the minutes read, "against giving
countenance, or assistance, by our conversation, conduct,
or property, to the shedding of human blood."[63] Quaker
periodicals were constant in their warnings to Friends not
to "rejoice in victory obtained by the sword," not to lend
their support to the exciting of hatreds and bloodshed.[64]

Suggestions were offered by individuals, by committees,
and by periodicals to conscientious objectors who might
be drafted. As an illustration, Quakers in Pennsylvania,
subject to the terms of the Militia Act, were recommended
to enroll and to give the information desired of them, and
to claim exemption on conscientious grounds, rather than
to send a substitute or to pay commutation money.[65]

---

[62] *Ibid.*, 6 mo. 13, 1863, p. 285.

[63] Min. of Indiana (Hicksite) Yearly Meeting quoted in the *Friends' Intelligencer*, XIX, pp. 566–568. See also Min. of the Meeting for Sufferings of New
York (Hicksite) Yearly Meeting, 10 mo. 6, 1862.

[64] *The Friend*, XXXVI, pp. 18, 35, 52, 135, 183, 307, 349, 375–376, etc.
*Friends' Intelligencer*, XIX, pp. 409, 436, 537–538, 566–568, etc.

[65] *The Friend*, XXXV, no. 51, pp. 403–404; no. 52, p. 414, and *Friends'
Intelligencer*, XIX, no. 27, p. 424. The New England and New York (Orthodox)
Yearly Meetings made the same recommendations to their members. See
Min. of the Meeting for Sufferings of New England Yearly Meeting, 7 mo. 30,
1863, p. 289, and Min. of the Meeting for Sufferings of New York (Orthodox)
Yearly Meeting, 8 mo. 6, 1863, pp. 182–184.

The form providing for such claims is illustrated on the following page. The names of those who were appointed to superintend the drafting in the several counties of Pennsylvania, and to whom application for exemption must be made, were also published.[66]

The year 1863 was a period of anxiety and hardship for noncombatants as well as for combatants in the North. The 37th Congress, which began its third session in December, 1862, had as one of its tasks the improvement of the military measures already enacted. The draft for 300,000 men had proved inadequate to meet the situation, and Federal conscription was deemed by many to be a necessity. The peace sects forsaw the liklihood of conscription and took what measures they could to oppose it.

The Meeting for Sufferings of the Philadelphia (Orthodox) Yearly Meeting was convened on February 23, 1863 "in consequence of a Bill being before the Congress of the United States which has passed the Senate enrolling all male Citizens for Draft in the United States Army, between the ages of 20 and 45." It was decided to refer the matter to a committee of seven Friends who might prepare a memorial to the President and Congress if the way should open for it. Such a memorial was prepared and approved by the Meeting, and Samuel Hilles, Charles Evans, James Emlen, and Charles Downing were requested to proceed to Washington to present copies of the memorial to the President, heads of departments, and members of Congress. The memorial set forth in detail the peace testimony of the Society of Friends and the reasons why commutation money could not conscientiously be paid.[67] Similar memorials were prepared and forwarded at this time by other Friends' meetings.[68]

---

[66] *The Friend*, XXXVI, no. 1, p. 6.
[67] Min. of the Meeting for Sufferings of Philadelphia (Orthodox) Yearly Meeting, 2 mo. 23, 1863, pp. 187–190.

No.

## CLAIM FOR EXEMPTION FROM MILITARY DUTY,

### Under the Enrollment and Draft of Militia ordered by the President of the United States, on the Fourth Day of August, 1862.

*Philadelphia, Sept._____ 1862.*

I,                                                    *aged                              years, by*

*occupation a* _____*residing at No.*

*Street, in the* _____*Precinct of the*_____*Ward*

*of the City of Philadelphia, in the State of Pennsylvania, do claim exemption from military duty under the enrollment and draft aforesaid, by reason of my conscientious scruples against bearing arms, either in self-defence, the defence of my country, or otherwise howsoever*

*Signed* _____

---

STATE OF PENNSYLVANIA,
    City and County of Philadelphia. } ss.

*Before me, Commissioner to superintend drafting for said City and County, personally appeared                              the claimant above named, who being duly affirmed, did depose and say, that he conscientiously scruples to bear arms, believes it unlawful to do so, whether in self-defence or in defence of his country, or otherwise howsoever: that the scruples and belief above stated have not been formed lightly, but carefully, deliberately and conscientiously, and are now declared and professed, not for the purpose of evading the military service of his country in the present exigency, but because he solemnly and religiously holds and maintains them, and in his conscience believes that it is his bounden duty to act in accordance with them on all occasions and under all circumstances.*

*Affirmed and subscribed before me, this,*
*day of September, 1862.*

                                    *Commissary.*

*Philadelphia, Sept.          1862.*

*To*

    *You are hereby notified that, having been exempted from military duty because of conscientious scruples against bearing arms, in accordance with Section 2, Article VI., of the Constitution of Pennsylvania, you will be held liable to pay to the Commonwealth such sum (as "an equivalent for personal service") as the Legislature may direct, by a law enacted for that purpose.*

*Commissioner.*

*I accept service of this notice on the date above stated.*

While these memorials and petitions were being presented, the debates on the Enrollment Bill were taking place in the Senate and House of Representatives. Senator Wilson, of Massachusetts, Chairman of the Committee on Military Affairs, offered an amendment on February 4th providing that any drafted militia man who should present an acceptable substitute should receive a certificate of discharge from such draft. This amendment was agreed to and was later incorporated in the final Act. The following day (February 5th) Senator Lane, of Indiana, moved to recommit the bill and pending amendments to the Committee on Military Affairs with a view to incorporate certain exemptions which would render the law equally effective and more acceptable to the people. These exemptions, however, did not include cases of conscience. Senator Howard, of Michigan, suggested that it would be well for Congress to be more specific in making provision for exemptions, because, "As this bill now reads such persons are to be exempt . . . therefrom by the existing laws of the United States," one of which excused "' . . . all persons who now are or may hereafter be exempt by the laws of the respective States.'"[69]

On February 9th the bill passed a second reading and on the 16th it was again debated in the Senate. In the evening session on this latter date Senator Ira Harris, of New York, proposed another exception to the second section for "persons who, being from scruples of conscience averse to bearing arms, are by the constitution of any State excused therefrom." He continued:

There are in some of the States persons who are so averse to bearing arms that they will not even pay a fine. There

---

[68] Meeting for Sufferings of New York (Orthodox) Yearly Meeting, 2 mo. 23, 1863, pp. 172–173, and Meeting for Sufferings of Baltimore (Orthodox) Yearly Meeting, 2 mo. 25, 1863.

[69] *Cong. Globe*, XLIII, Pt. 1, p. 737.

are the Shakers in my own State, with whom we had at one time a great deal of trouble on this subject. I do not want to be embarrassed in this thing by any conflict between this law and the State constitutions. By the constitution of New York this class of people are now entirely exempt from military duty; and while I do not feel inclined to make exemptions, I think it will be better not to make a law in conflict with our State constitutions.[70]

This proposal caused a great deal of comment. Senators Wilson, of Massachusetts, Clark, of New Hampshire, Ten Eyck, of New Jersey, and Lane, of Indiana, approved it but suggested going still further in the matter of exemptions so that the law would operate more justly. As Senator Lane explained:

This amendment would operate very unjustly on the people in the State of Indiana who are conscientiously opposed to bearing arms. They are not exempted either by the law or the constitution in our State. The provision of our constitution is, that those who are conscientiously opposed to bearing arms shall not be compelled to bear arms, but they shall pay a fine to be assessed by law, which has been fixed at $200, I think, in my State.... All persons having conscientious scruples should be excluded absolutely, or should be excluded upon the payment of a fine, and it should operate equally. The effect of this [proposed] amendment will be unequal and unjust.[71]

Senator McDougall, of California, protested against the whole idea of exempting conscientious objectors. He was joined by others when Senator Sumner, of Massachusetts, suggested that clergymen should also be covered by the amendment. After further discussion, Senator Harris was prevailed upon to withdraw his amendment.[72]

---

[70] *Ibid.*, XLIII, Pt. 2, p. 994.
[71] *Ibid.*, p. 994.
[72] *Ibid.*, p. 995.

When the debate on the Conscription Bill was taken up in the House of Representatives Thaddeus Stevens, of Pennsylvania, was the first to champion the rights of the conscientious objector. On February 24th, he said:

... There is a portion of this provision which I do not and cannot assent to ... There are in all countries exemptions for conscience sake, and it is right that there should be. In my own county a very large number of our best citizens, [Mennonites] our most loyal men, are conscientiously opposed to bearing arms. They are willing to pay their taxes; they would be willing to pay this amount to procure substitutes, but I do not believe that they should be forced to violate their conscientious and religious scruples which have existed from their birth, and which have descended to them from posterity; and I give notice that when the proper time comes I will offer the following amendment as a proviso to section thirteen:

'*Provided*, That no person, unless he provide a substitute, shall be exempt from service, except as hereinbefore exempted, who will not declare on oath or affirmation that he is conscientiously scrupulous against bearing arms, and that such is and has been his declared religion for more than __ years, before such draft.'

I will exempt nobody, so far as I am concerned, from serving his country, excepting those who are religiously opposed to that mode of doing it. The rich man who has no conscientious scruples, in my judgment, has no more right when he is drafted to refuse to go and fight the enemies of his country than the poor man who cannot raise $300. to pay for exemption.[73]

Accordingly, this above provision was recommended for adoption by Representative Stevens on the following day, with the addition that "the oath or affirmation may be administered by the person who superintends the draft." Stevens also suggested "more than one year" as the length

[73] *Ibid.*, p. 1261.

of time required for a person to have established his connection with a particular religious organization.[74] Representative Johnson, of Pennsylvania, moved that the
person's declared religion should be for a period of more
than three years, instead of merely one, which modification
Stevens readily accepted. The amendment was lost, however, when it came to a vote, 95 to 18;[75] and the Bill, as
passed by the House on February 25th, and as finally
approved on March 3rd, remained silent on the question of
exemptions for conscientious scruples.

This "Act for enrolling and calling out the national
Forces, and for other Purposes" was sweeping in its provisions. It included all able-bodied males between the ages
of 20 and 45, but divided them into two classes. The first
class was composed of all those between 20 and 35 and
unmarried men between 35 and 45, who were to be called
for service first. The second group included all others
subject to military duty. The sections which provided for
substitutes and commutation money were worded as follows:

> Sec. 13—*And be it further enacted*, That any person
> drafted and notified to appear as aforesaid, may, on or
> before the day fixed for his appearance, furnish an accept-
> able substitute to take his place in the draft; or he may pay
> to such person as the Secretary of War may authorize to
> receive it, such sum, not exceeding three hundred dollars,
> as the Secretary may determine, for the procuration of such
> substitute; which sum shall be fixed at a uniform rate by
> a general order made at the time of ordering a draft for any
> state or territory; and thereupon such person so furnishing
> the substitute, or paying the money, shall be discharged from
> further liability under that draft. And any person failing to
> report after due service of notice, as herein prescribed, with-
> out furnishing a substitute, or paying the required sum

---

[74] *Ibid.*, pp. 1291–1292.
[75] *Ibid.*, p. 1292.

therefor, shall be deemed a deserter, and shall be arrested by the provost-marshal and sent to the nearest military post for trial by court-martial, unless, upon proper showing that he is not liable to do military duty, the board of enrolment shall relieve him from the draft.

Sec. 17—*And be it further enacted*, That any person enrolled and drafted according to the provisions of this act, who shall furnish an acceptable substitute, shall thereupon receive from the board of enrolment a certificate of discharge from such draft, which shall exempt him from military duty during the time for which he was drafted; etc.[76]

The provision for the payment of commutation money in lieu of personal service was satisfactory to many non-combatants, but not to those who were most conscientious in their attitude toward military requirements. Quakers, especially, rightly surmised that the commutation money would be used for the purchase of substitutes and that payment of the fee was therefore a direct aid to the military authorities and virtually an equivalent to personal service.[77] Various arguments for and against payment of the commutation fee were offered by individual Quakers,[78] but, throughout 1863 and the years which followed, the attitude of the Society of Friends as a whole remained consistently opposed to the payment of commutation money or the procuration of substitutes.[79]

Friends in Pennsylvania at once took active measures to protest against the imposition of military fines for conscientious persons. A memorial had already been prepared

---

[76] *U. S. Statutes at Large,* (37 Cong., Sess. III, chap. 75), XII, pp. 731–737.

[77] *Ibid.,* XIII, p. 400 (Dec. 23, 1863).

[78] *Friends' Intelligencer,* XX, pp. 245–246, 277–278, 280, 292–294, 297–299, 325–327, 340–341, 342, 357–358, 360, 390–392, 408, 420–421, 470–472, 473–474, 614–616, 663–664, 692, etc.

[79] Shannon, Fred Albert. *The Organization and Administration of the Union Army,* II, pp. 253–254. See also Chap. VI of this study.

by a committee of the Meeting for Sufferings of the Philadelphia (Orthodox) Yearly Meeting and had been laid before Congress when the Conscription Bill was under consideration. On the 20th of March, the Committee which had been responsible for the preparation and presentation of this memorial reported back to the Meeting for Sufferings in the following words:

That we proceeded to Washington on the day after our appointment and found that the Bill under consideration had passed the House of Representatives a short time previous to our arrival, but with amendments requiring its return to the Senate for concurrence.

Having obtained a private interview with the President, we presented him with a copy of the Memorial, which he read aloud in our presence. After which some remarks were made inviting his attention to the views of Friends upon the subject of war, and the reasons why they could not engage in any military service as set forth in the Memorial. He received and heard us with apparent interest, and the interview though short was satisfactory.

Having met the Chairman of the military Committee of the Senate a copy of the Memorial was placed in his hands which he was requested to present to the Senate. This he willingly undertook to do informing us, however, that as the Bill was then situated, it was too late for any other amendments to be made than those proposed by the House of Representatives. The Memorial was presented, and printed copies were laid upon the desks of each Senator.

We called to see the Heads of nearly all the Departments and left copies of the Memorial for them; also for the Attorney General. A copy was likewise furnished to each member of the House of Representatives. In an interview with the Secretary of War his attention was directed to that part of the Bill which imposed a penalty on any one who shall discourage others from enlisting in the service of the United States; informing him that Friends,—parents and others—could not decline inculcating their well-known peaceable principles upon their children and their younger fellow-members. He assured us in reply that that provision of the Bill was not intended to be, nor would it be, applied to any such cases, and as it was well known that Friends had always held the principles of peace, they need have no apprehension of difficulty resulting to them from the law on that account.

In an interview with a Senator we learned that the bringing forward of this Bill had been designedly postponed until near the close of the session, with a view of hastening its enactment, and preventing as far as possible changes being made in it, and especially as its provisions should be made to apply to all classes, without respect to position or religious belief with the hope of making it more generally acceptable.

Although the short notice received of the character of this Bill prevented earlier measures being taken to obtain a modification in favor of Friends, yet we think there is reason to believe that good has resulted from thus spreading before the Executive and the members of Congress the Christian principles held by Friends upon the subject of war, and the reasons why they cannot consistently comply with the provisions of law in reference to military measures.

(Signed) Samuel Hilles
James Emlen
Charles Downing
Charles Evans[80]

Friends of both Philadelphia Yearly Meetings memorialized the Governor and Legislature of Pennsylvania, also on the subject of military fines.[81] These memorials called

[80] Min. of the Meeting for Sufferings of Philadelphia (Orthodox) Yearly Meeting, 3 mo. 20, 1863, pp. 202–204. A similar report was submitted to the New York (Orthodox) Meeting for Sufferings on 5 mo. 27, 1863, by the committee appointed by that body.

[81] Min. of the Meeting for Sufferings of Philadelphia (Orthodox) Yearly Meeting, 3 mo. 6, 1863, pp. 190–196, and *Friends' Intelligencer*, XX, no. 2, pp. 24–25.

attention, among other things, to the inconsistency of the Pennsylvania Constitution, which exempted conscientious objectors from bearing arms only upon the payment of some equivalent. One remonstrance said, "We ask no special favor or partial legislation, in our behalf; but equal liberty, as secured by the Declaration of Rights, for all who are conscientiously opposed to war and fighting."[82]

The committee of the Meeting for Sufferings of the Orthodox Yearly Meeting which submitted its report on March 20th, said:

> That having all except one Friend prevented by indisposition proceeded to Harrisburg they had the two[83] Memorials laid before the Senate and House of Representatives. In the former, that relative to the infliction of fines on those conscientiously scrupulous against bearing arms was read, and both the documents were referred to the respective Committees appointed by the two Houses to have the subjects referred to under care.
>
> In an interview with the Governor, the ground of the refusal of Friends to participate in any warlike measures was explained, and the objectionable features of the Bill proposed for the imposition of military fines were pointed out. He listened to our remarks with apparent interest and acknowledged the force of our objections made to the Bills under consideration . . . .
>
> Subsequently interviews were had with the Judiciary committee of the Senate and the Military Committee of the House, to which the Memorial respecting military fines had been referred, in both of which full opportunity was afforded for opening the views and feelings of Friends relative to the incompatibility of war with the spirit of the gospel, and their right to act in accordance with their conscientious convictions without subjecting them selves

---

[82] Min. of the Meeting for Sufferings of Philadelphia (Orthodox) Yearly Meeting, 3 mo. 6, 1863, pp. 192–196.

[83] A second memorial was presented at the same time, referring to the proposed exclusion of colored people from the State.

to punishment therefor. The unjust consequences that would attend the carrying out of the provisions of the law, were also pointed out. We were heard respectfully on both occasions, and the remarks made by several of the members gave reason to believe that should any law be enacted on the subject by this Legislature, care would be taken that its provisions should bear lightly upon Friends.

A visit was made to the Attorney General and he furnished with a copy of each Memorial . . . .

(Signed)  James Emlen<br>
Joel Evans<br>
Charles Downing<br>
Charles Evans[84]

On April 17th this same committee reported that a bill had passed the House but had failed in the Senate.[85] Friends in New York were active in the same way, memorializing and interviewing members of their legislative body[86] Friends became even more active as soon as actual drafting commenced. In Philadelphia the Society decided to present to the Provost Marshal of the district within which Friends might be enrolled a statement of the reasons why they could not comply with the requirements of the Conscription Act. The form of such statement follows:

To the Provost Marshal or other proper Officer—

The undersigned is informed that his name is included in a list of persons reported to be drafted in _____ _____ for service in the Army of the United States.

He respectfully represents that he is a member of the Religious Society of Friends and is conscientiously scrupulous against bearing arms or being otherwise concerned in war,

---

[84] Min. of the Meeting for Sufferings of Philadelphia (Orthodox) Yearly Meeting, 3 mo. 20, 1863, pp. 204–205.

[85] *Ibid.*, 4 mo. 17, 1863, p. 206.

[86] Min. of the Meeting for Sufferings of New York (Hicksite) Yearly Meeting, 4 mo. 6, 1863, and 5 mo. 25, 1863.

and on this ground he cannot conform himself to the draft, procure a substitute, pay the $300. provided by the law, or any other sum as a commutation for military service, and he respectfully asks to be released therefrom.[87]

A committee of twenty-three members was also appointed to assist drafted Friends in upholding their testimony against war. In New England Yearly Meeting a special meeting was called to consider what should be done about the draft. The provost marshals were asked to defer action on drafted Friends until "Friends should have time to meet together, and confer upon the subject." Apparently most of the provost marshals agreed to do this.[88] In Western and New England Yearly Meetings committees were appointed to proceed to Washington to appear before the proper authorities on behalf of drafted Friends.[89]

Religious denominations other than Friends were, in the meantime, not inactive. The Benedictine Order of Monks had already been released from military service as far back as November 28, 1862,[90] but in June, 1863, they appealed to President Lincoln on behalf of Catholic priests, who were not included in the original order of discharge.[91] There is no record of any action having been taken on this second appeal. The Religious Order of the Holy Cross likewise petitioned for relief on September 28, 1863, stating their willingness, however, to serve as chaplains and

---

[87] Min. of the Meeting for Sufferings of Philadelphia (Orthodox) Yearly Meeting, 7 mo. 22, 1863, p. 213. See also Min. of the Meeting for Sufferings of New York (Orthodox) Yearly Meeting, 8 mo. 6, 1863, p. 184, for similar action taken by that Meeting, and *The Friend*, XXXVI, no. 46, pp. 367–368.

[88] Min. of the Meeting for Sufferings of New England Yearly Meeting, 7 mo. 30, 1863, p. 286 et seq.

[89] Min. of the Meeting for Sufferings of Western Yearly Meeting, 7 mo. 21, 1863, pp. 61–62, and of New England Yearly Meeting, 8 mo. 19, 1863, pp. 289–290. See also *Report of Commission I*, pp. 38–39.

[90] *Official Records*, Series 3, III, p. 333.

[91] *Ibid.*, pp. 333–336; 341–345.

nurses.[92]   The Episcopal Church petitioned the Government for the relief of its ministers, but without success. Most of the smaller religious groups carried their appeals direct to the President, rather than to Congress or to the committees on military affairs, and their appeals were usually quite moderate in tone.[93]

The various interpretive circulars issued by the Provost Marshal General's office of the War Department from time to time all clearly showed that those conscientiously opposed to bearing arms could avail themselves of the commutation clause or the right of substitution, but in no other way could they be excused.[94] Of special interest was the opinion of Colonel Joseph Holt, Judge Advocate General of the Army, expressed in Circular #61 under date of August 1, 1863. The opinion read:

> 'Persons having conscientious scruples in regard to bearing arms are not on that account exempt. They are not found in the list of exempted classes, and the act expressly declares that no persons but those enumerated in that list shall be exempt. The Society of Friends, and others entertaining similar sentiments, if drafted, may find relief from their scruples in the employment of substitutes, or in the payment of the $300.'[95]

Toward the latter part of the year 1863 Secretary of War Stanton realized that there was a possibility of Congress passing a more stringent draft law and he sought some means of placating the Society of Friends should such a measure be passed. On November 6th, Colonel James B. Fry, the Provost Marshal General, in a report to Stanton, recommended that the commutation provision in the draft

---

[92] *Ibid.*, pp. 844–845.
[93] Shannon, Fred Albert. *op. cit.*, II, p. 256.
[94] Circulars #17 (June 2, 1863), #34 (June 30, 1863), #61 (August 1, 1863), and #82, amended (September 13, 1863).
[95] *Official Records*, Series 3, III, p. 606.

law should be abolished or at least limited to cases of those who could not conscientiously serve in a military capacity.[96]

When two members of the Society of Friends from the Baltimore (Orthodox) Yearly Meeting called on Stanton in reference to two conscripted Quakers early in November, he took the opportunity to make a proposal to the Society, which he hoped might be a way out of the difficulties under which he labored. As the report of the two Friends stated:

> The Secretary set forth with much feeling and stress the embarrassment which our position caused the Government, and our own Society, as well as himself personally in his efforts to grant us exemption unconditionally, for which he had no law. He spoke of a large draft which will soon be enforced, and the necessity of some definite settled course for him to pursue.
>
> He wished Friends to have a general Conference of their Committees to consider a proposition from him, 'which he believed would satisfy them and relieve him, and the Government.' And he expects to hear from them in relation to it. He proposes to create a Special Fund for the benefit of the Freedmen, and to exempt Friends from Military Service upon the payment of $300. into this fund. Such payment not to be as in other cases to the District Provost Marshal, but to his fiscal Agent at Washington to be credited on his books to the Freedmen, and that Friends can have the disbursement of it through their own agents, and laborers. He expressed deep interest in organized, and individual efforts of Friends to elevate the moral, and physical condition of the manumitted Slaves, and was 'willing to accept this medium as a relief for our members from the draft—the only legal mode in his power.'
>
> Our Committee informed him that they would convey the result of their interview to Friends generally. After a

---

[96] Report of Secretary of War and Postmaster General, 38th Cong., Sess. I, V, p. 113.

time of serious deliberation without entering upon the proposition itself, this Meeting [for Sufferings of the Baltimore (Orthodox) Yearly Meeting] concluded to lay the foregoing report before the several Meetings for Sufferings on this Continent inviting them to appoint Committees to meet in Conference in this City at 9 o'clock A.M. on 2d day 12th month [7th] 1863 to consider the whole subject believing that the time has come for our widely spread Society to have some definite, and settled understanding with the Government in relation to Drafts, that are now and soon will be ordered.[97]

Accordingly, committees from New England, New York, Ohio, Indiana, Western, and Baltimore Yearly Meetings met in Baltimore on December 7th to discuss the proposal of Secretary Stanton. Iowa Yearly Meeting could not be convened in time to send delegates, and Philadelphia Yearly Meeting took separate action.[98] It was the first time during the War that Friends had met in common to discuss their conscientious scruples.

The Conference united in adopting a minute which reemphasized the importance of Friends' testimony against war.

That to render other service as an equivalent, for or in lieu of requisitions for military purposes, is a compromise of a vital principle which we feel conscientiously bound to support under all circumstances, and notwithstanding any trials to which we may be subjected. But while thus recording our sense of obligation to maintain in all its fulness and purity, this testimony to our belief of the imperative duty of

[97] Min. of the Meeting for Sufferings of Baltimore (Orthodox) Yearly Meeting, 11 mo. 21, 1863, quoted in the *Bulletin of Friends' Historical Society*, IV, no. 1, pp. 15–16. See also Min. of the Meeting for Sufferings of Indiana Yearly Meeting, 12 mo. 1, 1863, pp. 327–329; of Western Yearly Meeting, 12 mo. 2, 1863, pp. 74–76; and of New England Yearly Meeting, 12 mo. 1, 1863, p. 291 et seq.

[98] Min. of the Meeting for Sufferings of Philadelphia (Orthodox) Yearly Meeting, 12 mo. 4, 1863, pp. 218–219.

abstaining from all wars and of regarding sacredly the rights of conscience, we have been introduced afresh into sympathy with those now in authority in the General Government, in the peculiar difficulties and trials in which they are involved. We gratefully appreciate the kindness evidenced at all times by the President and Secretary of War, when we have applied to them for relief from suffering for conscience' sake, and honor them for their clearly manifested regard for religious liberty.[99]

The minute went on to say that Friends had no intention of shirking the duties of good citizenship or of failing to relieve distress, especially among the freedmen, by the expression of the above sentiments.

A committee, composed of Francis T. King of Baltimore, Charles F. Coffin of Indiana, and Samuel Boyd Tobey of New England, was appointed to visit Washington in order to have an interview with Secretary Stanton. At an adjourned meeting of the Baltimore Conference, December 8th, this committee reported that a conference with the Secretary had been granted readily, that he had restated his original proposition and had even gone further.

He said that if any Meeting or body of Friends chose to place funds in his hands in advance, to a greater amount than would be requisite to cover all their members who would be likely to be Drafted he would receive their funds and would release all such as should be Drafted and apply the funds as previously proposed [i.e. to the relief of the freedmen]. He voluntarily observed that he would hold this plan open, and that the Society in general, or any Meeting or individual Friend, might avail themselves of it.

When he found that Friends firmly maintained their conviction that a commutation fee would be considered as infringing the rights of conscience:

[99] Min. of the Meeting for Sufferings of Indiana Yearly Meeting, 12 mo. 22, 1863, pp. 333–334.

He said he could understand no such abstraction as that
—that it was a work of mercy, and in accordance with the
commands of Christ, and that if our members did not
choose to accept so liberal an offer, he could do no more for
them, and the law would have to take its effect.[100]

The Conference then minuted its conviction that the
gathering had not been in vain. It exhorted young Friends
to be patient and to trust in God and exhorted older
Friends to give wise counsel and advice. A committee of
nine Friends from the various Yearly Meetings was appointed "to watch over the legislation of Congress and the
operations of the Draft and to act in such way for the
relief of Friends as Truth may direct, with full power, if
they deem it advisable, to call together again this conference."[101]

Strangely enough, there came soon after the close of this
Baltimore Conference of Friends a circular letter of instructions from the Adjutant General's office to each of
the assistant provost-marshal-generals, providing for the
parole of conscientious objectors until called for. This
was before Congress had taken any action on the subject
of exemptions. It was a distinct victory for Friends and
for those who sympathized with their views, and ulti-
mately proved a solution for most of Friends' conscientious
difficulties. The order was dated December 15, 1863, and
was worded as follows:

The Provost-Marshal-General directs me to inform you
that, in accordance with orders from the War Department,
persons who establish the fact before boards of enrollment
that they are conscientiously opposed to bearing arms and
to paying the commutation money for exemption from

[100] *Bulletin of Friends' Historical Society*, IV, no. 1, p. 21. Also Min. of Meeting for Sufferings of Indiana Yearly Meeting, 12 mo. 22, 1863, pp. 337–338.

[101] Min. of Meetings for Sufferings of Indiana Yearly Meeting, 12 mo. 22,
1863, p. 340; of New England Yearly Meeting, 1 mo. 1, 1864, p. 299; and of
New York (Orthodox) Yearly Meeting, 1 mo. 4, 1864, pp. 195–200.

draft, and that they belong to a religious society whose creed forbids them to serve in the Army or to pay commutation money, shall when drafted be put on parole by the provost-marshal of the district in which they were drafted, to report when called for.[102]

As a result of the Baltimore Conference and of the new Enrollment Bill, which came before the 38th Congress early in December, a new flood of memorials was sent to Lincoln and Congress by the Society of Friends and others.[103] The Amana Society of Iowa was the first to petition Congress, on December 23rd,[104] and the Society of Friends, through its various Yearly Meetings, memorialized Congress time and time again while the Bill was under debate.[105] One of these memorials is unusual in the stress which it laid on the dangers of the "hereafter" for those who performed military service. It said, in part:

Your Memorialists, whilst citizens of the United States, of well known loyalty, are also Christians, who feel bound to yield a literal obedience to the injunctions of Christ, and hence feel absolutely restrained, under the most solemn obligations, from all participation in war.

Your Memorialists submit that the paramount obligations of conscience are solemnly recognized in the Constitution under which it is our privilege to live, by the oath or affirmation prescribed for the President of the United States, and by all the officers of Government who make similar pledges of faithfulness. It is assumed that such obligations are binding and reliable, because their violation would inflict a *stain* upon the conscience, and affect our

[102] *Official Records*, Series 3, III, p. 1173.

[103] Min. of the Meeting for Sufferings of Philadelphia (Orthodox) Yearly Meeting, 12 mo. 18, 1863, p. 220; of Indiana Yearly Meeting, 12 mo. 22, 1863, p. 342; of Western Yearly Meeting, 12 mo. 31, 1863, pp. 80–82; of New England Yearly Meeting, 1 mo. 1, 1864, pp. 293–300; and Min. of Philadelphia (Hicksite) Yearly Meeting, 1864, pp. 16–19.

[104] *Cong. Globe*, XLIV, Pt. 1, p. 95.

[105] *Cong. Globe*, XLIV, Pt. 1, pp. 100, 144, 151, 205, and 262.

hopes of happiness in a future state. If then any such
officer were required by any act of Congress, to violate his
oath of office, he would undoubtedly refuse, and brave all
the consequences;—because his condition in this life is as
nothing compared with his happiness in eternity. It is
upon precisely the same grounds, and under the same obligations of conscience, that your Memorialists cannot perform military service; nor compound by the payment of
money, nor otherwise provide for a service from the performance of which they feel restrained by the law of Christ.
It would contravene a command which they consider binding upon *them;* and would become a stain upon their
conscience, and jeopard their hopes of happiness in eternity.[106]

The type and extent of action taken by various Quaker
delegations at Washington was well explained in a report
to the Meeting for Sufferings of the Indiana Yearly Meeting, at its meeting on June 22, 1864.

The committee appointed by the Baltimore Conference
to watch over the legislation of Congress, etc. gave prompt
attention to the meetings of Congress. Several of the Friends
visited Washington City repeatedly, and had interviews
with many of the members of Congress and collectively, had
at different times very interesting interviews with the Military Committees of both Houses of Congress. These Committees received our Friends kindly, and gave them ample
time fully to represent the views of Friends, and the grounds
upon which they are founded and heard them with much
politeness and interest saying that 'although they had much
unfinished business before them there was none of more importance than the rights of conscience' and they asked many
questions, not in controversy but for information. All the
Meetings for Sufferings which were represented in the
[Baltimore] Conference, had forwarded petitions to Con-

<hr>

[106] Min. of the Meeting for Sufferings of New York (Orthodox) Yearly
Meeting, 1 mo. 4, 1864, pp. 204–5.

gress asking for unconditional exemption on the grounds of the right of conscience. These were all before the Military Committee[s] and our Friends in their interviews maintained the same grounds. Some of the members were unhesitatingly opposed to granting the exemption, but a large majority seemed disposed to favor the views of Friends as far as they could consistently with their duty to their constituents; to many the position of Friends seemed new and strange and much interest was shown in the investigation of it.[107]

Another delegation, which reported even more promptly (January 25th) was one from New York. The report read:

We proceeded promptly to Washington, being joined on the way by a deputation from Baltimore Meeting for Sufferings, and subsequently by others from New England and Ohio. We had very free interviews with the Military Committees of both Houses—our Memorial was read in both, and received marked attention, especially the account of the treatment of our members who had been forced into the army, both North and South: many questions were elicited from the Committees, and full opportunity was given the deputations to explain and illustrate the Scriptural views of Friends on the subject of war. One member of the House was so much interested with our Memorial that he requested a copy should be sent to every Senator and Member of the House, which was done; and it was also duly presented to each House.

We had private opportunities with a number of Senators and Members of the House, and found a general feeling prevailed that Friends ought not be compelled to serve in the Army against their religious convictions; but difficulties presented as to their release by legislation.

We think the course taken by Friends generally in

[107] Min. of the Meeting for Sufferings of Indiana Yearly Meeting, 6 mo. 22, 1864, pp. 343–344.

memorializing Congress on this subject, has not been without its influence for good.[108]

The activity of these delegations, as evidenced by the preceding reports, could only have been exceeded by the patience of the legislators who had to listen to their pleadings.

The question of exempting ministers of the gospel was raised again in connection with the new Conscription Bill as it had been in the original Act of March 3, 1863. Senator Dixon, of Connecticut, asked leave of the Senate, on December 22, 1863, to amend further Section 2 of the Act by inserting the words, "all persons recognized as clergymen or religious ministers by the ecclesiastical authority of the denomination or communion of which they are members." He called attention to the fact that the original bill had been passed in a hurry toward the end of the last session, and that since that time public opinion had moved steadily in favor of the exemption which he proposed. Later in his speech he said, "I do not see any force in the argument that any exemption which would apply to the clergy may be equally claimed by any individual or sect alleging conscientious scruples. A clergyman's profession is a fact—a fact with certain consequences, recognized by the common judgment of mankind. The other claim of exemption is grounded on an opinion, which not only may be wrong, but in the common judgment of mankind is wrong." Dixon's amendment was rejected, however, by a vote of 33 to 9.[109]

When the question again rose in the Senate, on January 14, 1864, Senator James Harlan, of Iowa, proposed that conscientious objectors should be treated as noncombatants the same as ministers. The amendment to the act

---

[108] Min. of the Meeting for Sufferings of New York (Orthodox) Yearly Meeting, 1 mo. 25, 1864, p. 208.

[109] Cong. Globe, XLIV, Pt. 1, pp. 84–85.

then read as follows: "That ministers of the gospel and members of religious denominations conscientiously opposed to the bearing of arms may, when drafted into the military service, be considered non-combatants, and shall be assigned by the Secretary of War to duty in the hospitals or to the care of freedmen, or shall pay the sum of $300. to such person as the Secretary of War shall designate to receive it, to be applied to the benefit of the sick and wounded soldiers; and such drafted persons shall then be exempt from draft during the time for which they shall have been drafted."[110]

In the discussion which followed this proposed amendment, the attitude of the Society of Friends was best represented by Senator John C. Ten Eyck, of New Jersey. He explained clearly their opposition not only to military service, but to any substitute therefor.

One of the objects of the amendment is to relieve the religious Society of Friends from the burden of this bill, and the Senator from Rhode Island has stated very truly the difficulties to which members of that society have been heretofore subjected, and the persecutions, to adopt his language, that have been heaped upon them in regard to the performance of military service. If we intend to do them a favor and to relieve them from the consequences of this act, I respectfully submit that we must go further. We must not only relieve them from the draft, but from the liability of paying the commutation money, for I have always understood that Friends, as they call themselves, not only object to the performance of military service, but to the payment of any fine or commutation in lieu thereof; and many of them, even who were possessed of large estates, have lain for months in jail rather than violate what they understand to be a principle of their faith by paying a miserable fine. . . . In all the petitions and in all the proceedings as published coming from this very large

---

[110] *Ibid.*, p. 204.

respectable class of citizens in the United States, I have seen the objection raised to both features of the bill, and, to adopt their language, they bear testimony as strongly against the payment of the money as they do against going into the field.[111]

It was pointed out by other Senators that the question of military service among Friends was largely an individual matter, and that therefore it would be just as wrong to exempt the Society as a whole as it would be to exempt Unitarians, for example, just because their founder, Channing, wrote a profound and able essay on the terrible character of war. It was mentioned likewise that to exempt all ministers would excuse the entire Amana Society, of Iowa, because each member of that body was considered a minister. After further discussion, chiefly among Senators Henry B. Anthony, of Rhode Island, John Conness, of California, James H. Lane, of Kansas, James W. Grimes, of Iowa, James R. Doolittle, of Wisconsin, and James Dixon, of Connecticut, the amendment was adopted, with only slight changes.[112] Twenty-four voted in favor of the amendment: the noes were not counted.

On January 18th the question of exempting conscientious objectors was again raised in the Senate by Senator Anthony's proposal:

> That any person drafted into the military service of the United States, who is conscientiously unable to perform military service, or pay commutation therefor, by reason of his religious scruples against bearing arms, may apply by petition to any judge of any court of the United States for the circuit or district wherein he resides, setting forth the facts; whereupon the said judge shall proceed summarily to hear and determine the case; and if it shall appear that such petition is true, and that such petitioner shall

---

[111] *Ibid.*, p. 205.
[112] *Ibid.*, pp. 205–208.

have maintained a consistent character in accordance with his well-known religious professions, incompatible with military service, the judge shall certify the fact to the board of enrollment for the enrollment district in which such petitioner shall reside, and upon the receipt of such certificate the board of enrollment shall take no further proceedings, nor shall any proceeding whatever be taken to enforce such conscientious person into the military service of the United States under the draft, or for the period of three years from the date of such certificate.[113]

Senator TenEyck quoted from a memorial which he had received 'that morning from the Ohio Yearly Meeting of Friends, held January 8, 1864, at Damascus, to support his contention that Quakers ought to be exempted entirely, or not at all. The memorial stated, "' that the Society of Friends has from its rise been conscientious against fighting or bearing arms under any circumstances, or paying an equivalent in lieu thereof .... We therefore respectfully ask for exemption from military service, and from all penalties for the non-performance thereof.'" Senator Charles Sumner, of Massachusetts, supported the amendment proposed by Senator Anthony, and in doing so referred to a case of conscientious objection which had come to his attention, illustrative of the hardship which occurred under the existing law.[114] The proposal was lost, however, without any count having been made of the ayes and noes.[115]

The Act of February 24, 1864, as finally approved, provided under Section 17:

That members of religious denominations, who shall by oath or affirmation declare that they are conscientiously opposed to the bearing of arms, and who are prohibited

---

[113] *Ibid.*, pp. 254–255.
[114] See Chapter V of this study.
[115] *Cong. Globe*, XLIV, Pt. 1, p. 255.

from doing so by the rules and articles of faith and practice of said religious denominations, shall when drafted into the military service, be considered non-combatants, and shall be assigned by the Secretary of War to duty in the hospitals, or to the care of freedmen, or shall pay the sum of three hundred dollars to such person as the Secretary of War shall designate to receive it, to be applied to the benefit of the sick and wounded soldiers: *Provided,* That no person shall be entitled to the provisions of this section unless his declaration of conscientious scruples against bearing arms shall be supported by satisfactory evidence that his deportment has been uniformly consistent with such declaration.[116]

If Secretary Stanton and others hoped that the above provisions would meet all the demands of Friends, they were to be disappointed. Unquestionably many members of the Society of Friends, in common with other non-combatant sects, were entirely satisfied with the liberal allowances made for their conscientious scruples against bearing arms, and all Friends appreciated the motives behind the enactment of Section 17, but those who felt most deeply the conviction that military service, or any substitute therefor, was wrong, could not be satisfied even with hospital service or service with the freedmen. As an editorial in *The Friend* well expressed it:

While, therefore, we fully appreciate the good motives which, we doubt not, prompted the adoption of the section above quoted, and hail it as a cheering indication of the advance of correct views upon this important subject, we do not see how it can relieve our members, or they consistently avail themselves of any of its provisions; inasmuch as to be sent into the hospitals or serve as nurses, &c., or to be assigned to the care of freedmen, is just as much a penalty imposed for obeying the requisitions of our religion in not performing military service, as is the

---

[116] *U. S. Statutes at Large,* (38 Cong. Sess. I, chap. 13) XIII, p. 9.

fine of three hundred dollars. It matters not whether the commutation for military service is money or personal service in some other department; in either case it is an assumption on the part of the government of a right to oblige the subject to violate his conscience, or to exact a penalty if he elects to obey God rather than man.[117]

An editorial at this same time, in the *Friends' Intelligencer*, on the subject of the noncombatant provisions of the Conscription Act led to much misunderstanding among members of the Society, some interpreting it as a recommendation to take advantage of the terms of the Act, others protesting that its meaning was quite the opposite.[118]

In most instances Friends were allowed to act as they deemed best. The Meeting for Sufferings of the Indiana Yearly Meeting recorded that:

> . . . while some of our members may feel it to be their religious duty not to accept the provisions of our Government for the relief of Friends, there may be others who feel that they can, with consciences void of offense, avail themselves of the relief thus generously afforded, and it is the judgment of this meeting that Friends should exercise toward such a large measure of Christian charity and be forward to render them advice and pecuniary assistance as occasion may require. . . .[119]

It is also apparent that Western, Ohio, and New York Meetings for Sufferings made provisions for their members to exercise individual judgment as to how far they might conscientiously act under the exemption clause.[120]

Before many months had passed it was evident that another draft would be necessary to fill the ranks of the

---

[117] *The Friend*, XXXVII, no. 27, p. 215.

[118] *Friends' Intelligencer*, XXI, pp. 457–458; 518–519; 554; 599–600; 631–632; 679.

[119] Min. of the Meeting for Sufferings of Indiana Yearly Meeting, 9 mo. 27, 1864, pp. 351–352.

[120] *Friends' Intelligencer*, XXI, no. 40, pp. 631–632.

Union Army. A bill was therefore introduced in the House which abolished the commutation privilege but retained the provision for hiring substitutes. No mention was made of conscientious objectors in the original measure. On June 27, 1864, Representative Thaddeus Stevens, of Pennsylvania, offered a substitute measure, which embodied, in Section 9, a provision for those scrupulous of bearing arms. The section was worded as follows:

> Sec. 9. *And be it further enacted*, That the law with regard to persons conscientiously opposed to bearing arms shall not be altered or affected by this act, except so far as it regards the amount of money to be paid for exemptions.[121]

His substitute measure was voted down, however, after a lengthy debate in which Section 9 seemed to play no part. The following day Stevens again supported conscientious objectors by offering as an additional section to another substitute measure, then under consideration, the following:

> *And be it further enacted*, That nothing contained in this act shall be construed to alter or in any way affect the law relative to those conscientiously opposed to bearing arms.[122]

This proposed addition to the bill was carried by a vote of 79 to 64 with 39 members not voting, even though no agreement could be reached on the broader questions of commutation and substitution for personal service.[123]

Throughout the remaining debates on the bill the section relating to conscientious persons was not objected to. Even the committee of the two Houses, which put the bill in final form, made changes only in the wording of the provision. The Act became law on July 4th. The privilege of commutation was abolished, but Section 10 provided:

---

[121] *Cong. Globe*, XLIV, Pt. 4, p. 3316.
[122] *Ibid.*, p. 3354.
[123] *Ibid.*, p. 3355.

That nothing contained in this act shall be construed to alter, or in any way affect, the provisions of the seventeenth section of an act approved February twenty-fourth, eighteen hundred and sixty-four, entitled 'An act to amend an act entitled "An act for enrolling and calling out the national forces, and for other purposes,"' approved March third, eighteen hundred and sixty-three.[124]

The Government thereafter, and for the duration of the war, respected more and more the wishes of those conscientiously opposed to bearing arms, by not forcing them into any kind of service against their will. A circular letter from the Provost-Marshal-General's Office, under date of November 8, 1864,[125] shows that, officially, there was no relaxation of the law relating to noncombatants, but actually there were many instances reported by the Society of Friends in which drafted objectors were merely paroled until called for.[126] The situation was well summarized in an editorial in *The Friend*.

---

[124] *U. S. Statutes at Large*, (38 Cong., Sess. I, chap. 237) XIII, p. 380.

[125] The letter was worded as follows: "Drafted persons who claim the benefit of section 17 of the act approved February 24, 1864, and desire to avail themselves thereof, must first satisfy the board of enrollment in their respective districts that they are non-combatants, within the meaning of the law.

The provost marshal will then give a certificate to this effect to the drafted person, and upon presentation of this certificate, to the receiver of commutation money, he will receive the $300 (the amount fixed by the Secretary of War) and issue his receipt therefor in triplicate—the 'duplicate' thereof to be presented by the drafted person to the board of enrollment for their action.

Section 17 of the act approved February 24, 1864, prescribes that the commutation money paid by non-combatants shall be applied to the benefit of sick and wounded soldiers.

All funds received from those persons must, therefore, be deposited by receivers to the 'credit of the Treasurer of the United States on account of the appropriation for the benefit of sick and wounded soldiers,' and they must be particular to see that certificates of deposit are made out in accordance with these instructions.

JAMES B. FRY
Provost Marshal General"

[126] *The Friend*, XXXVII, no. 47, p. 375. See also Chap. V of this study.

So far as our knowledge extends, there has been no instance where a drafted Friend has faithfully and properly acted in conformity with the religion he professed, that the Government, on a representation of the circumstances, has not, sooner or later, ordered his discharge until called for. . . . We believe the ground on which Friends feel themselves restrained from participation in warlike measures, is generally better understood than heretofore, and their consistent course more fully estimated by reasonable men; . . .

We are persuaded that those Friends who have officially recommended their fellow members to acquiesce in the commutations proposed, 'as far as they can feel a freedom to do,' were hardly aware of the full extent and character of the service demanded in either position to which a drafted Friend may be assigned, or they would have hesitated before giving such advice.[127]

As the Presidential election of 1864 approached Friends were again disturbed by the question of voting. Some members of the Society were in no doubt as to their moral obligations. The writer of the following letter was among their number.

Here then we have the issue. Those who justify war for the extension of slavery, and desire to fill up our western Territories with slaves from Africa, will cast their votes for McClellan and his associates, whose voice and actions tend to this end. But they who wish . . . that, as far as possible, our vast territories may be peopled by a homogeneous free population, will cast their votes for Abraham Lincoln.

Members of the Society of Friends, who remember his kindness and sympathy for their brethren under trying circumstances, will not fail in the exercise of a gratitude which will, at the same time, accord with their principles of action.[128]

---

[127] *The Friend*, XXXVIII, no. 9, p. 71.

Many Quakers, however, were not so sure of their obligations as the writer of the above letter. Their dilemma was explained by the Editor of *The Friend*, and as usual in such cases, the matter was left to their individual consciences.

We have refrained from publishing anything sent to us respecting voting at the approaching Presidential election, believing the subject to be one better left to the serious consideration and conscientious action of Friends individually, rather than open the matter for discussion in the columns of our journal. Much may be said for and against our members availing themselves of their right to exercise the elective franchise at the present time, and under existing circumstances, but it is a question that should be settled by each one in accordance with his feeling of religious duty, which, judging from the communications received, we cannot but believe, differ widely in different honest-hearted individuals.[129]

The year 1864 closed and the year 1865 opened without any alteration in the status of the Northern conscientious objector. Apparently the method persued by the government of releasing such men on parole "until called for" worked satisfactorily from all standpoints. It was the belief of some Friends that unconditional exemption would have been granted had it not been for the effect such exemptions would have had on persons not conscientiously opposed to the bearing of arms.[130]

---

[128] Letter to *Friends' Review*, XVIII, no. 10, p. 157, from "T" (anon.), dated at New York, 10 mo. 24, 1864.

[129] *The Friend*, XXXVIII, no. 8, p. 63. See also *Friends' Review*, XVIII, no. 10, pp. 152–153 for editorial of a similar nature.

[130] In a report to the Meeting for Sufferings of the Baltimore (Orthodox) Yearly Meeting, 11 mo. 23, 1864, the special committee appointed to memorialize Congress made the following statement: "We feel satisfied that a majority of both Houses would have granted Friends unconditional exemption from Military Service, had they not believed it would embarrass the Government when the Draft was seriously resisted in several parts of the country."

The last enrollment act to be passed by Congress before the cessation of hostilities was called "An Act to amend the several Acts heretofore passed to provide for the Enrolling and Calling out the National Forces, and for other Purposes," and became a law on March 3, 1865. It contained no mention of those opposed to the bearing of arms on grounds of conscience.[131]

One of the last petitions for relief from military service to be presented to Congress was that of the Christadelphians, one of the smallest of the noncombatant sects. Its presentation was rendered unnecessary, however, by the cessation of hostilities.

*To the Senators and Republicans [sic] of the United States of America in Congress assembled.*

Gentlemen.—Your petitioners respectfully submit that they belong to a 'very small remnant' of that sect, which, in the days of the apostles, was 'everywhere spoken against,' because of its testimony 'against the world-rulers of the darkness of that age, and the spirituals of the wickedness in the high places of the State' (Eph. vi. 12). This has been their testimony in all ages of their standing before the powers that be. . . . The Enrolment Act recently passed provides no exemption for the brethren of Christ, who, owing allegiance only to him, positively refuse, under any circumstance whatever, to shed the blood of their fellow men in the service of any of the sin-powers of the world. The Divine Word teaches them, that wars and fighting comes of men's lusts. The brethren of Christ have no sympathy with such conflicts; and ask of the world-rulers, to be kind enough to let them alone. . . .

In conclusion, . . . your petitioners would add, that the brethren of Christ in Richmond, Lunenburg, and King William Counties, Virginia, and Jefferson County, Mississippi, have, under the influence of the principles herein avowed, refused to bear arms in the Confederate service,

---

[131] *U. S. Statutes at Large,* (38 Cong., Sess. II, chap. 79) XIII, pp. 487-491.

as we hereby do in that of the United States; and that a law was passed by the Confederate Congress recognizing their refusal as lawful and right.[132]

The last delegation of Quakers to be sent to Washington at the close of the war, was sent, not to protest against warlike measures, but to tender to President Johnson and his Cabinet their sympathy upon the occasion of Lincoln's death, and to express their own feeling of sadness at the loss of so true a friend. Delegations were sent from Baltimore, New England, Ohio, Indiana, and Philadelphia Yearly Meetings. Other Yearly Meetings, although unrepresented, heartily sympathized with the efforts of their fellow members to express their feelings of appreciation and sorrow.[133]

---

[132] Walker, C. C. *Christ and War*, pp. 27–28.

[133] Min. of the Meeting for Sufferings of Baltimore (Orthodox) Yearly Meeting, quoted in *Bulletin of Friends' Historical Society*, IV, no. 1, pp. 23–24; Min. of Meeting for Sufferings of Indiana Yearly Meeting (6 mo. 1, 1865), pp. 358–363, 364–366; Min. of the Philadelphia (Hicksite) Yearly Meeting, 1865, p. 16; and *Friends' Review*, XVIII, no. 39, p. 617.

# Chapter III

# Struggle in the South for Political Recognition

FROM the very beginning of the war the struggle for the recognition of the rights of conscience was more severe in the South than in the North. The reasons for this have already been mentioned.[1] It is true that the constitutions of Alabama and Texas exempted from militia duty those who were averse to the bearing of arms on grounds of conscience, but only upon the payment of an equivalent for personal service;[2] the constitutions of Mississippi, Tennessee, and Virginia left the matter in the hands of the legislature;[3] and the fundamental law of Arkansas, Florida, Georgia, Louisiana, North Carolina, and South Carolina made no provision at all for those scrupulous against military service.[4] Even in those states which legislated on the subject, the status of objectors was far from satisfactory.[5]

The warlike preparations of the Confederacy made those with peaceful principles deeply apprehensive, especially after the passage of the first important military measure by the Provisional Congress on March 6, 1861. This law was to provide "for the Public Defense" and for the enlistment of volunteers, but it had no direct effect on those who were opposed to the bearing of arms.[6]

On April 8, 1861, the Friends of the South took their

---

[1] Introduction, p. 4.

[2] Thorpe, Francis Newton. *The Federal and State Constitutions, etc.*, I, p. 105; VI, p. 3559.

[3] *Ibid.*, IV, p. 2059; VI, p. 3437; VII, p. 3845.

[4] *Ibid.*, I, p. 280; II, pp. 674, 791; III, p. 1421; V, p. 2791; VI, p. 3263.

[5] Weeks, Stephen B. *Southern Quakers and Slavery*, pp. 194–197.

[6] *Confederate Statutes at Large*, I, pp. 45–46 (Prov. Cong., Sess. I, chap. 26).

first definite action to provide for the coming conflict. At a stated gathering of the Meeting for Sufferings of North Carolina Yearly Meeting on the above date the following minute was recorded:

> This meeting being introduced into deep feeling on account of the disturbed condition of our country and the probability from a change in the laws of the State of new trials coming on friends—appoints the following committee to take the matter into consideration, and if they think best to prepare a short declaration of our principles particularly in regard to war for circulation among our members and others—Danl Barker, Ishan Cox, Jno Carter, Jonathan Harris, Nereus Mendenhall and Joseph Newlen.[7]

This committee prepared such an address for the members of the Yearly Meeting and others, but it was referred back to them by the Meeting for Sufferings for certain minor alterations.[8]  The address was finally approved on July 1, 1861, and "it was directed that each of the monthly meetings be furnished with a copy."[9]  At the same time the Meeting for Sufferings approved sending petitions to the Congress of the United States and the Confederate Congress, praying for a speedy restoration of peace. Neither of these petitions ever reached the body to which it was addressed.[10]

In September, 1861, the Goose Creek Monthly Meeting of Virginia prepared a statement of Friends' principles in order that there might be no misapprehensions as to the position they proposed to take.  Samuel M. Janney, Jesse Hoge, and Elisha Janney were appointed to lay the matter before the Fairfax Monthly Meeting.  The statement said:

---

[7] Min. of the Meeting for Sufferings of North Carolina Yearly Meeting, 4 mo. 8, 1861 (pages of minute book unnumbered).

[8] *Ibid.*, 6 mo. 3, 1861.

[9] *Ibid.*, 7 mo. 1, 1861.

[10] *Ibid.*, 9 mo. 16, 1861.

In as much as a state of war, now unhappily exists in this country, we deem it our religious duty to take no part in it; and to abstain from every act that would give aid in its prosecution.

Although laws might be passed, with which our principles and clear sense of religious duty would forbid our active compliance, even though there was connected therewith the heaviest penalty; yet the religion we profess, and as we conceive, the true spirit of Christianity, forbid our doing any act in opposition to the laws of the government under which we live. In all cases, not obviously and exclusively between ourselves and our Maker, we believe it to be our solemn duty, faithfully to comply with the laws of the land, or remain entirely passive under them, suffering all penalties.[11]

In the meantime, fighting had commenced, and all intercourse between the North and the South had practically ceased. Additional military measures were taken by the Confederate Government and by the various state governments. As the military measures of May 16 and August 8, 1861, allowed recruiting to be carried on by state agencies, and under state laws,[12] those conscientiously opposed to bearing arms addressed their own state legislatures for relief. North Carolina and Virginia were the states principally involved because these two states contained most of the Friends, Mennonites, and Dunkers of the South.

At a special session of the Meeting for Sufferings of the North Carolina Yearly Meeting, called on September 16, 1861, to consider petitioning the Legislature of North Carolina in reference to the military laws of the State, it was learned that a new law had already been passed similar to the one previously in force, "by which Friends

---

[11] Min. of Goose Creek Monthly Meeting, 9 mo. 10, 1861.

[12] *Confederate Statutes at Large*, I, pp. 114–116, 176 (Prov. Cong., Sess. II, chap. 20 and Sess. III, chap. 20).

and others conscientiously scrupulous against bearing arms [might] be excused."[13]  This law was exceedingly liberal in its provisions for conscientious scruples.  It exempted, in Section 5:

> Persons having scruples of conscience against bearing arms, who shall produce to the captains of their respective districts certificates, signed by the clerks of their respective churches, that they are regular members thereof, and shall make oath or affirmation, before a justice of the peace, that they are, from religious scruples, averse to bearing arms, and shall also produce a certificate from such justice of the peace that such oath or affirmation has been duly made, shall not be compelled to muster or perform military duty except in cases of insurrection or invasion, *or pay any tax for said exemption*,[14] but they shall be subject to taxation in time of insurrection, invasion or war, and also to furnish their quota of men or pay an equivalent.[15]

It was decided, therefore, merely to prepare an address to the members of the Yearly Meeting encouraging them to increased faithfulness in maintaining their testimonies on this and other subjects.[16]  Two Quakers, however,—William Nicholson and Joseph R. Parker, members of the Piny Woods Monthly Meeting,—went to Raleigh in May, during the sittings of the extra session of the Legislature, and interceded with various members in behalf of Quakers.  They 'ere later reimbursed $87.90 for their expenses in connection with this trip, even though the Yearly Meeting had not authorized it.[17]

Denominations other than Friends were also active at

---

[13] *Public Laws of the State of North Carolina*, Second Extra Session, 1861, chap. 17 (Militia Bill) Ratified Sept. 20, 1861.

[14] Italics mine.

[15] *Ibid.*, pp. 23–24.

[16] Min. of the Meeting for Sufferings of North Carolina Yearly Meeting, 9 mo. 16, 1861.

[17] *Ibid.*, 11 mo. 1, 1861.

this time in approaching state governments on behalf of their members. Benjamin F. Moomaw, of the Church of the Brethren, paid a personal visit to his representative in the Virginia Legislature, trying to arouse his interest in behalf of all the peace sects. A petition was also prepared jointly by the Brethren and Mennonites of Virginia, requesting exemption from service in the army.[18] On March 24th, of the following year, on a motion of Representative Gratton, the Virginia House of Delegates, "Resolved, that the committee for courts of justice enquire into the expediency of fixing a commutation to be paid by those persons whose religious tenets forbid them bearing arms."[19] The following day a bill was introduced in the House, providing for the exemption of certain parties on religious grounds,[20] but a substitute measure of Mr. Hopkins was adopted on the 27th, by a vote of 79 to 18, and became a law on March 29, 1862.[21] Section 1 of this Virginia law provided:

That whenever upon application for exemption to the board of exemption it shall appear to said board that the party applying for said exemption is bona fide prevented from bearing arms, by the tenets of the church to which said applicant belongs, and did actually belong at the passage of this act, and further, that said applicant has paid to the sheriff of the county or collector of taxes for the city or town in which said applicant resides, the sum of five hundred dollars, and in addition thereto, the further sum of two per cent of the assessed value of said applicant's taxable property, then the said board, on the presentation of the receipt of said officers for said moneys, and after the said applicant shall have taken an oath or affirmation that

[18] Sanger, Samuel F. and Hays, Daniel. *The Olive Branch*, p. 57.
[19] *Journal of the House of Delegates of the State of Virginia for the Session of 1861–62*, p. 308.
[20] *Ibid.*, p. 310.
[21] *Ibid.*, p. 319–320, 329.

he will sustain the confederate government, and will not in any way give aid and comfort to the enemy of the said confederate government, then the said board shall exempt the said applicant: provided, that whenever said party may be unable, or shall fail to pay the said sum of five hundred dollars, and the tax of two per centum on their property, he shall be employed (when liable to militia duty) in the capacity of teamster, or in such other character as the service may need, which does not require the actual bearing of arms: and provided further, that the persons so exempted do surrender to the board of exemption all arms which they may own to be held subject to the order of the governor, for the public use.[22]

Whem some of the Brethren and Mennonites were forced against their will to join the army in the latter part of the year 1861, before the passage of the above act, direct attempts were made to free them. "State officials were seen and army officers were written to and appealed to in person."[23] For example, Samuel Kline, a Dunker, who lived near Staunton, Virginia, went alone to Richmond on their behalf; in Botetourt and Roanoke Counties Elders Benjamin F. Moomaw, Peter Nininger, Jonas Graybill, and others championed them. In many places, especially in Rockingham and adjacent counties, the Mennonites and Brethren worked together.[24]

As another illustration of the action taken by these people, John Kline wrote a letter to a Colonel Lewis, from Rockingham County, Virginia, under date of December 16, 1861, saying:

'I now desire to approach you on another subject which I would like you to consider and use your influence with the generals and other officers in the army. The subject is

[22] *Acts of the General Assembly of the State of Virginia, Passed in 1861,* chap. 25, pp. 50-51.
[23] Zigler, David H. *A History of the Brethren in Virginia,* p. 98.
[24] *Ibid.,* p. 98.

this: We German Baptists (called Tunkers) do most solemnly believe that the bearing of carnal weapons in order to destroy life, is in direct opposition to the Gospel of Christ, which we accept as the rule of our faith and practice.

... We feel bound to pay our taxes, fines, and to do whatever is in our power which does not conflict with our obligation to God....'[25]

As in the North, the question of paying military taxes and fines was a vexatious one for members of the Society of Friends. The attitude of those in the Confederacy was probably best expressed in a document issued by the Half-Year's Meeting of Friends in Virginia, held October 7, 1861. This statement, which was later endorsed by the North Carolina Yearly Meeting,[26] read in part as follows:

Being thus careful to abstain from war, and everything connected with war, we cannot conscientiously pay any fines that may be imposed upon us, individually, for non-performance of military duty, but rather quietly submit to have the value of the same distrained by the proper officer; yet do we pay all taxes imposed on us as citizens, remembering the injunction, 'Tribute to whom tribute is due, custom to whom custom;' believing that upon the Government rests the responsibility of how they expend this tribute or custom; nor do our views prevent us from contributing our mite toward the relief of the sick and suffering, (soldiers as well as others), but on the contrary we feel it required of us, like the good Samaritan, to bind up the wounds of any we may find by the wayside, to feed the hungry, clothe the naked, and pray for our enemies even though they may have despitefully used and persecuted us.[27]

A new menace to Quakers arose in December, 1861,

---

[25] *Ibid.*, pp. 99–100.

[26] Min. of North Carolina Yearly Meeting, 1861, p. 7.

[27] Min. of the Meeting for Sufferings of North Carolina Yearly Meeting, 11 mo. 1, 1861.

through the attempted passage of an "Ordinance concerning Test Oaths and Sedition" by the Legislature of North Carolina, by which each free male person in the State above sixteen years of age would have been required to appear publicly and renounce all allegiance to the Government of the United States and also promise to "support, maintain and defend the independent Government of the Confederate States." The alternative was banishment in thirty days.[28] This measure was opposed by Friends, as a Society, and by Allen U. Tomlinson and Isham Cox in person. Despite the fact that it was defeated many Friends left the State before the end of the year and attempted to make their way to the North. Several parties of these emigrants were arrested and brought back.[29]

As the war increased in intensity and as the Confederacy required more men to fill the ranks of its armies, Quakers and other noncombatants were forced to assume more aggressive measures in order to protect their conscientious scruples against bearing arms. A special session of the North Carolina Yearly Meeting for Sufferings was held on March 17, 1862, at which a committee of fifteen was appointed to render assistance to any members of the Society who might be drafted, "and if Counsel should be required attended with expenses," they were directed to draw on the Treasurer of the North Carolina Yearly Meeting for the necessary money.[30] This committee rendered some aid, even before the passage of the Confederate Conscription Bill of April 16th, and they were continued for additional service throughout the war.[31]

---

[28] *An Account of the Sufferings of Friends of North Carolina Yearly Meeting*, p. 7.

[29] *Ibid.*, p. 7. See also Crosfield, Joseph. *North Carolina Before and After the War*, in *The Friends' Quarterly Examiner*, III, no. 9, pp. 29–41.

[30] Min. of the Meeting for Sufferings of North Carolina Yearly Meeting, 3 mo. 17, 1862.

[31] *Ibid.*, 4 mo. 14, 1862.

Eight Friends were also appointed to prepare a petition or memorial for the North Carolina Assembly on the subject of relief from military service.[32]  John Carter, Nereus Mendenhall, Isham Cox, Allen U. Tomlinson and William Nicholson were chosen as delegates to attend the legislative sessions with copies of the memorial.[33]  The memorial, which was dated April 14, 1862, was similar to most of the statements issued by the Society of Friends throughout the war period. It was addressed "To the Convention of North-Carolina, in Convention Assembled," and began: "Your petitioners respectfully show that it is one of our fundamental religious principles to bear a faithful testimony against all wars and fightings, and that in consequence we cannot aid in carrying on any carnal war." The memorial went on to explain how this principle of the Society existed from its foundation, and also how the number of members of the Society of Friends in the Confederate States were fewer than 10,000 as compared with some 200,000 in the North. "We may further show that, according to the best information we can obtain, until the present time, Friends of North-Carolina have not been called on to aid in the battle-field or military camp; but now our peaceful principles are in a measure disregarded, *and many of our members are drafted to take part in the conflicting armies, while we understand our brethren in the United States are not.*" The memorial concluded with a plea for the recognition of the religious principles already enunciated.[34] As a result of these efforts the State Government of North Carolina again exempted Friends from military duty, but only upon the payment of a $100. fine.[35]

---

[32] *Ibid.*, 3 mo. 17, 1862.

[33] *Ibid.*, 4 mo. 14, 1862.

[34] Moore, Frank (Editor of) *Rebellion Record*, Supplement, I, p. 752.

[35] *An Account of the Sufferings of Friends of North Carolina Yearly Meeting,* p. 7.

About this same time (April 4, 1862) Jonathan Worth, a Senator, and afterwards State Treasurer, wrote to Allen M. Tomlinson, of the Society of Friends, suggesting work in the State Salt Works as a possible substitute for military service. He said, "I felt extreme solicitude to relieve such of your Society as were drafted, and from Morehead City and Wilmington earnestly pressed it upon the Govr. to allow such as would labor at the Salt Works or send a substitute as a laborer, at a liberal rate of wages, to be excused from military service. He cheerfully assented to it."[36] Apparently this substitution was no more agreeable to Friends than the payment of commutation money, because Worth proceeded to say, "It never occurred to me that you would have any scruples about adopting this plan of relief. . . . I am greatly disappointed and mortified at your decision. . . . If we have unconsciously placed you in a worse position than you were, I hope you will at least allow us credit for the best intentions . . . I sincerely hope you will re-consider your decision—at least so far as to allow such members to accept the proposed alternative without censure from his Society."[37]

On April 16, 1862, the regulation of the draft was removed from individual state control and placed under the jurisdiction of the Confederate Government by the passage of "An act to further provide for the public defense." By this measure substitutes were allowed under conditions to be prescribed by the Secretary of War, but no specific provision was made for conscientious objectors.[38]   On April 12th, however, a few days before the passage of the above act, Senator William L. Yancey, of Alabama, introduced in the Confederate Senate a bill for exempting certain persons from enrollment for service in the army,

---

[36] *The Correspondence of Jonathan Worth*, I, p. 165.
[37] *Ibid.*, p. 166.
[38] *Confederate Statutes at Large*, II, p. 29 (First Cong., Sess. I, chap. 31).

which was referred to the Committee on Military Affairs.[39] The measure finally went to a compromise committee of the two Houses before becoming a law on April 21st.[40] By its terms, ministers of the gospel were exempted in addition to many other enumerated classes.[41] This act only covered cases of conscience on the part of recognized ministers, such as John B. Crenshaw in the Society of Friends, so that the noncombatant sects at once turned their efforts from petitioning the various state governments to petitioning the Confederate Government for relief.

The Friends of North Carolina directed John Carter, Allen U. Tomlinson, Nereus Mendenhall, and Joseph Newlin, "if the way should open for it," to have an interview with the Secretary of War and others in authority, "either personally, by letter or an attorney in regard to military service."[42] This committee corresponded with the Secretary and learned that he had no objection to assigning Friends to service "not requiring them to shed the blood of their fellow men," but he said that no general order to that effect could be made. The committee found that they could take no further action in this direction, and they were therefore released.[43]

Four other Friends were appointed to prepare a memorial to the Confederate Congress, "praying that body to legislate for our relief from Military service."[44] Such a memorial was prepared and approved by the Meeting for Sufferings on August 8th, and Nereus Mendenhall, John Carter, Thomas Kennedy, and Jonathan Harriss were

---

[39] *Journal of Confederate Congress*, II, p. 158.

[40] *Ibid.*, pp. 206, 219, 221.

[41] *Confederate Statutes at Large*, II, pp. 51–52 (First Cong., Sess. I, chap. 74).

[42] Min. of the Meeting for Sufferings of North Carolina Yearly Meeting, 7 mo. 21, 1862.

[43] *Ibid.*, 8 mo. 18, 1862.

[44] *Ibid.*, 7 mo. 21, 1862.

chosen as delegates to present the petition to Congress.[45] On August 26th, William T. Dortch, of North Carolina, presented this memorial in the Senate, and the following day James R. McLean, also of North Carolina, presented it in the House. In each case it was referred to the Committee on Military Affairs for their consideration.[46] Two days later Senator Edward Sparrow, of Louisiana, moved "That the Committee on Military Affairs be discharged from the further consideration of the . . . Memorial of the Society of Friends, of North Carolina, asking to be exempted from the operation of the conscription law." It was so ordered.[47]

On the same day (August 29th) a committee of Friends, composed of John B. Crenshaw, Isham Cox, Nereus Mendenhall, John Carter, and Allen U. Tomlinson presented their case before the Military Committee, of which Mr. Miles, of South Carolina, was Chairman.[48] This same delegation visited Jefferson Davis, who received them with courtesy, but gave them no satisfaction.[49]

The Mennonite and Dunker Churches were also active during the summer of '62. Benjamin F. Moomaw and Jonas Graybill visited their representative in Congress in order to get him to use his influence in behalf of their brethren, "'which he seemed to take a pleasure in doing. He also secured the assistance of a member of the Senate, one of Virginia's ablest men, who, we were informed, made one of the grandest speeches in this case that was ever delivered in a legislature'."[50] A letter was also addressed

---

[45] *Ibid.*, 8 mo. 18, 1862.

[46] *Journal of Confederate Congress*, II, p. 239; V, p. 320.

[47] *Ibid.*, II, p. 246.

[48] *Diary of John B. Crenshaw*, Aug. 29, 1862. Weeks, Stephen B. *Southern Quakers and Slavery*, p. 305.

[49] Cartland, Fernando G. *Southern Heroes*, p. 127.

[50] Moomaw, B. F., quoted in Sanger and Hays, *op. cit.*, p. 57. I have found no record of the speech, referred to above.

by John Kline to Representative John B. Baldwin, of Virginia, on July 23rd, urging that the Virginia State exemption law be recognized by the Confederate Congress. In reply, Baldwin suggested that a petition on the subject might be effective.[51] Such a petition was therefore prepared. It was worded, in part, as follows:

> It may not be amiss to state here, that under the excitement of the hour, indiscreet, and inconsiderate persons, have preferred the charge of Disloyalty, against our Churches, this charge, has not the Semblance of truth in fact, and has doubtless originated, from our faith against bearing arms. We would further state, that Most of our members, embraced in said act of the General Assembly of Virginia, have already payd[sic] the penalty of $500 & 2 per cent, to the officers of the state, and thus fulfilled our contract, and have complied with the law. We only ask Congress, so far to *respect our Rights, our Consciences, and the Act of the state of Virginia, as to Ratify the same*, and we will ever Pray.[52]

This petition was presented in the House by Baldwin on September 1st, but was referred to the Committee on Military Affairs without being read.[53]

Another petition was presented to Hon. B. F. Anderson by Elders Moomaw and Graybill after they had secured the signatures of more than one hundred church members in the Virginia counties of Botetourt, Roanoke, and Franklin.[54] Representative Baldwin presented two additional memorials of the Society of Friends and Dunkers on September 12th, but they were merely referred to the Committee on Military Affairs, as in the case of all such memorials.[55] About the same time, Senator James L. Orr,

---

[51] Zigler, D. H. *op. cit.*, pp. 115–117.
[52] *Ibid.*, p. 118 (facsimilie of the petition).
[53] *Journal of Confederate Congress*, V, p. 336.
[54] Zigler, D. H. *op. cit.*, p. 120.
[55] *Journal of Confederate Congress*, V, p. 379.

of South Carolina, and others presented memorials of the faculty of the Theological Seminary, at Columbia, South Carolina, praying for the exemption of theological students from conscription.[56]

These various petitions and memorials seemed to have the desired effect, because when "An act to amend an act to exempt certain persons from enrollment for service in the Army of the Confederate States, approved April 21, 1862" was under consideration in the Senate, Senator Sparrow, on September 17th, moved to amend the bill by inserting the words "all persons who have been and now are members of the Society of Friends and the Association of Dunkers, in regular membership in their respective denominations." The motion was carried.[57]  On September 30th, Representative Thos. S. Ashe, of North Carolina, urged in the House that exemption to Friends and Dunkers be granted only upon the furnishing of a substitute or the payment of $500. into the Treasury of the Confederacy.  His proposal was readily agreed to.[58] The same day Representative Smith, of North Carolina, moved that the Mennonite Church be included in the provisions of the act.  This was also agreed to.  Finally, the Committee on Conference of the two Houses added the "Nazarines" to those exempted on religious grounds, and the addition was accepted, apparently without debate.[59]

When the bill became a law on October 11, 1862, Section VII, which was the one providing for conscientious objectors, read as follows:

> . . . all persons who have been and now are members of the society of Friends, and the association of Dunkards,

---

[56] *Ibid.*, II, pp. 230, 236, 241, 253.
[57] *Ibid.*, II, p. 289.
[58] *Ibid.*, V, p. 460.
[59] *Ibid.*, II, p. 410; V, pp. 460 and 490.

Nazarenes, and Mennonists, in regular membership in their respective denominations: *Provided*, Members of the society of Friends, Nazarenes, Mennonists, and Dunkards shall furnish substitutes or pay a tax of five hundred dollars each into the public treasury; . . .[60]

A small pamphlet, published at this time, may have had some influence likewise on the members of Congress in providing for the exemption of those denominations. It was called *Non-resistance, the patience and the Faith of the Saints*, and was written and published at Charlottesville, Virginia, by William Thurber, a conscript in the Confederate Army.   As an editorial in *The Friend* explained:

> Being a non-resistant in principle, he refused to take up arms, and was exempted by the authorities at Richmond, Virginia. He afterwards wrote and published this Tract on the subject of non-resistance.   Copies were sent to the members of the Richmond Congress, and it is said the arguments used had much influence in inducing them to pass a law exempting from military service those who are conscientiously opposed to bearing arms.   The arguments are presented in a sober, devout, strain, and are almost entirely scriptural. . . .[61]

Several days after the passage of the Exemption Act a special officer was chosen to collect exemption money from members of the exempted sects, as the following letter from the Adjutant and Inspector General's Office explains:

Richmond, October 15, 1862.

Col. A. C. Myers
  Quartermaster-General, Richmond:
Sir.: The Secretary of War directs that you select some suitable officer of your department in this city to receive

---

[60] *Confederate Statutes at Large*, II, p. 78, (First Cong., Sess. II, chap. 45) and *Official Records*, Series 4, II, p. 161.
[61] *The Friend*, XXXVII, no. 42, p. 332.

the sums paid in by members of the Dunkard Society to secure exemption from military service. This officer will perform this duty until further orders. This order will include also the members of the societies of Friends, Mennonites, and Nazarenes.

Very respectfully, &c.,

S. Cooper

Adjutant and Inspector General.[62]

On November 3rd a general order was issued by the same office explaining in greater detail the procedure to be followed by members of the enumerated religious sects, in claiming their exemption under Section VII of the Act of October 11th. The order stated:

Friends, Dunkards, Nazarenes, and Mennonites

All persons of the above denominations in regular membership therein on the 11th day of October, 1862, shall be exempt from enrollment on furnishing a substitute, or on presenting to the enrolling officer a receipt from a bonded Quartermaster for the tax of $500 imposed by Act of Congress and an affidavit by the bishop, presiding elder, or other officer, whose duty it is to preserve the records of membership in the denomination to which the party belongs, setting forth distinctly . . . etc.[63]

The terms of the Exemption Act apparently satisfied the conscientious scruples of most members of the Mennonite and Brethren Churches, even though the payment of the exemption money caused considerable hardship for some.[64] As one author expressed it, "Before the close of the year the government designated persons to receive the fines, and the Brethren, on their part, raised the necessary money to pay them. This was the cause of a deep feeling of gratitude throughout the churches in Virginia,"

---

[62] *Official Records*, Series 4, II, p. 122.

[63] *Ibid.*, p. 166.

[64] Sanger and Hays, *op. cit.*, p. 58, and Zigler, D. H. *op. cit.*, p. 121. See also Chap. VI of this study.

and January 1, 1863, was appointed as a day of thanks-giving.[65] The dangers which threatened the Brethren and Mennonites thereafter arose chiefly from the difficulty of enforcing the provisions of the Exemption Act and the danger of the law's repeal.[66] In a letter from Benjamin F. Moomaw to John Kline, dated December 16, 1862, he said, "I will here inform you that our military authorities are so construing the exemption bill as to deprive those few brethren that are in the army under the conscript act, from its benefit. I have just written to the Secretary of War upon the subject. If his answer is unfavorable, I will petition congress for an amendment, as soon as it convenes."[67]

Many members of the Society of Friends were not so well satisfied, however, with conditional exemption. At a Meeting for Sufferings of the North Carolina Yearly Meeting, held October 31, 1862, eleven Friends were asked "to take into consideration the subject of the Tax imposed by the Congress of the Confederate States upon the members of the Society of Friends who come under the requisitions of the Conscription act passed by said Congress, and report their judgment thereon to next sitting."[68] The North Carolina Yearly Meeting, which met a few days later, gave the matter their attention, and came to the following conclusion:

> We have had the subject under serious consideration, and while in accordance with our last yearly meeting we do pay all taxes imposed on us as citizens and property-holders in common with other citizens, remembering the injunction, 'tribute to whom tribute is due, custom to whom custom', yet we cannot conscientiously pay the specified tax, it being

---

[65] Zigler, D. H. *op. cit.*, pp. 122–123.

[66] See Chapters IV and V of this study for illustrations.

[67] Facsimile of this letter is given in Zigler, D. H., *op. cit.*, p. 124.

[68] Min. of the Meeting for Sufferings of North Carolina Yearly Meeting, 10 mo. 31, 1862.

imposed upon us on account of our principles, as the price exacted of us for religious liberty. Yet we do appreciate the good intentions of those members of Congress who had it in their hearts to do something for our relief; and we recommend that those parents who, moved by sympathy, or those young men who, dreading the evils of a military camp, availed themselves of this law, shall be treated in a tender manner by their monthly meetings.[69]

Even those members of the noncombatant denominations who felt they could conscientiously pay for exemption from the draft wondered if they would be required to pay both the state and Confederate exemption fees. In North Carolina, for example, Joseph Newlin, a Quaker, wrote to Senator Worth on December 6, 1862, saying, "There is one subject to which I wish to call thy attention. Not knowing whether it would be advisable at the present time to agitate it, which is the subject, of Friends paying the $500.—the price of exemption under the Conscript Act, whether it releases them from the ordinance requiring the payment of the $100. I have my own views in relation to it, but I do not know whether they are correct, . . ."[70] In some cases Brethren who had already paid their exemption money to the State of Virginia were told that they must also pay the Confederate Government.[71]

The constitutionality of the Confederate Conscription Act was not decided without a bitter struggle,[72] but the courts finally supported the Confederate Government, and a special Alabama case decided the matter so far as conscientious objectors were concerned. In this case a man by the name of Levi M. Stringer applied for a writ of *habeas corpus* to obtain his discharge from the custody of Major W. T. Walthall, commandant of a camp of instruc-

---

[69] Min. of North Carolina Yearly Meeting, 11, mo. 3, 1862, p. 8.

[70] *The Correspondence of Jonathan Worth*, I, p. 207.

[71] Zigler, D. H. *op. cit.*, p. 121.

[72] Moore, Albert Burton. *Conscription and Conflict in the Confederacy.*

tion near Talladega, Alabama. He alleged that, as a member of a "Christian Church," and having conscientious scruples against bearing arms, he was entitled to exemption from military duty under the provisions of the Alabama State Constitution (Art. IV, Sec. 2) upon the payment of an equivalent for personal service. The court ruled, however, that he was not entitled to exemption unless he was a member of one of the religious denominations, enumerated in the Act of October 11, 1862, because this act superceded the laws of the individual states.[73]

Although there were constant rumours that the Confederate Government would revoke or restrict the numerous statutory and class exemptions,[74] actually no change was made in the political status of conscientious objectors during the year 1863. Congress continued to be flooded with petitions for exemption from military service from workmen in gas and water works, physicians, mail carriers, railroad employees, "all those engaged in printing and binding school books," dental surgeons who had been in practice ten years, certain types of farmers, manufacturers of tableware, editors, and others,[75] but not from the noncombatant sects, as in the preceding year.

When the Act of May 1, 1863, was passed, repealing certain clauses of the Act of the previous October, no mention was made of Quakers and the other peace denominations. Instead of preparing memorials to the Government, the Meeting for Sufferings merely directed "that the several Monthly Meetings composing the North Carolina Yearly Meeting appoint in their respective Monthly Meetings committees to assist the Clerks of said

---

[73] *Ex Parte Stringer*, 38 Ala., p. 457.

[74] *Journal of Confederate Congress*, III, p. 44. Moore, Albert Burton. op. cit., p. 72.

[75] *Journal of Confederate Congress*, VI, pp. 51, 52, 126, 523, 586, 696, 707, 759. Moore, Albert Burton, *op. cit.*, p. 70.

meetings in making out certificates for applicants who may apply for them in order to avail themselves of the exemption by paying the tax imposed by act of Congress."[76] The Clerk was directed to furnish each monthly meeting with a copy of this minute. By this action the Yearly Meeting definitely allowed its members to avail themselves of the exemption privilege if they could conscientiously do so.

By this time the oversight of the draft had been assumed by the Bureau of Conscription, which was organized on December 30, 1862, but this Bureau functioned in an administrative rather than in a legislative or judicial capacity.[77]

During the year 1863 Friends were again agitated by the question of military taxes; this time by a "tax in kind." The North Carolina Meeting for Sufferings was convened on July 20th to discuss the question. A committee was appointed to prepare an essay on the subject and to report to the next meeting.[78] Their report was worded in part as follows:

> ... When taxes have been imposed for the purpose of buying guns, drums, colors or for other warlike purposes— Friends have not felt at liberty to pay such taxes. Such we think should be the case with the demand for the tenth part of the produce of our lands. We believe that this is designed for the direct support of the army. It is strictly a *war measure*. Hence believing as we do that all wars are contrary to the Spirit of the Gospel of our Lord and Savior Jesus Christ, and that by the payment of this tithe, we are directly aiding to prolong these evils; it is the sense and judgment of this meeting that we cannot consistently pay said tithe.[79]

---

[76] Min. of the Meeting for Sufferings of North Carolina Yearly Meeting, 4 mo. 13, 1863.

[77] Jones, J. B. *A Rebel War Clerk's Diary*, I, p. 233, et seq.

[78] Min. of the Meeting for Sufferings of North Carolina Yearly Meeting, 7 mo. 20, 1863.

[79] *Ibid.*, 8 mo. 3, 1863.

However, the matter did not rest there. Soon a committee of fourteen Friends was appointed "to take the whole subject of taxation into weighty consideration and report their sense and judgment thereon to next sitting."[80] This new committee came to the conclusion that no further action could be taken and the matter was therefore dropped for the time being.[81]

When the first Confederate Congress assembled for its fourth session on December 7, 1863, President Davis, in his Message, proposed drastic changes in the conscription laws. He said:

> In view of the large conscription recently ordered by the enemy and their subsequent call for volunteers, to be followed if ineffectual by a still further draft, we are admonished that no effort must be spared to add largely to our effective force as promptly as possible. The sources of supply are to be found by restoring to the Army all who are improperly absent, putting an end to substitution, modifying the exemption law, restricting details, and placing in the ranks such of the able-bodied men now employed as wagoners, nurses, cooks, and other employees as are doing service for which negroes may be found competent.[82]

Naturally these suggestions again aroused the anxiety of exempted classes. Measures were taken by Elder John Kline, on behalf of the Church of the Brethren, to secure the support of members of Congress against any repeal of the law so far as religious exemptions were concerned.[83] He wrote to various members of Congress concerning the threatening danger, but a reply from Colonel Baldwin, on January 28, 1864, gave a forecast of the sentiment of Congress, which was opposed to any repeal at that time.

---

[80] *Ibid.*, 10 mo. 30, 1863.

[81] *Ibid.*, 11 mo. 4, 1863.

[82] Richardson, James D. *A Compilation of the Messages and Papers of the Confederacy*, I, p. 370.

[83] Zigler, David H. *A History of the Brethren in Virginia*, p. 141.

Another letter from Judge John T. Harris said, " 'The exemption on religious grounds stands firm in Congress.' "[84]

Nevertheless, the year 1864 was one of intense anxiety for noncombatant sects in the South. Those who were drafted, and who refused to serve in a military capacity, were subjected to great hardships. Those who had thus far been exempted were never sure that their scruples against fighting would be respected by the military authorities.[85]

On February 17, 1864, the Confederate Government passed another military measure, entitled "An Act to organize forces to serve during the war." Section four provided "That no person heretofore exempted on account of religious opinions, and who has paid the tax levied to relieve him from service, shall be required to render military service under this act."[86] In reality this was a great favor to those scrupulous against bearing arms because the decline in the value of Confederate money made the $500. exemption fee easier to meet than would have been a payment in kind.[87]

Since the act extended the limits of the draft to all those between the ages of 17 and 50, it was not clear whether the exemption provisions of Section 4 included or excluded those noncombatants between the ages of 17 and 18 and 45 and 50. For this reason a committee of Friends was appointed to take up the matter with the proper authorities. The committee produced a memorial which they presented to President Davis, after securing the endorsement of Assistant Secretary of War, Campbell.[88] Friends were not satisfied, however, with petitioning the

---

[84] *Ibid.*, p. 141.

[85] See Chap. V of this study.

[86] *Confederate Statutes at Large*, II, p. 211. *Official Records*, Series 4, III, p. 178.

[87] Brooks, Robert P. *Conscription in the Confederate States of America*, p. 425.

[88] Min. of the Meeting for Sufferings of North Carolina Yearly Meeting, 4 mo. 11, 1864.

President. They also sent copies of the memorial to the House of Representatives, where it was presented by John A. Gilmer, of North Carolina, on May 16, 1864.[89]

The memorial and endorsement were worded as follows:

To Jefferson Davis, President of the Confederate States.

The undersigned were appointed by the Meeting for Sufferings representing the North Carolina Yearly Meeting of Friends to wait on the proper authorities on behalf of those of our members who by the late law are liable to be brought into suffering on account of their Religious principles.

Those between the ages of 18 and 45 have heretofore been exempt from military service upon the payment of a tax of $500 and from information received from some members of Congress being induced to believe that it was the intention of the late law to leave the subject of our further exemption discretionary with the President, we are desirous of knowing whether the law will be so construed as to allow those between the ages of 17 and 18 and 45 and 50 the same privilege, and if not whether they will be exempt under that part of the law which allows the Secretary of War under the direction of the President, to exempt such persons as he may be satisfied ought to be exempt on account of public necessity.

While Friends cannot consistently enter into a contract to perform anything in lieu of personal service in the army, we can confidently state our belief that they will be of more real service to the country if allowed to pursue their usual occupations of farming, &c. than if forced into the army, when according to one of their primary principles they could not in any event bear arms.

We trust that the Confederate Government in Christian Charity will not be behind the Federal Government which we have good authority for saying does not attempt to force Friends to bear arms; but exempts them on their affirmation that they are members of our Society.

---

[89] *Journal of Confederate Congress*, VII, p. 66. No mention is made of the memorial being presented in the Senate.

The Confederate Government may well be liberal towards Friends when according to the best of our information and belief there are at least eighty men at the North to one at the South, who are restrained by our Religious principles from taking any part in this war. It may be worth while to consider too what the Confederacy would really gain by disregarding our religious scruples when we state that the whole number of our members rendered liable by the late law probably does not amount to 125 persons.

Nereus Mendenhall)
Isham Cox          )   Comt.
Jonathan Harriss  )

Bureau of Conscription

The Department, upon the general principle of Justice, Equity and necessity is disposed to relieve the persons embraced in this application from Military service, or enrollment for that object. When they are in a condition to be detailed for agricultural pursuits, it may be done under the conditions imposed upon other classes of producers. When there are clerical employments, or artisan, or mechanical labors that they can perform they may be selected for those objects.

The Department recognizes the force of their Appeal and refers it to your bureau for appropriate action.

By order,
J. A. Campbell
ASS. W.[90]

The Bureau of Conscription took action on the matter by issuing on March 22nd, Circular No. 11, Section 2 of which read:

Upon general principles of justice, equity, and necessity the Government is disposed to relieve persons between seventeen and eighteen and forty-five and fifty, members of the Society of Friends, Dunkards, &c. When they are in a condition to be detailed for agricultural pursuits it may be

[90] Min. of the Meeting for Sufferings of North Carolina Yearly Meeting, 4 mo. 11, 1864.

done under the conditions imposed upon other classes of producers. When there are clerical employments or artisan or mechanical labors that they can perform they may be selected for those objects. Every case, however, should be referred to this Bureau for its action, allowing the parties to remain at their employments until action is taken.

By command of Col. John S. Preston, superintendent:

Thos. Goldthwaite,

Acting Assistant Adjutant-General[91]

In order to clarify further the procedure of exempting conscientious objectors, a bill was introduced in the House of Representatives, known as "An Act to amend so much of an act entitled 'An act to organize forces to serve during the war' approved February seventeenth, eighteen hundred and sixty-four, as relates to the exemption of certain religious denominations." This was reported out of the Committee on Military Affairs on May 26th, was passed by both Houses without amendment, and was signed by President Davis on June 7th.[92]

Its terms provided:

That the Secretary of War shall be authorized to grant exemptions to the various denominations of Christians mentioned in the exemption act of the eleventh of October, eighteen hundred and sixty-two, who, at that time, belonged to the same, and who were in regular association therewith, upon the terms and conditions specified in that act, or upon such other terms and conditions as he is authorized to allow exemptions or grant details under any of the clauses of the act approved February seventeenth, eighteen hundred and sixty-four, to which this is an amendment.

Sec. 2. That the Secretary of War be, and he is hereby, authorized, to revoke any such exemptions under the act aforesaid, when the same have been obtained by any fraud, misrepresentation or error.[93]

[91] *Official Records*, Series 4, III, p. 240.
[92] *Journal of Confederate Congress*, IV, pp. 96, 97, 161, 167; VII, pp. 99, 168.
[93] *Confederate Statutes at Large*, II, p. 261 (Second Cong., Sess. I, chap. 24).

This amendment extended only to persons who were members of the various sects on October 11, 1862. Judge Campbell, the Assistant Secretary of War, claimed that the membership of these denominations had been largely augmented since October from families not previously connected with them. "This has been a cause for distrust," he said, in a circular, dated June 27th, "and probably led to the adoption of the precise language of the act. The Department [of War] has exercised a liberal indulgence in favor of those who held or were supposed to hold conscientious scruples upon the subject of bearing arms, but there is no reason for affording any countenance to efforts to avoid the performance of public duty by hypocritical pretenses of a religious belief, which has no root in the conscience or influence upon the conduct."[94] The Bureau of Conscription called the attention of all officers of conscription to this communication as furnishing the rules and principles by which they should be guided in dealing with persons within military ages who were members of the religious denominations referred to in the act.

Apparently Secretary Campbell's position was well taken because there is evidence among the records of the noncombatant societies themselves that many applications were received for membership after the beginning of the war. The following letter, for example, written by Joseph Newlin to John B. Crenshaw on July 20, 1863, illustrates the situation in the Society of Friends.

Esteemed Friend,
    There seems to be quite a looking, and leaning to our Society in this part of the land, quite a number of men and women, have requested to become members, and some have been received, these are mostly such, as have in some measure been connected with Society, and thus seems to have

---

[94] *Official Records*, Series 4, III, p. 515. Moore, Albert Burton, *op. cit.*, p. 89 (footnote).

been awakened to a sense of duty by the calamities of the present war. Now I wish to enquire through thee of the Secretary of War, whether, those who have become members since the passage of the exemption act can be allowed to pay the exemption tax . . .

I feel very well aware that a heavy responsibility, rests on our Society in regard to receiving members, as well as many other things, and I do hope that all of our Different Monthly Meetings every where may be enabled to judge aright in these matters, . . .[95]

Friends, in order to qualify for exemption on religious grounds, were required to submit to the proper enrolling officer a statement showing that they were members of the Society in good standing. An illustration of such an affirmation follows:

> Guilford Co., North Carolina,
> 11th mo. 9th, 1864

This is to certify that William H. Watson is a member of the society of Friends. He was admitted into membership with Friends at his own request in the year 1863. It is proper to state that his Mother had a birthright in Friends Society she being born and reared a Friend.

> Lewis Starbuck / Clerk

of Dover Monthly Meeting

State of North Carolina)
Guilford County        )

Personally appeared Lewis Starbuck before the subscribing Justice for the County of Guilford and made affirmation in due form of Law that he is Clerk of Dover Monthly Meeting of Friends and that the foregoing certificate is true, and that the above signature purporting to be his is genuine.

November 9th, 1864        A. H. Lindsay, J.P.

---

[95] North Carolina Yearly Meeting Collection of Crenshaw Correspondence.

North Carolina )
Guilford County)

I, Lynd [?] Swain, Clerk of Guilford County court, do certify that A. H. Lindsay, Esq. whose genuine signature appears to the foregoing certificate is an acting Justice of the Peace in aforesaid County, and that full faith and credit are due to his official acts as such.

Wts my hand and official Seal, at office,
Nov. 10th 1864      Lynd [?] Swain, A.C.C.[96]

The situation was made still more critical for those who sought exemption on conscientious grounds during 1864 by the issue of General Orders #77 from the Adjutant and Inspector General's Office at Richmond on October 8th. It provided that all details previously granted under authority of the War Department to persons between the ages of 18 and 45 years should be revoked, "and all such detailed men, together with those within the said ages who hold furloughs or temporary exemptions by reasons of pending applications for detail, will be promptly assembled at the camps of instruction and appropriately assigned among the armies for service; except that men detailed and now actually employed as artisans, mechanics or persons of scientific skill (and those detailed and now engaged in the manufacture, collection, and forwarding of indispensable supplies for the Army and Navy) will be continued in their present employments until their respective details be revised."[97]

Friends were not willing to resign without a struggle the rights of their members, who joined the Society after October 11, 1862, to exemption from military service. Various methods were taken to secure these rights. On November 1, 1864, *The Southern Friend*, in an editorial, reviewed the entire legislative situation, in so far as it

[96] *Ibid.*
[97] *Official Records*, Series 4, III, p. 715. *Southern Friend*, I, no. 2, p. 15.

applied to Friends and to other noncombatant peoples. It called attention especially to General Orders #73 of the Adjutant and Inspector General's Office, under date of September 22, 1864, which said, in Section 4:

> All applications for exemption and detail will be transmitted, through the generals of reserves, to the superintendent of the Bureau of Conscription for decision. The office of Congressional district enrolling officer is abolished, and communications from local enrolling officers will be transmitted through the commandants of conscripts to the generals of reserves. An officer may be assigned to duty in each Congressional district by the generals of reserves as inspector of conscription.[98]

The editorial concluded with the statement:

> There seems at present no relief for those who have joined since 1862.[99]

On November 9th, a committee, to whom had been referred the question of memorializing the Confederate Government in reference to recently joined members of the Society of Friends, produced such a memorial at a session of the Meeting for Sufferings of the North Carolina Yearly Meeting.[100] Another committee, composed of John Carter, Nereus Mendenhall, Isham Cox, Jonathan Harriss, and Allen U. Tomlinson, was chosen to visit Congress and those in authority with the memorial, "asking relief in regard to the conscription of the members of our society, and to labor as way may open to obtain the objects in view." John B. Crenshaw, of Richmond, was also asked to serve with the delegation.[101]

---

[98] *Official Records*, Series 4, III, p. 675.

[99] *Southern Friend*, I, no. 3, p. 21.

[100] *Ibid.*, I, no. 5, pp. 38–39.

[101] Min. of the Meeting for Sufferings of North Carolina Yearly Meeting, 11 mo. 9, 1864.

On November 24th Senator William A. Graham, of North Carolina, presented in the Senate the memorial of the Society, "praying that certain persons who have been received into the membership of the society since the 11th day of October, 1862, may be exempted from military service," which was referred to the Committee on Military Affairs.[102] The following day Representative Wickham, of Virginia, presented the same memorial in the House, where it was likewise referred, without discussion, to the Committee on Military Affairs.[103] Nothing came of this petition, so that those members of the Society of Friends who had joined since 1862 continued to suffer in the military camps and elsewhere for their scruples of conscience, except in individual cases where appeals on their behalf to the military or civil authorities were successful.[104]

The year 1865 would doubtless have increased the difficulties of Southern objectors had the war continued much longer. On March 7th the Bureau of Conscription was abolished and the Generals of Reserves in the several states took over the task of enforcing conscription and of granting all exemptions and details.[105] Likewise bills were introduced in both Houses revoking certain exemptions from military service. In fact, on March 18th, the last day Congress met, the Senate approved a bill of the House supplemental to an act entitled "An act to diminish the number of exemptions and details,"[106] but the cessation of hostilities soon after made all such acts inoperative.

---

[102] *Journal of Confederate Congress*, IV, p. 288.

[103] *Ibid.*, VII, p. 299.

[104] See Chapters IV and V of this study.

[105] *Official Records*, Series 4, III, pp. 1176–1177; Brooks, Robert P. *Conscription in the Confederate States of America*, p. 430.

[106] *Journal of Confederate Congress*, VII, p. 796.

# Chapter IV

## Attitude of the Civil Authorities Toward Conscientious Objectors

WITH very few exceptions, those highest in civil authority in the Federal Government were sympathetic to, or at least tolerant of, the conscientious scruples of the noncombatant sects. Religious objectors to military service were particularly fortunate in having President Lincoln and Secretary Stanton show a friendly attitude at all times.

Lincoln's position with regard to religious objectors was a most difficult one. Apparently he sympathized greatly with their scruples of conscience for he used his prerogative on numerous occasions to parole or pardon those cases which came to his personal attention,[1] but he did not feel that he should recommend to Congress specific measures for relief.[2]

One of Lincoln's first acknowledgements of the many letters, petitions, and memorials which were addressed to him by the Society of Friends throughout the war was on January 5, 1862, when he replied to an address of the Iowa Quakers, sent to him through Senator Harlan. He wrote:

> It is most cheering and encouraging for me to know that in the efforts which I have made, and am making, for the restoration of a righteous peace to our country, I am upheld and sustained by the good wishes and prayers of God's people. No one is more deeply than myself aware that without his favor our highest wisdom is but as foolishness, and

---

[1] Shannon, Fred Albert. *The Organization and Administration of the Union Army*, II, p. 252.

[2] Nicolay and Hay. *Abraham Lincoln—A History*, VI, p. 327.

that our most strenuous efforts would avail nothing in the shadow of his displeasure. It seems to me that if there be one subject upon which all good men may unitedly agree, it is in imploring the gracious favor of the God of Nations upon the struggle our people are making for the preservation of their precious birthright of civil and religious liberty.[3]

At the time of the Mason and Slidell controversy between the United States and Great Britain, Friends in both countries took measures to support their respective governments in seeking a peaceful solution of the difficulty. In America these measures took the form of letters and memorials to the President.[4] In reply to the memorial of the New England Quakers, he said:

Engaged, as I am, in a great war, I fear it will be difficult for the world to understand how fully I appreciate the principles of peace, inculcated in this letter, and everywhere, by the Society of Friends.

Grateful to the good people you represent, for their prayers in behalf of our common country, I look forward hopefully to an early end of war, and return of peace.

Your obliged friend,

A. Lincoln[5]

Probably Lincoln's feelings were best expressed in a letter which he wrote to Eliza Paul Gurney (Mrs. Joseph John Gurney) on September 4, 1864. Mrs. Gurney, together with John M. Whitall, Hannah B. Mott, and James Carey, had visited Lincoln in October, 1862. About a year later (August, 1863) Lincoln made a special request, through Isaac Newton, United States Commis-

---

[3] *Ibid.*, VI, pp. 327–328.

[4] Min. of the Meeting for Sufferings of Western Yearly Meeting, 1 mo. 9, 1862, pp. 43–44; Min. of the Meeting for Sufferings of New England Yearly Meeting (1842–1887), pp. 266–268.

[5] Min. of New England Yearly Meeting, 1862, pp. 18–19, or Nicolay and Hay, *op. cit.*, VI, p. 328. The letter was dated at the Executive Mansion, Washington, March 19, 1862.

sioner of Agriculture, that Mrs. Gurney write to him, which she did on August 18, 1863.[6]

In his reply, Lincoln said:

My Esteemed Friend: I have not forgotten—probably never shall forget—the very impressive occasion when yourself and friends visited me on a Sabbath forenoon, two years ago; nor has your kind letter, written nearly a year later, ever been forgotten. In all, it has been your purpose to strengthen my reliance on God. I am much indebted to the good Christian people of the country for their constant prayers and consolations, and to no one of them more than to yourself. The purposes of the Almighty are perfect, and must prevail, though we erring mortals may fail to accurately perceive them in advance. We hoped for a happy termination of this terrible war long before this; but God knows best, and has ruled otherwise. We shall yet acknowledge his wisdom, and our own error therein. Meanwhile we must work earnestly in the best lights he gives us, trusting that so working still conduces to the great ends he ordains. Surely he intends some good to follow this mighty convulsion, which no mortal could make, and no mortal could stay. Your people—the Friends—have had, and are having, a very great trial. On principle and faith, opposed to both war and oppression, they can only practically oppose oppression by war. In this hard dilemma, some have chosen one horn and some the other. For those appealing to me on conscientious grounds, I have done, and shall do, the best I could and can, in my own conscience, under my oath to the law. That you believe this I doubt not; and believing it, I shall still receive, for our country and myself, your earnest prayers to our Father in Heaven.

Your sincere friend,
A. Lincoln[7]

---

[6] *Memoir and Correspondence of Eliza P. Gurney*, pp. 307–313.

[7] A facsimilie of the above letter is contained in *Ibid.*, pp. 316–317. The original is in the Pennsylvania Historical Society. See also *Quaker Biographies*, Series 2, II, pp. 123–124 and Nicolay and Hay, *op. cit.*, VI, pp. 328–329.

On September 9, 1864, Eliza Gurney again wrote to Abraham Lincoln, but it was her first letter that was found in his pocket at the time of his assassination, seven months later.

Lincoln's sympathetic attitude towards those who actually suffered for conscience' sake is well illustrated by the case of Henry D. Swift, a member of the Society of Friends, and a resident of South Dedham, Massachusetts.[8] Swift was drafted in 1863, and when he went to Concord, where the conscripts were being mobilized, he was ordered to take part in the military drills.

This he resolutely refused to do, it being contrary to the dictates of his conscience. For this he was put into the guard-house, but he adhered to his determination and refrained from all military activity at Concord, as well as later on, when sent to Long Island, and to Boston Harbor. From here troops were being constantly sent south to replenish armies in the field. While at Long Island he gladly helped in hospital services, but refused all remuneration for his services. He was 'bucked down' and was finally told by the officers he would be shot for refusal to obey orders. He was then taken from the guard-house and made to witness an execution, and was told that that would be his fate if he persisted in his insubordination; but he still remained firm. He was tried by court-martial and sentenced to be shot.

During his stay at Long Island, he was visited by Stephen A. Chase, of Lynn, and Charles R. Tucker, of New Bedford, both prominent members of the Society of Friends. They went to Washington and stated the facts of Henry D. Swift's case to President Lincoln and Secretary Stanton. When the matter was considered by the President he di-

[8] The account of Henry D. Swift's experiences was first published in the Worcester, Mass. *Gazette*, March 1, 1916, and afterwards reprinted in condensed form in the *Bulletin of Friends' Historical Society*, VII, no. 1 (5 mo. 1916) pp. 37–38; also in Jones, Rufus M. *The Later Periods of Quakerism*, II, p. 735.

rected that an honorable parole be made out. This was
done and delivered to Henry Swift shortly before the time
he had been informed his execution was to take place. This
was in the fall of 1863. 'It is needless to say he was never
called upon.'

Words of appreciation for the President's sympathetic
attitude towards those conscientiously opposed to bearing
arms were frequently expressed by official Quaker bodies.
For example, the Conference of Friends, held in Baltimore
in December, 1863, stated, "We gratefully appreciate the
kindness evidenced at all times by the President and
Secretary of War, when we have applied to them for
relief from suffering for conscience' sake, and honor them
for their clearly manifested regard for religious liberty."[9]
As another illustration, the New York (Orthodox)
Yearly Meeting of 1864 made a minute to the effect that,
" 'Through the exertions of the committees who have
visited Washington at various times, on behalf of conscripted members of our Society, several of them have
been released by direction of the Heads of the Government, for which favors we are much indebted to the
President and his advisers.' "[10]   Or again, in an address
to President Johnson, after the cessation of hostilities,
the Philadelphia (Hicksite) Yearly Meeting said, "We
feel greatly thankful that his [Lincoln's] heart was im-
bued with a regard for conscientious scruples in relation
to war, and for the relief that he extended to us therein."[11]
The New England Yearly Meeting of 1865 also said,
"We mourn the violent death of our beloved Chief Magi-
strate, the late Abraham Lincoln, by the hands of wicked
men. We acknowledge the deep debt of gratitude due from

---

[9] Min. of the Meeting for Sufferings of Indiana Yearly Meeting, 12 mo. 22,
1863, p. 333.

[10] Quoted in *The Friend*, XXXVII, no. 47, p. 375.

[11] Min. of Philadelphia (Hicksite) Yearly Meeting, 1865, pp. 18–19.

us, as a religious society, to him for his tender regard to our conscientious scruples against bearing arms; . . ."[12]

Edwin M. Stanton, Lincoln's Secretary of War, was also sympathetically inclined toward those scrupulous against bearing arms, and he at all times showed an unusual degree of patience in dealing with matters of conscience. As one author expresses it, "It is known that Stanton used his influence to secure even greater concessions to this class [of conscientious objectors] than were ever granted by Congress."[13] When application was made to him, he more than once secured the release of Quakers who, when drafted, refused to bear arms. Petitions for his personal intercession were not at all uncommon. The following case is a typical one.

> Philadelphia Quarterly Meeting reports, that two members of the Southern District Monthly Meeting were drafted into the United States Army. 'One was released on account of physical disability, the other was drafted for Military Service 7th mo. 27th 1863. He was respectfully treated by the Provost Marshall, and was not restrained of his liberty. The Secretary of War, upon being informed that he was conscientiously scrupulous against bearing arms, or paying an equivalent therefor, granted him a furlough through the Provost Marshall.'

(Signed) Joseph Scattergood
Nathan Kite
James R. Greeves[14]

In another instance he ordered the release of three Quakers who were drafted about the first of October, 1862, and who were confined at camp for about two weeks. Apparently no fine or penalty was required of them, although mention is made of a sum of $67., which was the

---

[12] Min. of New England Yearly Meeting, 1865, pp. 13–14.

[13] Shannon, Fred Albert, *op. cit.*, II, p. 260.

[14] Min. of the Meeting for Sufferings of Philadelphia (Orthodox) Yearly Meeting, 4 mo. 14, 1865, p. 253.

amount of expense incurred by them in securing their discharge.[15]

One further illustration of the type of memorial which Stanton received and of the kind of suffering which some religious objectors underwent in the Northern Armies prior to their release is contained in the following application, addressed to the Secretary by four citizens of Massachusetts.

'The following facts in relation to the young man we have from such authority as leaves us no doubt of their substantial correctness. He has from boyhood been a non-resistant, and regarded all war as criminal, and has entirely abstained from voting as a religious duty. Since then he has done everything in his power to aid the Government against the assaults of the slaveholders. Drafted in October last, the authorities of the camp on Long Island appreciated his religious scruples against bearing arms, and treated him with kindness and respect. But in Virginia, the officer in charge, a Major Cook, of Gloucester, Massachusetts, has endeavored to force him to yield his conscientious convictions. He has been tied up in the woods with mules, suspended by his hands after the manner of slaves, until he could hardly stand alone, deprived of shelter, food, and finally put in the guardhouse, where he has been for six or seven weeks. All this the soldier has borne with great courage and patience. His health is seriously impaired by such exposure and severity.

You have already generously discharged several Quakers who have been drafted into the Army. This leads us to hope that you will not hesitate to discharge from military service this young man who is suffering from his adherence to the same principles as theirs.'[16]

The most notable action of Stanton on behalf of ob-

[15] Min. of the Meeting for Sufferings of Indiana Yearly Meeting, 9 mo. 27, 1863, p. 324.
[16] *Congressional Globe*, XLIV, Pt. 1, p. 255.

jectors was his order, in December, 1863, through the office of the Provost Marshal General, to parole all such persons until called for.[17] Equally sincere, however, was his attempt during the winter of 1863–64, to provide, through legislation, for the scruples of members of the Society of Friends.[18] It was at his direct instigation that the Baltimore Conference of Friends was convened to discuss his proposals. As he explained to the Committee of this Conference, which called on him December 7, 1863, "he had great respect for their conscientious scruples, and should be very sorry to oppress them," but he was unable to grant them what they wanted, namely, unconditional exemption from military service.[19]

Possibly the Secretary's attitude was best expressed in a reply which he made to a delegation of Friends who visited him on May 5, 1865, shortly after Lincoln's assassination. One member of the delegation explained to him that "they felt unwilling to leave the city without calling to express their thankfulness to him for the uniform kindness and consideration with which he and his Department had treated Friends; . . . . They were grateful not only for the relief afforded Friends, but especially for his and the Government's recognition of the rights of conscience, and the respect they had manifested for religious scruples. Several other members of the delegation expressed similar views."[20] Stanton replied, apparently with much feeling. "He said that he deeply appreciated the sentiments which had been expressed, and that in the administration of his department he had ever sought to respect the religious views of the Society of Friends and other religious bodies, and had been careful from the moment that he solemnly

[17] *Official Records.* Series 3, III, p. 1173.
[18] See Chap. II of this study, pp. 71–75.
[19] *Bulletin of Friends' Historical Society,* IV, no. 1, p. 20.
[20] *Friends' Review,* XVIII, no. 39, p. 617.

assumed the duties of his office, to endeavor to do no act which could, by displeasing the Almighty, bring his displeasure upon his country."[21]

Again, in answering another delegation of Friends on June 1, 1865, he said, "He [Lincoln] and myself felt that unless we recognized conscientious religious scruples, we could not expect the blessing of Heaven."[22]

If would have been strange indeed if Friends had not made some acknowledgment of Stanton's kindness, as they did in the case of Lincoln. The records show, however, that appreciation was frequently expressed even though the Secretary was not always notified personally of the action taken on his account. For instance, the Meeting for Sufferings of the Philadelphia (Orthodox) Yearly meeting learned at one of its meetings that:

> Some cases of Friends in Pennsylvania, members of the Ohio Yearly Meeting, were also brought under the notice and care of the Committee, as being Citizens of the same State, and the release of all of them obtained. One of these was taken to the Army and treated with great severity by a subordinate officer. Information of his sufferings being transmitted to the Committee in Philadelphia, a letter briefly stating the case was written to the Secretary of War. Some delay took place ere this letter reached him, but immediately on its reception, he telegraphed to the writer of it, saying, 'Your letter has just reached me; N. B. shall be immediately discharged, and if the name of the officer or officers who maltreated him are furnished he or they shall be dealt with in such manner as will prevent any repetition of such conduct.'

The Friend soon after this left the army and reached his home in safety. The Committee mentions this case in order

---

[21] *Ibid.*

[22] Min. of Philadelphia (Hicksite) Yearly Meeting, 1866, pp. 12–14. See also Min. of the Meeting for Sufferings of New York (Orthodox) Yearly Meeting, 5 mo. 31, 1865, pp. 222–26 and of New England, 6 mo. 10, 1865, pp. 310–14.

to show the friendly disposition manifested by the Government toward our Society; and feel bound to acknowledge with gratitude that whenever it has been necessary to appear before its officers they have uniformly been treated with respect, and generally a kind consideration for our conscientious scruples has been manifested.[23]

Or again:

The Committee appointed to aid such of our members as might be Drafted for Military service made the following report, which was read. The kind consideration manifested by the Officers of the Government especially the Secretary of War for the conscientious scruples of Friends and the exemption from Suffering which our members generally have experienced during the unsettled state of our country is cause for thankfulness.[24]

The attitude of the other members of Lincoln's Cabinet is not clearly known, but one incident, which has been preserved, would tend to show that Secretary Seward had far less patience with objectors than did Stanton. A Quaker, by the name of Ethan Foster, while visiting Washington on behalf of several New England young Friends who had been conscripted, said:

Soon after we entered the War Office, the Secretary of State (William H. Seward) came in and took a seat. He remained silent until our conference with Secretary Stanton was concluded; when Charles Perry (who had an impression that Seward, when Governor of New York, had recommended the passage of a law to exempt from military service those who were consciously opposed to war) turned to him expecting a word of sympathy and encouragement, and remarked that he would perceive why we were there; upon which he suddenly and with much vehemence of manner

---

[23] Min. of the Meeting for Sufferings of Philadelphia (Orthodox) Yearly Meeting, 4 mo. 14, 1864, p. 239.

[24] *Ibid.*, 4 mo. 14, 1864, p. 237.

asked, 'Why don't the Quakers fight?' Charles replied, 'Because they belive it wrong, and cannot do it with a clear conscience.' He reprimanded us severely because we refused to fight. After a little pause I said, 'Well, if this world were all, perhaps we might take thy advice;' to which he responded, 'The way to get along in the next world is to do your duty in this.' I replied, 'That is what we are trying to do; and now I want to ask thee one question, and I want thee to answer it; whose prerogative is it to decide what my duty is, thine or mine?' He did not answer the question, became more angry and excited; asked, 'Why, then, don't you pay the commutation?' We told him we could see no difference between the responsibility of doing an act ourselves and that of hiring another to do it for us. On this he sprang from his seat and strided around in a circle of some eight or ten feet across, exclaiming, *'Then I'll pay it for you,'* and thrusting his hand into his coat pocket, added, *'I'll give you my check!'*

Immediately after this exhibition, we took our leave in much sadness, at treatment so opposite to that we had expected from Secretary Seward.[25]

In general, the attitude of Senators and Representatives in the Federal Congress was cordial towards conscientious objectors. This fact was fully recognized by Friends and others of the noncombatant sects. Although the section of the Conscription Act of February 24, 1864, which provided for the exemption of those opposed to serving in the military forces did not afford relief for those most conscientious in their opposition, Friends, nevertheless, expressed their appreciation through their representatives at the Baltimore Conference, of the preceding December, in the following words:

> While this section is not all that we could desire we feel that Friends should gratefully appreciate the kind consideration of our Legislators toward us as a people, and we

---

[25] Foster, Ethan. *The Conscript Quakers*, pp. 14–16.

look upon it as a growing appreciation of the rights of conscience when such a provision can be adopted in the midst of
a great conflict, involving the most momentous consequences of any event of modern times. We are realizing the
great privilege of living in a government whose legislators
and rulers appreciate and respect our conscientious scruples.[26]

Mentioned has been made already in this study[27] of the
attitude of various members of Congress. Those who were
most favorably inclined toward religious objectors were
Senators Anthony, of Rhode Island, Clark, of New Hampshire, Doolittle, of Wisconsin, Harlan, of Iowa, Harris,
of New York, Lane, of Indiana, Lane, of Kansas, Pomeroy,
of Kansas, Saulsbury, of Delaware, Sumner, of Massachusetts, TenEyck, of New Jersey, Wilson, of Massachusetts, and Representative Stevens, of Pennsylvania.
All of these men either initiated or supported measures
for the relief of conscientious objectors at various times
during the war.[28]    In addition to these men, Senators
Dixon, of Connecticut, Johnson, of Maryland, Morgan,
of New York, Morrill, of Maine, and Ramsey, of Minnesota, presented on various occasions to the Senate memorials from the Baltimore, New England, and New York
Yearly Meetings of the Society of Friends, and Senator
Grimes, of Iowa, presented a similar petition of the Amana
Society.[29]

As one example of the attitude of this group, Senator
Clark, of New Hampshire, said, on February 16, 1863:

I think it may be trifling with grave matters to compel
people to fight whose consciences forbid them to do it.
These Quakers and Shakers, so far as I know them, are

---

[26] Min. of the Meeting for Sufferings of Indiana Yearly Meeting, 6 mo. 22,
1864, pp. 345–346.
[27] Chapter II.
[28] *Cong. Globe*, XLIII, Pt. 2, pp. 994, 1261, 1291–1292; XLIV, Pt. 1, pp. 204,
206, 208, and 255.
[29] *Ibid.*, XLIV, Pt. 1, pp. 95, 100, 144, 151, and 262.

among our most patriotic people; and you shock their religious feeling and their religious sense if you compel them to bear arms; but if you excuse them from military service they will pour out of their subsistence to aid the country, and their blessings to help your cause. They had better be excused.[30]

As another illustration of their attitude, Senator Saulsbury, of Delaware, said (December 22, 1863): "I confess that I, for one, am in favor of exempting the members of that Society [Society of Friends]. I would not require them to do military duty when they have been brought up from their early childhood in opposition to bearing arms."[31]

Those who were most outspoken in their opposition to relief measures were Senator Conness, of California, and Senator McDougall, also of California. The former claimed, ". . . that no citizen, be he Jew or Gentile, be he Quaker or Catholic, be he what he may, to whatever religious persuasion he may belong, can perform a higher duty, nor, in my opinion, a more ennobling one, than to go to the field and to fight this great battle of civilization for the preservation of human liberty; and I am opposed to every amendment of this kind. There is a means proposed by which persons may become exempted, . . . but I am opposed to this exemption for conscience' sake."[32] Later he said, "I think more of the country than I do of their consciences."[33]

His colleague, Senator McDougall, assumed that, "If the Government has the right as well as the power to call its citizens into the military service, let it be exercised; and if they cannot afford to fight they must pay."[34] Others

[30] *Ibid.*, XLIII, Pt. 2, p. 994.
[31] *Ibid.*, XLIV, Pt. 1, p. 204.
[32] *Ibid.*, XLIV, Pt. 1, p. 205.
[33] *Ibid.*, p. 206.
[34] *Ibid.*, XLIII, Pt. 2, p. 994.

opposed to granting exemption on grounds of conscience were Senators Dixon, of Connecticut, Davis, of Kentucky, and Henderson, of Missouri.[35]

The real grounds for conscientious objection to military service were not always clear to the legislators, even among those who were most favorable. As an illustration, Senator Lane, of Kansas, said in a speech on December 22, 1863:

> I have had some dealings with Quakers, and I desire to say, for the edification of the Senator from California [Conness] that it is perfectly rediculous to attempt to force a Quaker into the ranks of the Army. It cannot be done, or if you should succeed in doing it, he would be worthless as a soldier. Besides, the attempt to collect money from the Quakers in lieu of military service will cost the Government ten dollars where they obtain one, if they get it at all. But if you adopt the proposition of the Senator from Iowa [Harlan] giving them the privilege of serving in hospitals, and permitting them to pay their money in lieu of hospital service, they will promptly and cheerfully come forward and pay that money, their conscientious scruples not being violated by such payment.[36]

Senator Powell, of Kentucky, saw at once the weakness of the above argument, for he said:

> I cannot understand the subtile logic of gentlemen who seem to think that if you compel a Friend to pay $300. commutation money in lieu of hospital service he can do it conscientiously when he cannot pay the money in lieu of military service .... Assigning them to hospital service and to military service is in effect the same.[37]

In this same connection Senator Anthony, of Rhode Island, pointed out, "A great many of them object to

---

[35] *Ibid.*, XLIII, Pt. 2, p. 995; XLIV, Pt. 1, p. 85.
[36] *Ibid.*, XLIV, Pt. 1, p. 206.
[37] *Ibid.*, p. 206.

rendering any service which relieves another man from the obligation of that service and enables him to go into the Army."[38]

With the exception of Representative Thaddeus Stevens, of Pennsylvania, there were few opinions expressed in the House on the subject of religious objectors, although ministers of the gospel entered into the discussions many times.

The governors of those states which contained large numbers of non-resistants also took a favorable attitude. In 1862, Governor Kirkwood, of Iowa, recommended the exemption from draft of those who could not conscientiously perform military duty, upon the payment of a commutation fee.[39] Governor Morton, of Indiana, was instrumental in relieving certain individuals from the draft,[40] and it was largely through his efforts that the Federal Government fixed the amount of the commutation tax in connection with the Militia Bill of July 17, 1861.[41] Again his attitude can be illustrated by an incident which occurred later in the war. When a Quaker, by the name of Allen Jay, was drafted and refused to serve, Governor Morton spoke to Lincoln in an effort to prevent Jay's farm from being sold. In this effort he was apparently successful.[42]

Governors Tod, of Ohio, and Andrew, of Massachusetts, also acted favorably when the subject was brought to their attention. In 1861, without waiting even for well-defined authority, Tod exempted from the provision of the Militia Act, upon the payment of $200., members of religious

[38] *Ibid.*, XLIV, Pt. I, p. 255.

[39] Shambaugh, Benjamin F. *Messages and Proclamations of the Governors of Iowa*, II, pp. 316–317.

[40] Foulke, William Dudley, *Life of Oliver P. Morton*, I, p. 199.

[41] *Official Records*, Series 3, II, pp. 587, 588, 589, and 590.

[42] Holder, Charles Frederick. *The Quakers in Great Britain and America*, p. 567.

denominations whose creeds forbade their taking up arms.[43]    Governor Andrew wrote to Brigadier General Buckingham in 1861 asking him if "Quakers, and the like" should not be exempt from military duty.[44] As another illustration of his attitude, Senator Sumner, of Massachusetts, on January 18, 1864, referred to a letter which he had just received from Andrew regarding a case of conscientious objection to military service. Sumner said, " . . . And the Governor in his communication to me especially asks me to interest myself in this case and to present it to the Government; . . . "[45]

Further evidence of the conciliatory attitude of governors in the North is contained in the unique account of Ira Whipple, a Rogerene,[46] born in Ledyard, Connecticut. Whipple was drafted twice, but refused to serve.   "He was obliged to appeal to the Governor of the State, and with his Bible in his hand, with the Mayor of the City of Norwich by his side, he addressed him, reading passages from the New Testament.   After he had finished the Governor said, 'Go home and do not worry for no soldier leaves the State against my wishes and you will not be required to do military duty.' "[47]

The attitude of some of the other Northern Governors during the period of the war is not well known, but the instances cited above leave no doubt as to the fairmindedness of many of them on this subject.

The attitude of some of the less important civil authorities in the North and of the people in general is much harder to judge largely because of the more widely scat-

---

[43] *Official Records*, Series 3, II, pp. 650, 662. See also Chap. II of this study, p. 53.

[44] *Ibid.*, p. 319, and Chap. II of this study, p. 53.

[45] *Cong. Globe*, XLIV, Pt. 1, p. 255.

[46] Only one other reference to a Rogerene refusing military service was found —in Foster, Ethan. *Conscript Quakers*, p. 7.

[47] *The Peacemaker*, XXII, no. 9, p. 194.

tered material from which such evidence must be gathered. It seems significant, however, that Quakers and other non-resistants were unmolested by civilians in the pursuit of their ordinary occupations, in the holding of their religious gatherings, and in their petitioning for relief from military service.[48] It also appears to be significant that a periodical such as *Harper's Weekly*, which ordinarily took a very belligerent attitude towards the Confederacy, printed in 1862, a very fair editorial on the subject of "The Quakers and the War." It said:

> The Legislature of Rhode Island lately debated a proposition not to exempt Quakers from military duty. The ground of those who wished that they should serve like other citizens was that the Quakers enjoyed all the benefits of the Government, sued in the courts, and shared a protection which rested at last upon the bayonet; and that consequently to release them from the duty of supporting that Government, in the last resort, was to be guilty of class legislation.
>
> The reply to this was, that non-resistance was a tenet of the sect, and that to compel them to fight was to interfere with that religious liberty and equal respect of sects which the fundamental law guarantees.
>
> The proposition was lost by a heavy majority.
>
> Yet the ground of the defense seems to be unsound. To excuse the Quakers, as a religious sect, from duties which are imposed upon all other sects, is evidently a very unequal respect for sects. The only true ground of excuse should be not that the man is a Quaker, but that he is a non-resistant. For by what just law can a non-resistant Quaker be excused from military service, and a non-resistant Baptist or Methodist compelled to serve? Suppose that a new sect should appear with a new tenet of non-resistance, to the effect that governments should be supported by voluntary

---

[48] For one exception to this statement, see Smith, C. Henry. *Mennonites of America*, p. 315.

contributions, should the members of the sect be excused from taxation? And if the members of the sect, then why not all citizens who hold similar opinions?

Unless, therefore, all persons who conscientiously object to fighting are to be released from military duty, there is no good reason why any of them should be.

The law in regard to the exemption of Quakers is of no great importance in itself, because they are not a large class, and because many of them practically disregard it, and are as gallant soldiers as any in the field. But the principle of the law is very important. It favors one sect. It discriminates between equal citizens. It is really a law of privilege, and ought to be repealed. Then if it shall be thought wise to excuse all citizens who have true conscientious scruples against fighting, let a law be made to secure their release.[49]

It was this same periodical that humorously pointed out at the time of the first draft in New York City that "One of the most singular Phenomena of the day is the remarkable increase of Quakerism in the Sixth Ward in this City." An accompanying picture showed ruffians in Quaker broad-brimmed hats brawling together.[50]

Much less can be said about the attitude of the civil authorities in the South during the conflict. Many of the records of the period are either silent on the subject or have not been preserved with as great care as in the North; furthermore, the direct contacts between conscientious objectors and the civil authorities were fewer in the Confederacy than in the North.

Religious objectors, to begin with, were not as fortunate as those in the North in having a sympathetic President. Jefferson Davis turned over to his subordinates all ques-

[49] *Harper's Weekly*, VI, p. 579.

[50] *Ibid.*, VI, p. 560. Other periodicals which were investigated and which contained no mention of those scrupulous against bearing arms were the Atlantic Monthly, Harper's New Monthly Mag., Living Age, and North Amer. Review. No attempt was made, however, to cover adequately this field of the press.

tions involving rights of conscience, and, in addition, was far more sparing than Lincoln in his expressions of opinion.[51] When a delegation of Friends visited him during the summer of 1862 he received them courteously but "remarked that he regretted to learn that there was within the limits of the Southern Confederacy a body of people unwilling not only to fight, but if needful to die in defense of their country."[52] Certain it is that Friends depended little upon his sympathy, and there are no statements by the Society of gratitude for his interest or efforts in their behalf.[53]

Quakers and other non-resistants were very fortunate in having John A. Campbell as Assistant Secretary of War during the greater part of the conflict. Unquestionably, he did more than any other person in the Confederate Government to alleviate the sufferings of conscientious objectors, and the appeals which came to him, mostly through John B. Crenshaw, of the Society of Friends, were always given careful consideration. Even after the Bureau of Conscription took over the administration of the draft, Assistant Secretary Campbell continued to be the real directing force, as he was already the dominating personality in the War Department.[54]

Campbell was formerly an Associate Justice of the United States Supreme Court, but after the war commenced he took no direct part in it until George W. Randolph, who was then Secretary of War, offered him in

---

[51] Davis, Jefferson. *The Rise and Fall of the Confederate Government*, (2 vols.) and Rowland, Dunbar *Jefferson Davis, Letters, Papers, and Speeches*, (10 vols.) were examined for evidences of Davis' attitude, but nothing was found.

[52] Cartland, Fernando. G. *Southern Heroes*, p. 127.

[53] Margaret E. Crenshaw, daughter of John B. Crenshaw, who lived in or near Richmond throughout the war period states that Davis had no patience with Quaker beliefs on the subject of non-resistance.

[54] Jones, J. B. *A Rebel War Clerk's Diary*, II, pp. 428 and 442. Moore, Albert Burton *Conscription and Conflict in the Confederacy*, p. 208.

October, 1862, the position of Assistant Secretary of War, "stating that there was in the War Department a large accumulation of business of a civil nature requiring the attention of an experienced lawyer."[55] Campbell accepted reluctantly. His appointment was approved October 21, 1862, and was confirmed by the Senate the following April.[56] Judge Campbell himself said of his appointment and subsequent work in office:

'This application was without any agency on my part .... The country was then suffering all the calamities of invasion. Much of the business and the feelings and the sensibilities of the country were concentrated in the War Office, for conscription had placed the whole military population under it and impressments were doing the same in regard to property. The courts were debilitated. Military rule dominant. The office of Assistant Secretary did not give me any control over military operations or organizations. It did not charge me with the subsistence, movement, or employment of troops; or with the conduct of the war. It gave me no control, custody, oversight, care, or responsibility in regard to prisoners of war. I had no charge of regular or irregular enterprises of war, or of any secret service or the employment of money. I decided a vast number of cases for the exemption of citizens from military service. I made details in cases of justice, equity, and necessity, and granted exemptions on that account, on appeal from the subordinate officers. I revised a vast number of cases of arrests by subordinates. I superintended the current correspondence of the office. I made a great variety of orders and decisions in particular cases. The office was one that imposed irksome, uncongenial, and in most cases, trivial labor. But I do not doubt that I alleviated much distress, mitigated the severities of the war to some persons, enforced justice and order in many instances, and won the respect of those

---

[55] Connor, Henry G. *John Archibald Campbell*, p. 158.
[56] *Journal of Confederate Congress*, III, p. 166.

having connection with the office, by a firm, impartial, and benevolent administration.'[57]

Many examples of Campbell's kindness to Quakers might be cited. Several of the following, taken from the Diary of John B. Crenshaw, will serve as illustrations:

2/7/63 I went to Richmond this morning and interceded for M. H. Bradshaw, who the Asst. Sec. of War agreed to pass as a Friend. I paid the Tax, and brought him out here this evening.

3/1/63 I went to Richmond today and succeeded in getting the Asst. Sec. of War to pass Wm. A. Wills as a friend and I paid the Tax for him and arranged to get his discharge. I should have written this in 2d.

10/15/63 I went to see Judge J. A. Campbell who wished to see me about the Hockett boys. He wished to send them north. I wrote tonight to their father for advice. 11/3/63 Received discharge for Hocketts and sent on to them by mail.

Judge Campbell first tendered his resignation as Assistant Secretary of War soon after his appointment in the fall of 1862. This he did because of Secretary Randolph's withdrawal from the War Department. He thereafter offered his resignation time and again, but it was not until 1865 that it was accepted. At each application to resign he was told that his services could not be dispensed with, and the last time nearly all of the members of Congress appealed to him to remain. His own conclusion was that he made little impression upon the events of the war but that he was able to do a great amount of good and to diminish " 'the weight of the heaviest calamity that ever befell a country, to many; ... ' "[58]

It is small wonder that the Meeting for Sufferings of the

---

[57] Connor, Henry G. *op. cit.*, pp. 158–159.

[58] *Ibid.*, p. 160.

North Carolina Yearly Meeting of Friends prepared a petition on behalf of Judge Campbell after he was imprisoned by the Federal authorites at the close of the war. The Meeting united in preparing the following minute:

> A petition in behalf of John A. Campbell now imprisoned for his post in the late rebellion being read and deliberately considered in view of the kind aid heretofore rendered by him to us as a Society in our late trials under said rebellion, and our being convinced that the facts set forth in said petition are true, the Clerk is directed to sign it on behalf of the meeting.[59]

As most of the questions of conscription and conscience were handled in the Confederacy by Assistant Secretary Campbell there were only a few cases in which Secretary of War Seddon took action. One famous instance was the case of Tilman R. Vestal, a Quaker from Tennessee, who was conscripted at the age of eighteen. The following petition, which was addressed to President Davis, gives part of the story of Vestal's trials and of the action finally taken in his case.

> We desire respectfully to present the case of Tilman R. Vestal whose Mother is a member of the Religious Society of Friends, a native of North Carolina, but now a resident of Tennessee. His father, not being a Friend, he does not come under the law allowing exemption to such, but his mother having carefully instructed him in the principles of said Society, it appears he has endeavored faithfully to maintain them. When conscribed and taken to the Western Army he was offered the privilege of the exemption Act, but declined to avail himself of it at that time, supposing that such would be the course of Friends generally. He was afterward moved to the Army of Genl. Lee, where after having endured many trials, he was finally Court-Martialed and sen-

---

[59] Min. of the Meeting for Sufferings of North Carolina Yearly Meeting, 6 mo. 19, 1865.

tenced to imprisonment during the War, for declining to perform military duty. When Vestal had opportunity of communicating with friends in North Carolina Yearly Meeting of which his Mother is a member, and learned that said meeting, had by Minute granted to its members the liberty of availing themselves of the law of exemption for non-combatants, he also wished to be allowed the same privilege. The case was brought by appeal before the Honl. James A. Seddon Secretary of War, who declined to allow him the privilege because he had once refused it. We hope it may be the pleasure of the President to allow said Vestal exemption on the payment of the tax, seeing that his refusal in the first instance to pay such tax arose from his separation from the body of the Society and ignorance of what action they had taken in the matter.

We would further mention that this young man is a Potter by trade, and if released would be a useful member of the Community and we are sure a peaceful and law-abiding Citizen. In support of the facts above mentioned we respectfully refer to papers on file in the Office of the Adjutant General at Richmond.[60]

---

[60] *Papers of Thomas Ruffin*, III, pp. 365–366. The papers, above referred to, in the Office of the Adjutant General at Richmond, were transferred to the War Department at Washington after the War. They are of interest because they throw additional light on the attitude of the civil and military authorities in the case of Vestal. They include the following:

Record of Tilman R. Vestal
  Co. I, 14 Tenn. Inf.
Appeared on Co. Muster Roll, July and Aug. 1863. Taken Aug. 12, 1863. In arrest for refusing to do duty, says he is of Quaker belief. (Sept. and Oct.) Would not draw any pay or clothing (Nov. and Dec. '63). "Imprisoned for during the war for refusing to duty as a soldier by sentence of Genl. Court Martial A. N. V. Claimed to be of Quaker belief." Mar. 10, 1865. Taken oath. Trans. furnished to Phil. Pa.

Mar. 16, '64

Sp. Orders No. 63 Par. XXXIII
  So much of the sentence of the military court 3 Corp. Army of Nor. Va. held Feby 6/63 as condemns Private *Tilman R. Vestal* Co. I 14 Tennessee Regt. to imprisonment for the War, is remitted & He will, accordingly, be released from confinement, & is assigned to work, during the War, with David Parr & Sons, Richmond, but without pay and allowance from the Government.

Earnestly craving the guidance of best wisdom for Thee as our Ruler and submitting the above petition to thy clemency, we are respectfully—

> Peter Adams
> N. H. D. Wilson
> C. A. Boon
> Sheriff Guilford County, N. C.
> Andr. J. McAlpin
> Discharged Soldier—from 1st
> Regt. La. Vols.
> Cyrus P. Mendenhall
> President Farmers Bank
> Joab Hiatt
> A. P. Eckel
> Mayor
> James Sloan
> Major and Chf. Coms.
> John A. Gilmer

Under a decision of Judge Campbell the man is entitled to exemption provided the Statements made are Correct.

> (Signed)    J. H. Anderson
> Capt. and E. O. 6th Dist.

James T. Morehead
Jesse H. Lindsay

The attitude of legislators in the Confederacy towards religious objectors must be judged almost entirely from their actions rather than from their words. The fact that they were willing to exempt Friends, Mennonites, Dun-

---

Letter from H. E. Peyten, Maj. to Gen. (?) H. Chilton, dated Headquarters Ar. N. Va. Sept. 23, 1863

"As instructed I have made an investigation of the facts in the case of private Thos. R. Vestal—a conscript Co. I 14 Tenn. Regt. referred to in the accompanying papers from the War Dept. . . . etc."

"In compliance with the order the Col. of his Regt. had him punctured with bayonets—as stated in the enclosed letter of Vestal, but not with the severity he represents. The Surgeon present certifies that the punctures were in the fleshy part of the buttocks and *very slight* except in *two* places where the bayonet entered not *over* $\frac{1}{2}$ an inch. The punishment did not at all unfit him for duty."

kers, and Nazarenes from military duty in October, 1862, was in itself not remarkable considering the comparatively small numbers in these denominations and the many other classes of persons who were exempt for other reasons. It is significant, however, that as the war proceeded and as exemptions were curtailed the conscientious scruples of these religious sects were still recognized.

There seem to have been no outstanding supporters of conscientious objectors in the Confederate Congress at Richmond as there were in the Federal Congress at Washington, with the possible exceptions of Senator Preston, of Virginia, and Representative Miles, of South Carolina. In the report of the committee, which was appointed by the North Carolina Yearly Meeting to present a memorial to the Confederate Congress and to President Davis in July, 1862, Preston and Miles were mentioned especially. The Committee reported:

> We were treated with respect by everyone with whom we conversed on the subject, and by some with tenderness of feeling. We may particularly mention William B. Preston, of Virginia, chairman of the committee on military affairs for the Senate, and William Porcher Miles, chairman of a similar committee for the House. On an interview with the former, he told us to make ourselves entirely easy on the subject; that the Senate Committee, in acting upon it, were unanimous in recommending an entire exemption. He said that some were for requiring us to furnish substitutes, but that he was well aware that we could not conscientiously do that, and that nothing but a clear and full exemption would meet our scruples. Miles, chairman of the House committee, invited us to a hearing, in their room, before the committee at large, and took pains to arrange the sittings as much as possible to suit our convenience. We had the very acceptable company and assistance of John B. Crenshaw who labored faithfully in word and doctrine.[61]

---

[61] Min. of North Carolina Yearly Meeting, 11 mo. 3, 1862, pp. 6–8.

In the states of the Confederacy in which the non-resistant sects were most numerous, namely Virginia and North Carolina, some of the Governors and higher civil authorities seemed to be in sympathy with their pacific principles. This was especially true of North Carolina, the stronghold of Quakerism in the South. In that State, for example, Governor William Graham, in a speech delivered to the State Convention, which at the time (December 7, 1861) was considering the passage of a Test Act,[62] said, " 'This ordinance wholly disregards their [the Quakers'] peculiar belief, and converts every man of them into a warrior or an exile. True, they are allowed to affirm, but the affirmation is equivalent to the oath of the feudal vassal to his lord, to "defend him with life and limb and terrene honor". . . . This ordinance, therefore, is nothing less than a decree of banishment to them . . . . Upon the expulsion from among is of such a people, the civilized world would cry, shame!' "[63]

Jonathan Worth, at various times a member of the Legislature, Treasurer, and Governor of North Carolina, frequently interceded on behalf of distressed Quakers. On April 3, 1863, for example, he wrote to Governor Zebulon B. Vance presenting some cases of extreme hardship under the Act of Assembly conscripting free negroes to work on fortifications. Among other cases he cited that of "Felix Walker, who has a good farm, and who is working at the State Salt works to avoid military service, has several children of tender years. His wife has recently become insane and is in the Asylum here. I am informed that Lewis Phillips, a free negro and his only hand, is taken." Worth concluded with these words, "Looking to the extreme hardship of the cases and the urgent necessity that grain be made, I respectfully petition in behalf of the

---

[62] See Chap. III of this study, p. 98.
[63] Weeks, Stephen B. *Southern Quakers and Slavery*, pp. 304–305.

parties that these free negroes be allowed to return to their employers."[64]

On June 17, 1863, three Quakers by the names of Nere Cox, Seth Cox, and Eli Macon wrote to Jonathan Worth in the following manner: "There is three in Camp Holmes members of the society of Friends and we want thee to come over immediately on receiving these lines in order to pay our exemption tax and let us go home if thee cannot furnish us with the money we want thee to come and see us any how."[65] On June 6, 1863, Worth received a communication from another Friend by the name of Delphina E. Mendenhall regarding a Quaker conscript. She said, "Since I wrote O. C. Gordon has been twice arrested and twice discharged. I suppose his exemption is now secure. Lt. Anderson stays at Greensboro and expressed his regret that the Militia officers had arrested Gordon the second time. Gordon will pay for thy services. He is a worthy young man. Send me the bill and I will present it to him . . . "[66]

Finally a letter which he himself wrote to John B. Crenshaw on November 3, 1864, stated in no uncertain language his attitude towards religious objectors. He said, "Yours of the 29th ult. was received in yesterday's mail, but the numbers of the 'Southern Friend,' which you said you would mail to me, containing the law touching such cases as those in relation to which I wrote you, have not come to hand. I regret it, as I would gladly excuse from war all whom I may believe conscientious in their scruples against bearing arms; and my duties, public and private, have been so pressing that I have neglected to keep properly posted . . . ."[67] Doubtless Worth's sympathy for Friends

[64] *Correspondence of Jonathan Worth*, I, pp. 229–230.
[65] *Ibid.*, I, p. 242.
[66] *Ibid.*, I, p. 241.
[67] Cartland, Fernando G. *Southern Heroes*, pp. 145–146.

arose partly from the fact that his mother was a member of that religious Society. Worth, himself, however, was not affiliated with any denomination.

Thomas Ruffin, a justice of the Supreme Court of North Carolina for many years prior to the war, was also appealed to by Delphina E. Mendenhall on January 23, 1864, on behalf of Tilman R. Vestal.[68]  Among other things she said:

> Please be so kind as to write a letter to President Davis, recommending the bearer of the Petition, Judith J. Mendenhall, and respectfully asking the release of T. R. Vestal on the ground stated in the Petition, and on account of his having been from his infancy remarkable for the purity of his life, the tenderness of his conscience, and the devotedness of his piety from early boyhood.  For the truth of which I hereby pledge my word and honor . . . .
>
> We are advised that a letter of this kind from thee, will have much weight with President Davis, and ask it as a very great favor.
>
> This occasion opens the way for me to ask another favor which has been resting on my mind for many months.
>
> At the time the Quaker Bill was before our Legislature, (or Convention) my cousin T. J. Wilson of Forsyth County, told me that the Society of Friends ought to have the speech made by thee on the subject—Because it was the Speech that set forth most forcibly the reason why they ought to be exempt from military service. As there may be future Legislation on the subject, not only in this, but other lands, please be so good as to write out the substance of that speech, not for *me*, my much esteemed Friend, but for the innocent, the meek and lowly, of this and other lands—of this and other days—perhaps for generations yet unborn.[69]

In Virginia, when the Militia Bill of 1862 was being debated by the Legislature, the Chairman of the House of Delegates made a speech in favor of exempting non-

---

[68] See pp. 142-144.

[69] *Papers of Thomas Ruffin*, III, pp. 364-365.  No record was found of the speech referred to above.

resistants in that State. He pointed out the folly of attempting to force them into the army, and, on the other hand, the advantages of allowing them to remain at home to produce crops for other people. All would be lost and nothing gained, he claimed, for " 'they will fold their arms and take your enemies' fire' "[70] Other members of the Virginia Legislature to plead for religious objectors were Representatives Gratton and Hopkins.[71]

As in the North, so in the South, the attitude of civilians is harder to judge than the attitude of particular individuals, especially if those individuals were prominent in civil life. There were undoubtedly many Southerners, outside the ranks of the Army, who lost patience with the conscientious scruples of non-resistants, and treated them with scant respect, but, on the other hand, it is certain that many persons sympathized with their point of view.

One example of severe justice is contained in the following letter, written by N. T. Perkins to John B. Crenshaw in November, 1863.[72]

Brother Calvin is still there [Salisbury prison] he was brought to the gate of the Garison and I allowed to speak about ten words to him we were then separated—I have been there three times during his nine months imprisonment and each time my interview has been equally as short as the last—Calvin had the promise of being exchanged some months ago but they refuse to carry out their promise. In the sixth mo. last I sued out a writ of Habeas Corpus in his favor—they confessed on trial that they had no charges against him yet the Judge put off the trial for about ten days pretending they might find something against him—during this time the President declared martial law—there the Judge said that put a stop to the case. Some three

[70] Sanger and Hays, *The Olive Branch*, p. 57.

[71] *Journal of the House of Delegates of the State of Virginia for the Session of 1861–62*, pp. 308, 310.

[72] From North Carolina Yearly Meeting Collection of Crenshaw Correspondence.

months ago the President was petitioned for his release there was nothing found against him there the Secretary of War ordered his release more than two months ago—The commander of the prison requires a bond of $5000.00 for his good behavior and take the oath of allegiance to the Southern Confederacy before he releases him—he says he will stay there until the end of the war before he would do either.

Another letter, which was published in *The Friend* summarizes excellently the attitude apparently assumed by many non-Friends, both North and South, and accounts for the impunity which so many Quakers enjoyed during the heat of the conflict. The letter said:

> The unkind efforts of some editors to create an issue between the people at large, and the Society of Friends, with regard to the performance of military duties, compares but poorly with the consideration accorded by the leaders of the rebellion to the views and feelings held by Friends in the South, or with that of a Georgia slaveholder who, while riding with a Friend in North Carolina, acknowledged to having six sons in the army, but was nevertheless glad to find that there was one Society opposed to *all* wars; expressing the hope that they would continue firm in their principles; also with the testimony of a distinguished member of the Philadelphia Bar, . . . who says, 'it would be a lasting disgrace to this or any other community, to disregard the real, unaffected, conscientious feelings of such as are opposed to *all* wars.'
>
> The question is not, may members of the Society of Friends as such, be exempted from military duties—for I blush to acknowledge there are some in membership with us, who appear to have little or no scruple about murder and plunder when legalized, and combined under the name of war—but the question is, may such individuals of whatever name, as are raised above these baneful lusts . . . be forced to violate their highest obligations?[73]

---

[73] *The Friend*, XXXVI, no. 5, p. 38.

# Chapter V

## Attitude of the Military Authorities Toward Conscientious Objectors

APPARENTLY more cases of conscience came to the attention of those highest in civil authority in the Federal Government than to those highest in military rank. It is largely for this reason that the attitude of the military leaders is not so well known as is the attitude of the civil authorities and the military officers of lower rank. Such evidence as there is points to the fact that the Generals in the Northern Armies were more considerate in their treatment of conscientious objection to military service than were some of the officers and privates who came more directly in contact with individual cases of objection.

On September 28, 1863, for example, when the Religious Order of the Holy Cross petitioned President Lincoln for exemption from military service, both Generals Grant and Sherman endorsed the request. The petition read in part:

We most respectfully venture to ask of Your Excellency the privilege of being exempted from military service, or rather from bearing arms. Not, indeed, because we are opposed to the measures which our rightful Government thinks proper to adopt and enact for the vigorous prosecution of the war—for that is, we sincerely believe, the speediest way to crush down rebellion and restore peace to the nation —but on account of our true devotion to the Union and the constant support we have willingly and cheerfully given to the Government in sending with our armies six priests as chaplains, . . . and in our army and navy hospitals nearly forty sisters as nurses. To serve as chaplains or nurses we always willingly do, as it is in conformity with our vocation;

but to bear arms even in a war we deem right and just is very repugnant to our religious and sacred calling; nay, more, priests or clerics cannot shed blood without *ipso facto* incurring the censures of the church.

General Grant appended to this petition the following words:

I would respectfully represent that the order herein applying for exemption have contributed largely of their services to the support of the war, and if any class is to be exempt from the present or any future draft, they have fully entitled themselves to such benefit. Respectfully referred for the consideration of the President, hoping that, if not inconsistent with law or the policy of the Government, that the favor asked will be granted.

General Sherman merely added:

I concur, but do not commit myself as to the legal questions involved.[1]

General Halleck, when General-in-Chief of the United States Army, was evidently confronted with the problem of what to do with conscientious objectors who came under his jurisdiction, because Major-General John A. Dix wrote him the following letter from the Headquarters Department of the East, New York City, on October 24, 1863:

The cases of Quakers who have conscientious scruples in regard to bearing arms or paying money as a commutation for military service may be provided for without injury to the public or objection on their part by assigning them to duty as nurses and attendants in hospitals.

They do not object to being employed in nursing the sick and disabled, as it is a duty of humanity and of men capable of bearing arms, without any sacrifice of principle on the part of the Government. Several cases have occurred in this department, and I take the liberty of suggesting the

[1] *Official Records*, Series 3, III, pp. 844–845.

adoption of the above rule to meet them and all others of the same character.[2]

It seems likely that General Halleck would have been sympathetic with cases of conscience because, owing to an oversight caused by his removal to the West, he remained a member of the Friends' Meeting at Newport, Rhode Island, throughout the war.[3]

It was not unusual for those in the North opposed on conscientious grounds to bearing arms to receive courteous treatment when in military hands. Apparently there were many Federal officers who both understood and respected the scruples of Quakers and other non-resistants. The following account illustrates the liberal treatment which many received.[4]

At the time of the 'Civil War,' I was living six miles North of Dayton, Ohio, and was there drafted.

As Secretary of War Stanton had issued a statement in regard to the release of conscientious objectors, I immediately went to Commissioner Young (who conducted the draft), and made affidavit that I was conscientious against bearing arms. He very willingly took my affidavit and forwarded it to Secretary Stanton, and told me to remain at home while he went with the drafted men to Camp Denison at Cincinnati.

In some way the army officers at Camp Dayton learned that I had not gone to Camp Denison with the others, and so sent a squad of soldiers out to arrest me, and also to find a 'deserter' from the regular army. They had no trouble in getting me, and then proceeded to search for the 'Deserter' until after midnight, when we reached Camp Dayton (they failed to find the deserter).

They reported to the 'Captain of the Day' that they had a 'Prisoner' (a boy from the country). They had treated

[2] *Ibid.*, p. 922.
[3] Cartland, Fernando G. *Southern Heroes*, p. 129.
[4] Letter from A. M. Jenkins to the author under date of August 1, 1928.

me kindly and so introduced me to the captain, who said it was a shame to put a decent man in the guard house, as there had been a fight in camp that day, and the guard house was full of the worst characters in camp. And so he took me up to his quarters. In the morning he told me to go get my breakfast 'that the boys all helped themselves,' there was no restraint placed upon me.

After three days, Commissioner Young came out to camp, and calling me to come out where he and the colonel were talking, said to me 'This is a mistake that you are here. I never gave orders for you to be brought here. You can go home, and report to me later.' He then criticized the colonel for arresting me and told him that he was attending to my case. I reported to him the following Monday, together with another young Friend who had been 'Drafted' from another county. As my discharge had not been received, he said I would have to report at Camp Denison.

The Commissioner went with us and was very kind and jovial with us. He frequently introduced us to army officers stating that we were a couple of 'young Quakers,' that we could neither 'fight nor run.' When we reached Camp Denison, he gave us the same introduction to the Colonel, who replied that if we would not run, he would soon have us drilling. He said 'he wanted to see how Quakers would look drilling.'

He refused to give us furlows back home (as Comissioner Young had expected him to do), and so we remained in Camp for three days until our discharges, were brought to us by a friend. When presented to the colonel, he replied that they had come too soon, as he wanted to see 'Quakers drilling,' but added 'that he could give us an "honorable discharge," as we had maintained our "conscious principles," ' and so we were permitted to return home.

. . . I was never mistreated, and my 'conscious principles' were respected.

The draft occurred in the fall of 1862 when everything seemed to be at the darkest period of the war, and there was a strong 'secession element' in Dayton, Ohio, which made the situation there very critical.

Another illustration of a liberal attitude on the part of military authorities is found in the case of Barclay Stratton, an Ohio Quaker who was drafted on September 23, 1864.[5] He was ordered to appear at Alliance, a gathering-point, about eighteen miles from his home, from which place he wrote:

> The officials did not doubt the sincerity of my views, and, were it in their power, would gladly release me, but, as it is, they will be obliged to forward me to Todd's Barracks, Columbus.

While at Todd's Barracks he wrote:

> I made my way to the major's office about eight o'clock, found him very busy, but willing to entertain me a moment, so I inquired about Dr. Stanton (a relative of the Secretary of War who had some connection with Friends), who, he said, had left here to fill a position in Cincinnati. I now felt to be altogether upon my own resources, and showed him my affidavit, which he hastily read, and agreed himself to forward to Secretary Stanton, but said I was now in the service, and would have to put on my soldier's clothes and drill with them, perhaps be sent to the front before Stanton could be heard from, but that the Secretary would undoubtedly release me, yet it would require some time, probably a week, before the thing could be accomplished.

Stratton's first real conflict with the authorities came when he refused to put on his soldier's clothes. He described his experience in the following words:

> The major, as they called him, was then called in, from whom I had reason, from my previous interview, to expect some harshness, but, calling me into an adjoining room,

---

[5] This account is taken from the letters of Barclay Stratton, which were printed in full in *The Friend*, LXVIII, nos. 28, 29, 30.

with two or three others, conversed very feelingly, and differently from what I was expecting. He instanced one other case of the kind from the same district, which, on account of public sentiment, was occasioning them some trouble, and that they had to use a great deal of caution in such cases. I then briefly stated to him the circumstances under which I was here, what my principles had long been on the subject of war, and why I declined putting on the clothing, after which, placing his hand on my shoulder, he said, 'My friend, I admire your candor. You just put on the pants and jacket, and remain here until we can hear from the Secretary of War, who will relieve you, and you shall be exempt from any service during the interval, but will have to remain here, as we dare not relieve you, except at his instance, and it will not do for you to remain long inside the barracks in citizens' clothing. I replied that I felt under great obligations to him and other officers for their kindness to me, but that consistency with my views would require that I should decline putting them on myself, but if they considered it their duty to put them on me, they could easily do it. He then told the clerk to put them on me, which he did in a very good-humored style, saying he did not blame me in the least for not doing it myself. They have given me the privilege of being in this office whenever I see proper, which I regard a great privilege.

Later on, in the same letter, Stratton said:

As, from what I can learn, officers are going to be governed very much by public opinion in the vicinity where the individual is known. Isaac Cadwallader (another Friend from the same quarter) arrived here yesterday. He says he met with as favorable a reception as he could expect. The major, however, told him that, unless he furnished the best of evidence respecting his consistency with his views, he would have to send him to the front.

On still another occasion he said:

I have been eyed a great deal since being here and de-
tected several times as a Quaker, even since parting with
my peculiar garb, yet on no occasion have I been spoken to
rudely or uncivilly on that account.  At one time, the ser-
geant having care of the barracks where I stay, came to me,
saying he had orders to take the names of all in his barracks,
that he would take my name, but would see that it should
not be transferred to the muster-clerk; that I might still
remain where I was; . . .

Speaking again about his major, he said:

He certainly made fair, and, I thought, candid, promises
that I would be relieved, and I must gratefully acknowledge
that his assurances that I would not be called upon to *drill*,
*muster*, or be *forewarded* to the front, as hundreds have been
since I came here, have *all* been realized thus far.

Later Stratton, and his friend, Isaac Cadwallader, were
sent South.  They were given the opportunity of doing
hospital service as an alternative to military service, but
they remained faithful to their pacific principles and did
not accept the offer.  They were treated apparently with
continued kindness by most of the officers and men, and
were finally paroled until called for after they had been
some time with the army in front of Richmond, Virginia.

It was not at all uncommon for military officers to mis-
understand the motives underlying the objection to
military service of Quakers and members of the noncombatant religious sects.  Until such misunderstanding
was cleared up the treatment of the objectors was likely
to be harsh, but, in the following case at least, the attitude
of the authorities changed as soon as it was learned that
the objector was a Friend. Joseph G. Miller, a resident of
Brooklyn and a member of the New York (Hicksite)
Monthly Meeting of Friends, was examined several times
by the local enrollment board before being taken to a

military camp on Rikers Island. At the camp he was forced to put on soldiers' clothing; he also was subjected to rough treatment by the officers and suffered from exposure to the weather.

But when it became known that he was a Friend and was actuated by conscientious scruples their manner towards him underwent an entire change. After a detention of about three weeks on this Island he was on the 23d of 10th month removed to Governors Island, where he was furnished with a comfortable Bed in the Hospital, was permitted to resume his own clothes, and was required to do nothing contrary to his feelings, on the 11th of Eleventh Month he was liberated under parole.[6]

Some religious objectors, when called upon to perform military service, stated to the authorities in advance their reasons for non-compliance. In such cases the attitude of the military authorities varied considerably, but for the most part the treatment which the objectors received was not severe.

William P. and Edward G. Smedley, cousins who lived in Delaware County, Pennsylvania, took such a course upon the advice of their friends. A paper was prepared, setting forth their views, and was addressed "to the Provost Marshal and Board of Enrollment or other Proper Officers."[7] It said:

The undersigned is informed that his name is included in a list of persons reported to be drafted for service in the army of the United States.

He respectfully represents that he is a member of the Religious Society of Friends, and is conscientiously scrupulous against bearing arms, or being otherwise concerned in war, and on this ground he cannot conform himself to the draft,

---

[6] Min. of New York (Hicksite) Monthly Meeting, 4 mo. 6, 1864, and Cox, John, Jr. *Quakerism in New York City*, p. 48.

[7] *The Friend*, LXXXI, no. 49, p. 390.

procure a substitute, pay the three hundred dollars provided by law, or any other sum as a commutation for military service, or for the free exercise of his natural right to
liberty of conscience.

He feels that he is truly and entirely loyal to the government of the United States, and is willing to obey the laws, to
bear his full share of the civil burdens and to perform all the
other duties of a peaceable and good citizen, so far as these
things are not inconsistent with his religious obligations
.... He respectfully asks that this paper may be filed among
your records as evidence that he is not a deserter in fact,
although the law may designate him by this appellation.

(Signed) Edward G. Smedley

In telling of his later experiences, Edward Smedley
wrote:

... We were sent to Philadelphia in charge of Lieutenant
Joseph G. Cummins, of Media, also a schoolmate of mine,
and who treated us as kindly as he could, it being much
against his will to take us .... When we were turned over to
the officers ..., and they were informed of the circumstances of our declining from conscientious motives to participate in any warlike measures, they utterly repudiated
such notions, commanded our immediate compliance with
their orders, and when we quietly declined, manifested
great resentment by wordy abuse and threatenings of
punishment. After their passions were pretty well spent,
we were sent to the third floor of the building, turned in
with some hundreds of drafted men and substitutes, and left
to make the best we could of the situation till morning.

As the cousins refused to carry their own knapsacks
their guard had to carry these burdens for them all the
way to their destination in Philadelphia. Upon their
refusal to take up these knapsacks, upon their arrival at
the barracks, their officers threatened to tie them up in
ropes. They were given five minutes in which to obey,
or be bound. Before the threat could be carried out, how-

ever, they were hurried off to make way for a number of substitutes who had just come in, and who might be demoralized by seeing resistance to orders so early in their military careers.

The lieutenant who had brought the Smedleys to Philadelphia pled with their officers not to send them to the Potomac with the squad which was leaving the following day, but urged that they be held in camp. A committee of Friends, being notified of their plight, wrote to Secretary Stanton and interviewed General Hatch, who "treated them very courteously, but did not see how any relief could be obtained, as the law gave no discretionary powers to officers; he, however, consented not to send them off that day." The same Friends called on a Colonel Kellogg, who was in charge of the barracks where the Smedley cousins were stationed, to see what could be done for them.

These men were held in the barracks for a period of seventeen days, with short releases from time to time. For refusing to "fall into line" they were at first placed in the guard-house, but in the latter days of their imprisonment the officers grew so tired of forcing them into line that they were unmolested. Their three meals a day were supplied by outside friends through the Colonel's office and by means of a basket lowered from a window in the barracks to the street below.

As in similar cases they wondered how far they should carry out their principles of non-cooperation with the military authorities. On one occasion they wrote, "Our situation is one requiring close watchfulness. I think we both earnestly desire to be directed aright. The men were scouring the floor this afternoon with sand and heavy flat stones, drawn by ropes back and forth; when they came near to us we took hold without being asked and helped a little."

Their confinement was not severe as is shown by the fact that one was able to attend his brother's wedding and both were allowed to see friends in the Colonel's office. About the time that they were threatened with being sent South an order came for their parole upon the condition that they report daily until further order. About a month later they received their liberty under a special order of the Secretary of War, which said, "Edward G. Smedley and William P. Smedley, drafted men, at Philadelphia, Pa., are hereby honorably discharged from the service of the United States."[8]

Another case of somewhat the same kind was that of William Shaw, who was drafted for service in 1864.[9] Upon being notified of his call to arms, he said:

I went to the Provost Marshal previous to the time specified and had an opportunity to lay before the officers assembled there the reasons why I could not comply with the order. That I was conscientious against taking the life of my fellow men, believing it to be in direct opposition to the command of our Lord 'Thou shalt not kill' and therefore I did not expect to report myself at the time proposed.

He was afterwards sent to a concentration camp at Columbus, where he said, "I soon found we were in the hands of unprincipled men . . . ." When he refused to drill or to obey other military commands he was taken before the Major General in command of the barracks.

When we came before him, we found a man tremulous with rage. After he had spent himself railing out against us my friend was about to reply when he forbade him saying, 'Not a word out of your mouth. Your stubbornness may

---

[8] *The Friend*, LXXXI, no. 51, p. 405.

[9] This account was written by William Shaw for *The Day Star*, printed at Mt. Vernon, Iowa, in 1884, but the proof sheets were copied into a scrap book by his daughter, Ellen Shaw Taber, and were loaned for the purpose of this study.

even be the means of causing a mutiny among my men, but you are not to have your way,' and closing with, 'Now go back to your quarters and when you are commanded to drill, *Drill!* You will have to do it, even if we have to place two bayonets before and two behind you, or if we have to run them into you.'

William Shaw and his friend, William Nichols, were later consigned to the guard house for refusing to form in line with the other conscripts. Shaw found that their guard in this latter place was sympathetically inclined, for he said to the two Quakers:

Men I do pity you, as it is such a filthy place and such hard cases to be your company but I do like to see men live up to their principles. I said Perhaps thou hast felt condemnation for wrong-doing and contrary a glow of satisfaction when thou doest well. He replied he had. Well now said I live up to this, and thou mayest be brought into as tight a place as we are. He said 'I want to do so.' And giving us a cordial shake of the hand he bid us farewell.

Another unsuccessful attempt was made to force Shaw to drill before an order arrived from Secretary Stanton for his release. Shaw described his release in the following words:

We were repeatedly visited by a cousin of the Sec. of War Stanton. He being a wise and humane man took us before a notary public and had me to give my views as to my conscientious scruples against war signing his name as a witness then allowed me to write stating that I would endeavor to bear whatever sufferings were permitted to befall me until Providence made way for my deliverence. This instrument of writing was sent to Washington and probably occasioned my discharge . . . . In a few days an order came from Sec. of War ordering the officer to release me from the prison, and from being confined at Todd Barracks. Thus was I relieved from the hands of unprincipled men and restored to the bosom of my family with a reward of *peace*. All praise to Him that enabled me to endure the cross and despise the shame to His glory.

Another unusual case was that of a young Northerner who refused to serve personally in the army or to hire a substitute, but who, after considerable hesitation, paid the commutation fee of $300. under written protest. The protest was addressed "To the governmental authorities of the United States and their constituents" and was worded, in part, as follows:

... The undersigned, John Lowell Heywood of Hopedale, in the town of Milford, in the eighth congressional district of Massachusetts, respectfully maketh solemn declaration, remonstrance, and protest, to wit:

That he has been enrolled, drafted, and notified to appear as a soldier of the United States, pursuant to an Act of Congress approved March 3, 1863, commonly called the Conscription Law.

That he holds in utter abhorrence the rebellion which the said law was designed to aid in suppressing and would devotedly fight unto death against it if he could conscientiously resort to deadly weapons in any case whatsoever.

But that he has been for nearly nine years a member in good and regular standing of a Christian Community whose religious confession of faith and practice pledges its members 'never to kill, injure, or harm any human being, even their worst enemy.'

That with such principles, scruples, and views of duty, he cannot conscientiously comply with the demands of this Conscription Law, either by serving as a soldier or by procuring a substitute. Nor can he pay the three hundred dollars of commutation money which the law declaratively appropriates to the hiring of a substitute, except under explicit remonstrance and protest that the same is virtually taken from him by compulsion for a purpose and use to which he could never voluntarily contribute it, and for which he holds himself in no wise morally responsible.

And he hereby earnestly protests not only for himself but also in behalf of his Christian associates and all other orderly, peaceable, taxpaying, non-juring subjects of the government of whatever domination or class, that their conscientious scruples against war and human life-taking, ought, in justice and honor, to be respected by the legislators and administrators of a professedly republican government; and that, aside from general taxation for the support thereof, no person of harmless and exemplary life who is conscientiously opposed to war and deadly force between human beings, and especially no person who for conscience sake foregoes the franchises, preferments, privileges, and advantages of a constituent citizen, ought ever to be conscripted as a soldier, either in person or property.[10]

An additional case, in which the commutation fee of $300. was paid for the conscripted person without his consent, was that of William P. Bancroft. He said:[11]

I went to Smyrna to see the Board that had charge of the matter, told them that I did not feel that I could do any one of the three things, and that I expected to remain at home about my usual occupations, and could probably be found there. Leonard E. Wales, who was a member of the Board, tried to reason with me, perhaps as to the necessities of war, but I could not say much. I was not sent for, and someone, without my knowledge, and I think I may say without being my desire, paid the commutation money for me. I believe one of my father's brothers did it. If I had been arrested I do not think I would have been treated harshly. It was not the disposition of the authorities to do so.

The only other member with Friends drawn here at the time, so far as I recollect, was Ashton Richardson, a member

[10] *Autobiography of Adin Ballou*, pp. 449–451.
[11] In a letter to Thomas A. Jenkins, from Wilmington, Delaware, dated 4th mo. 14, 1917.

of the other Meeting. His case resulted as mine did,—a relative, secretly I believe, paying the commutation money.

An example of more severe treatment is found in the case of Cyrus Pringle, who, on July 13, 1863, was drafted with two other Quakers, of Charlotte, Vermont, for service in the army.[12] In relating his experiences, after he was taken with his regiment to the battle-front, he says:

This morning the officers told us we must yield. We must obey and serve. We were threatened great severities and even death. We seem perfectly at the mercy of the military power, and, more, in the hands of the inferior officers, who, from their being far removed from Washington, feel less restraint from those Regulations of the Army, which are for the protection of privates from personal abuse.

Later he suffered a great deal from actual ill treatment. "Two sergeants soon called for me," he says, "and taking me a little aside, bid me lie down on my back, and stretching my limbs apart tied cords to my wrists and ankles and these to four stakes driven in the ground somewhat in the form of an X."

"I was very quiet in my mind as I lay there on the ground [soaked] with the rain of the previous day, exposed to the heat of the sun, and suffering keenly from the cords binding my wrists and straining my muscles."

As in so many other cases Pringle was finally released by order of the President and Secretary of War.

Occasionally a delay in the execution of military orders resulted temporarily in the suffering of those scrupulous against bearing arms. Such suffering occurred in the case of three New York Friends in the fall of 1863. Members of the Meeting, to which the drafted Friends belonged,

---

[12] The account of his experiences is given in full in Pringle, Cyrus. *The Record of a Quaker Conscience* (Cyrus Pringle's Diary).

learning of their confinement in the Camp on Long Island in Boston Harbor, hastened "to approach the President through a third party whose social relations, as they learn-[ed], [gave] him access to the President at times when released from official cases."[13]  The parole of the men was ordered but for some unknown reason the order was not immediately executed.  In the meantime the men were sent to Culpepper, Virginia, where, upon their refusal to bear arms, muskets were strapped on them, and they were forced to march under heavy loads and without food or water about four miles to camp.  On the way one of them was forced to give up from exhaustion.  "They were then required to perform duty which they could not comply with, and in consequence of their refusal they were arrested and bound in painful position, and told they *must* submit, being threatened with fearful punishment."  Their case was again taken up with the authorities at Washington with the result that they were released and sent to Alexandria, where they were visited by several members of the home Meeting.  After being placed temporarily in Douglass Hospital, where no military service was required of them, they were liberated and allowed to return to their homes.[14]

It is perhaps astonishing that Friends in the North were allowed to carry on their peace propaganda during the latter part of the war.  In one case at least the military authorities, not only knew of this activity of Friends, but actually expressed approval of the sentiments involved.  As the committee in charge of Quaker publicity in the Indiana Yearly Meeting expressed it in one of their reports:

---

[13] Min. of the Meeting for Sufferings of New York (Orthodox) Yearly Meeting, 9 mo. 28, 1863, p. 190.

[14] *Ibid.*, p. 190.

We have found an increasing demand for tracts on war; even among prominent military men, these have been kindly received and read.  A Major-General in the United States Army, to whom one of our tracts on War, was presented by a Friend, carefully read it, and remarked: 'That tract is true, and the doctrine right, but we must wait to put it in practice, until after the war closes.'[15]

In the South, as in the North, there were instances in which the higher military authorities showed unexpected leniency in their attitude towards conscientious objectors. It was General T. J. Jackson, for example, who, in referring to the Dunkers and Mennonites, said:

'There lives a people in the Valley of Virginia, that are not hard to bring to the army.  While there they are obedient to their officers.  Nor is it difficult to have them take aim, but it is impossible to get them to take correct aim.  I, therefore, think it better to leave them at their homes that they may produce supplies for the army.'[16]

In one case at least General Polk also showed great consideration.  Tilman R. Vestal, an eighteen year old Quaker, was conscripted in Tennessee and placed under his command.  "General Polk heard with kindness and sympathy his earnest declaration that he could not perform military service without violating his conscience, and sinning against his God, and for that reason, gave him a discharge and sent him home to his parents."[17]  No record has come to light, however, of the attitude of General Robert E. Lee, and others of his associates.

In a similar manner, some of the military officers of lower rank showed a considerable degree of patience with, and consideration for, the conscientious scruples of

---

[15] Fourteenth Annual Report of the Central Book and Tract Committee of the Indiana Yearly Meeting in the Min. of Indiana Yearly Meeting, 1864, p. 29.

[16] Quoted in Zigler, David H. *A History of the Brethren in Virginia*, p. 98.

[17] *Papers of Thomas Ruffin*, III, p. 364.

certain individuals. In March, 1862, two groups of about ninety Mennonites and Dunkers fled from their homes in the Valley of Virginia and attempted to make their way to the West. However, they were easily captured and returned, one group of eighteen to Harrisonburg, Virginia, and the other group of seventy to Richmond, Virginia.[18] While in prison, and awaiting the action of the military authorities, they were examined by Sydney S. Baxter, of the War Department, who submitted the following favorable reports:

March 31, 1862.

I have examined a number of persons, fugitives from Rockingham and Augusta Counties, who were arrested at Petersburg, in Hardy County. These men are all regular members in good standing in the Tunker [Dunker] and Mennonite Churches. One of the tenets of those churches is that the law of God forbids shedding human blood in battle and this doctrine is uniformly taught to all their people. As all these persons are members in good standing in these churches and bear good characters as citizens and Christians I cannot doubt the sincerity of their declaration that they left home to avoid the draft of the militia and under the belief that by the draft they would be placed in a situation in which they would be compelled to violate their consciences. They all declared they had no intention to go to the enemy or to remain with them. They all intended to return home as soon as the draft was over. Some of them had made exertions to procure substitutes. One man had sent the money to Richmond to hire a substitute. Others had done much to support the families of volunteers. Some had furnished horses to the cavalry. All of them are friendly to the South and they express a willingness to contribute all their property if necessary to establish our liberties. I am informed a law will probably pass exempting these persons

---

[18] Hartzler, J. S. and Kauffman, Daniel. *Mennonite Church History*, pp. 209–211; Smith, C. Henry. *Mennonites of America*, pp. 317–319; Sanger, Samuel F. and Hays, Daniel. *The Olive Branch*, pp. 61–65, 72–73, 108–111.

from military duty on payment of a pecuniary compensation. These parties assure me all who are able will cheerfully pay this compensation. Those who are unable to make the payment will cheerfully go into service as teamsters or in any employment in which they are not required to shed blood. I recommend all the persons in the annexed list be discharged on taking the oath of allegiance and agreeing to submit to the laws of Virginia and the Confederate States in all things except taking arms in war.

S. S. Baxter

In addition to these cases I report the case of Peter L. Goode, a broken-legged man, whom I believe to be incapable of Military duty, and of John Sanger, a youth of sixteen years. Both these persons were arrested. They seem to have partaken in the Tunker panic and fled with the others. I believe both of them are faithful and loyal to Virginia and the Confederate States. I recommend they also be discharged from prison here on taking the oath of allegiance and reporting themselves to the proper officer of the regiment of Virginia milita to have their claims of exemption acted on.

S. S. Baxter[19]

April 2, 1862.

Since my last report I have seen the copy of the law passed by the Legislature of Virginia on the 29th of March, 1862. It exempts from military duty persons prevented from bearing arms by the tenets of the church to which they belong on condition of paying $500. and 2% on the assessed value of their taxable property, taking an oath to sustain the Confederate Government and not in any way to give aid or comfort to the enemies of the Confederate Government, with the proviso that if the person exempted is not able to pay the tax he shall be employed as teamster or in some character which will not require the actual bearing [of] arms, and surrender any arms they possess for public

---

[19] *Official Records*, Series 2, III, p. 835.

use. I renew my recommendation that these persons be discharged on taking the oath of allegiance and an obligation to conform to the laws of Virginia.

S. S. Baxter[20]

Another account, by an individual Mennonite, named John A. Showalter, gives additional evidence of the liberal attitude sometimes assumed by the military authorities of the South. Showalter said:

'In the month of June, 1861, I was drafted for service in the war; but I refused to go for two reasons; First, I was conscientiously opposed to war; second, I claimed exemption on the ground of bad health. So I remained at home until I was forced to go. When I arrived at camp, I refused to bear arms, again claimed exemption, was examined, and placed on the sick list by order of the doctor of the regiment; but I was compelled to remain in camp. Within three weeks, I took the measles, and through the influence of the captain of the company, I got a furlough to come home for ten days. The captain told me to go home and stay there until he sent for me. So I came home and remained till December of the same year, when I was forced to go back to the army, contrary to the captain's orders. After reaching camp again, I was taken before a court of inquiry and court-martialed, and sentenced to be drilled alone two hours a day for a certain number of days. I again refused to drill or learn the art of war. For this I was threatened to be punished severely; but I still refused to bear arms. Finally, I was asked if I would assist in cooking for the company. To this I consented, and I was not punished.'[21]

William Peters, of Seven Fountains, in the valley called the Fort, Virginia, had quite a different experience from that of John Showalter, but his story emphasizes the fact that the military authorities, in some instances at least,

---

[20] *Ibid.*, p. 837.
[21] Quoted in Sanger and Hays, *op. cit.*, pp. 105–106.

were more liberal in their attitude towards conscientious objectors than were civilians. "'As to myself, I never was in the army,'" he said.

'They made about four attempts to take me, but never got me away from home. In the fall of '61, the conscript officers came to take me. I told them I could not go and gave them my reasons. They finally went away and left me. Then during that winter and the next spring they came three different times to take me at the point of the bayonet, saying they had orders to take me dead or alive. I told them that if dead men were of any service to them, and they saw fit, they could use me; but that was the only way they could get any service out of me in the army . . . . I reasoned with them kindly, and every time they went away and left me. But citizens and "bushwackers" threatened to take my life, and as my life was in danger I was advised to go into the army. I, however, replied that I could not take up arms even if it would be the means of saving my life. I never went to the woods or the mountains for concealment as some did to get out of the way, . . . . Finally, I paid my fine. Still I was accused of being a Union man, and my life was threatened. Three of my neighbors were shot, being accused as Union men; and a number left their homes and went North to save their lives. I remained at home at my post, and I am still here, thank the Lord, who is our Strength, and to whom belongs all honor and praise.'[22]

Another exceptional case was that of Rufus P. King. While serving in the Confederate Army at the age of nineteen, he became convinced of the evils of war, and therefore refused to carry a gun or to drill. He was treated with kindness, however, largely through the influence of his lieutenant, and was assigned to ambulance duty. During the retreat from Gettysburg King was made a prisoner and was sent to Point Lookout Prison at the mouth of the Potomac River. In 1864 he was exchanged with other

[22] Quoted in *Ibid.*, pp. 106–107.

prisoners, but was again forced into the Southern Army. Again no military duty was required of him. Finally he escaped to the Union lines and joined a company of refugees bound for Indiana.[23]

In most instances conscientious objectors in the South were treated with much greater severity than were their brethren in the North. Many accounts of severity on the part of the military authorities leave no doubt on this question. The North Carolina Yearly Meeting of the Society of Friends made a determined effort to preserve some of the experiences of its members during the period of the war. On June 19, 1865, it appointed a committee under the chairmanship of Isham Cox, to prepare a statement of the sufferings of members of the Yearly Meeting. This committee reported, and was continued, from time to time, until finally, under the direction of Francis T. King, it prepared and had printed *An Account of the Sufferings of Friends of North Carolina Yearly Meeting, in Support of Their Testimony Against War, from 1861 to 1865*.[24] In this account the individuals who suffered are divided for convenience into three groups: first, those who suffered previous to the passage of the exemption act, or under irregular proceedings; second, those who joined the Society of Friends during the war; and, third, those who could not conscientiously pay the commutation tax.

The first group included the largest number of cases, but not the greatest amount of suffering. Those included in the group were subjected to rude arrests, short and uncertain imprisonments, violent threatenings; some were even hung up by their thumbs for several hours at a time, some escaped to the West, some engaged in the North

---

[23] *Quaker Biographies*, Series 2, II, pp. 177–181. See also Cartland, Fernando G. *Southern Heroes*, pp. 290–298.

[24] This official report is the basis of such books as Cartland's *Southern Heroes*, Jones' *The Later Periods of Quakerism*, and Hirst's *Quakers in Peace and War*.

Carolina State Salt Works or in other protective employments, and many suffered even after the exemption law
was passed and even though they had their exemption
papers.[25]

A group of Friends in the northern part of Virginia were
especially the victims of the strong feelings which were
aroused by the outbreak of hostilities. As the minutes of
one of their meetings reads:

> The first summer of the war a few of our young men were
> forced out in the Militia, and placed to work on fortifica-
> tions, but through favor of a kind Providence were soon
> enabled to obtain their enlargement and escaped as refu-
> gees into the loyal states, and in no case that we are aware of
> was our testimony against war compromised by our mem-
> bers. Some of our members not subject to conscription
> were arrested by Military authority on account of their
> known Union sentiments, and held under guard in a loath-
> some guard house, or in camp, without a tangible charge,
> until, released through the interposition of personal friends.
> All were subject to taunts, and reproaches by a vindictive
> and unscrupulous soldiery, countenanced, and encouraged
> by sympathising citizens, purely on account of their con-
> scientious sentiments in opposing the Rebellion, and the
> mad ambition of its leaders . . . . Freedom of speech, and
> transmit from place to place was greatly abridged and as a
> consequence our regular religious Meetings were interfered
> with and social intercourse nearly destroyed.[26]

The second group, which included those who had only
been members of the Society of Friends a short time, was
treated by the military authorities with greater harsh-
ness. Apparently the officials were particularly suspicious
of individuals whom they knew to be recent members of a
noncombatant denomination. The letter which follows,

---

[25] *An Account of the Sufferings of Friends of North Carolina Yearly Meeting,*
pp. 8–9.
[26] Min. of Hopewell Monthly Meeting, 3 mo. 7, 1866.

and which was written by Joseph Newlin to John B. Crenshaw from New Market, North Carolina, on September 15, 1864,[27] illustrates the attitude of some of the local enrolling officers.

> ... We understand here that the Secretary of War has made some provisions for the relief of our new members, but our enrolling officers say that no such instructions have reached them, therefore they can do nothing. The consequence is that several other of our new members have since been forwarded to the army and I presume quite a number of others will have to follow, unless the authorities do something for their relief. If thee can do anything for the alleviation of their suffering condition the favor will be reciprocated.
>
> P. S. I have just learned that they have conscribed several new members who have paid out, and ordered them to camp. They call them Bogus Members. I wonder who are the better judges, they or the Monthly Meetings? J.N.

That which was true of recently convinced members of the Society of Friends also was true of the other noncombatant sects of the South. For instance, Henry Davis, a member of the Church of the Brethren, was conscribed and held in the army on the pretext that he joined the Church the same day the exemption act was passed. Davis managed to return to his home, but he was again claimed by the military officials. He again secured his release, and this time fled from the country.[28]

Another instance of intolerance on the part of local officers was given by Elder Benjamin F. Moomaw, in a letter written to Elder John Kline, August 31, 1863.[29]

'The Brethren in Roanoke have been until lately much annoyed by the quartermaster in that county, refusing to

---

[27] North Carolina Yearly Meeting Collection of Crenshaw Correspondence.
[28] Zigler, David H. *A History of the Brethren in Virginia*, p. 130.
[29] Quoted in *Ibid.*, pp. 131–132. See also Sanger and Hays, *op. cit.*, p. 58.

allow them the benefit of the exemption. At length, however, I reported him to President Davis. He sent the case to the Secretary of War. He ordered him [the quartermaster] to report to Richmond and give an account of his conduct. I afterward met him in Salem, when he made a furious assault on me, cursing and threatening violently. I calmly told him I disregarded him; dispised his threats; that he must understand that he could not intimidate me and when he interferes with our rights I will attend to him. Since that time the Brethren have been unmolested.'

Another instance of ill treatment of a recently converted Quaker is found in the story of Jesse Buckner, of Chatham County, North Carolina. At the beginning of the war Buckner was a Baptist and a colonel in the militia. After actively aiding in the military preparations of the Confederacy he became interested in Friends' doctrines of peace, and finally decided to apply for membership in their Society. This he did, not long after being drafted in the year 1862. His application for membership was received and favorably acted on. He paid his commutation tax of $500. but early in the spring of 1863 his exemption papers were declared void by a sub-officer; he was arrested and was sent to Camp Holmes near Raleigh, and then to Wilmington, where he suffered much abuse. Friends did all they could to release him, but without success. He escaped from the army and returned to his home, but he was captured and taken back to Wilmington, where his treatment was more severe than before. He soon afterwards was taken very ill, and was discharged from the army. As soon as he recovered he was again conscripted and taken from camp to camp as a prisoner. "At each new place the trying experiences were repeated, from the attempt to force him to bear arms; but amid sneers and taunts and cruel treatment, he persevered. When the officers and men came to understand the grounds of his objections, many treated him kindly."[30]  For the balance of the war he endured privations and hardship because of his refusal to fight. He was finally released when Johnston's Army surrendered to General Sherman in the spring of 1865.[31]

One of the few deaths which is indirectly traceable to ill treatment on the part of military authorities occurred in the case of Seth W. Laughlin, "a member of the Society [of Friends] only a few months before he was arrested and taken to a military camp near Petersburg, Virginia."[32] The officers at the camp attempted by severe measures to make Laughlin yield his conscientious scruples against bearing arms.

First they kept him without sleep for thirty-six hours, a soldier standing by with a bayonet to pierce him, should he fall asleep. Finding that this did not overcome his scruples, they proceeded for three hours each day to buck him down. He was then suspended by his thumbs for an hour and a half. This terrible ordeal was passed through with each day for a week. Then, thinking him conquered, they offered him a gun; but he was unwilling to use the weapon. Threats, abuse and persecution were alike unavailing, and in desperate anger the Colonel ordered him court-martialed. After being tried for insubordination he was ordered shot. Preparations were accordingly made for the execution of this terrible sentence. The army was summoned to witness the scene, and soldiers were detailed. Guns, six loaded with bullets and six without, were handed to twelve chosen men. Seth Laughlin, as calm as any man of the im-

---

[30] Cartland, Fernando G. *Southern Heroes*, p. 149.

[31] *An Account of the Sufferings, etc.*, pp. 13–14; Cartland, Fernando G. *op. cit.*, pp. 146–150.

[32] *Southern Friend*, I, no. 22, pp. 171–172. Only one other death of this type recorded was that of Job Throckmorton, who, according to one account, "while on his way to attend the Monthly Meeting at Hopewell, . . . was arrested by the soldiery, and with many other prisoners who had not been bearing arms, he was subjected to fatiguing marches and great privations which resulted in his death." See Min. of Baltimore (Hicksite) Yearly Meeting of 1862, p. 232, and *Friends' Intelligencer*, XIX, no. 36, p. 571 and XX, no. 16, p. 244.

mense number surrounding him, asked time for prayer, which, of course, could not be denied him. The supposition was natural that he wished to pray for himself. But he was ready to meet his Lord; and so he prayed not for himself but for them: 'Father, forgive them, for they know not what they do.'

Strange was the effect of this familiar prayer upon men used to taking human life and under strict military orders. Each man, however, lowered his gun, and they resolutely declared that they would not shoot such a man, thereby braving the result of disobeying military orders. But the chosen twelve were not the only ones whose hearts were touched.

The officers themselves revoked the sentence, and:

He was led away to prison, where for weeks he suffered uncomplainingly from his severe punishments. He was finally sent to Windsor Hospital at Richmond, Va., where he was taken very sick, and after a long, severe illness, . . . he passed quietly away, leaving a wife and seven children.[33]

The third group of objectors, mentioned in the official report of the North Carolina Yearly Meeting, endured the most severe treatment of any of the religious objectors. They refused not only to pay the commutation tax of $500. but they also refused to perform any form of alternate service. The experiences of the three Hockett brothers, all Quakers, are illustrative of the treatment of this last group.

William Hockett was drafted in September, 1862, and was taken to Greensboro, the seat of his county. Several times he was furloughed home after reporting to the military authorities, but finally "on the 30th of May [1863] he was conscripted by the Raleigh guard and taken to a Methodist meeting-house called the 'Tabernacle,' which was used as

---

[33] *An Account of the Sufferings*, etc., p. 17, and Cartland, Fernando G. *Southern Heroes*, pp. 211–213.

a rendezvous for conscripted men." Later he was sent to
Camp Holmes, Raleigh, where he was assigned to the 21st
North Carolina Regiment, then stationed in the northern
part of Virginia. When Hockett was sent to join his regiment, and refused to drill he was ordered to be shot. However, as in the case of Laughlin, soldiers could not be found
to carry out the order. Later an officer tried to ride over
him with his horse, but the horse could not be made to
harm him. Several additional attempts were made to force
him to carry a gun, but without success. After the battle
of Gettysburg, in which he took no part, he was captured
by the Federal forces, and sent to Fort Delaware. Shortly
afterwards he, together with other conscientious objectors
who were confined in Fort Delaware, were released through
the instigation of Friends.[34]

Most of the sufferings of Himelius and Jesse Hockett
occurred when they were imprisoned for conscience' sake.
As in other instances, their fellow soldiers sympathized
with them more than their officers did, as the following
petition to Jefferson Davis demonstrates:

State of North Carolina
    Randolph County

                            To Jefferson Davis
May 1863    president of the Confederate States of America
    Your petitioners Respectfully request of you to Exempt
your Conscripts prayer in this petition Himelius M. Hockett and Jesse D. Hockett Simeon Barker & Isiah Cox they
are all in feeble health not able to stand a camp life the all
have helpless families to support no person to work on their
farms but themselves the 2 Hocketts is now in Kinston N.
C. prisoners your petitioners pray that you will duly consider this petition and if adjuded Expedient will exempt they
four persons above stated as we believe they can render this

---

[34] Cartland, Fernando G., in *Southern Heroes*, quotes from William Hockett's
Diary. See pp. 232–251. William Hockett, Jr., of Richmond, Virginia, also
substantiated the story told by Cartland.

Government more service at home on their farms your petitioners on duty bound ever pray

[Ten names follow][35]

In a few instances the sufferings of conscientious objectors continued up to and even after the cessation of hostilities. In a letter from Joseph J. Neave to Francis T. King, written from Norfolk, Virginia, April 12, 1865, he said:

W. T. Hales, from Wayne Co. came to J. B. Crenshaw's last Seventh day, having been walking most of the week. He has been consistently refusing to bear arms (with some eight or ten more) for about six months, and has suffered a good deal of punishment, such as having his hands tied, being fed on bread and water, tied up by his thumbs for three hours and bucked down for three hours alternately. He was made to keep up with the flying Confederates and walked off to J. B. C.'s not knowing what became of the other Friends.[36]

Taking all things into consideration, it is apparent that the cases of extreme severity in the South were the exception rather than the rule. Where such cases did occur the responsibility for the harsh treatment usually rested on the shoulders of subordinate officers and not on those of the higher officers or the privates.

[35] North Carolina Yearly Meeting Collection of Crenshaw Correspondence.
[36] *Friends' Review*, XVIII, no. 37, p. 588.

# Chapter VI

# Official Attitude of the Non-combatant Sects

IN THE preceding chapters it was shown how the attitude of the civil and military authorities towards conscientious objectors varied from one of real leniency to one of great severity. Doubtless these extremes in the treatment and understanding of such objectors were partly the fault of the noncombatant sects themselves in not supporting more uniformly their testimony against war. Certainly individual divergences from the official attitude of each sect were common enough to confuse the authorities.

The relative consistency of these denominations might appear if it were known what proportion of their drafted members refused to serve on grounds of conscience. Any attempt to tabulate the numbers of such persons, however, is fraught with difficulties. Most of the denominations kept no formal record of the actions of their members and even the records of the Society of Friends, which are more elaborate and systematic than those of the other sects, are frequently deficient, or at least indefinite, on this point. Nor is it possible to separate the number of those who conscientiously refused to bear arms from those who opposed the war, but who nevertheless felt that they could consistently pay the commutation fee or procure a substitute when drafted. On the other hand, it is difficult to tell with any degree of certainty the number of men in these noncombatant denominations who served voluntarily in a military capacity contrary to the established principles of their sect.

Government records are only of partial assistance in judging the numbers of noncombatants involved in the war. In the North, Provost-Marshal-General James B. Fry reported to Secretary Stanton on November 15, 1864, that a total of $25,584,599.25 had been received as commutation money up to November 1st of that year,[1] but there is no means of knowing what proportion of this represented the payment of those opposed to serving on grounds of conscience. In the same report Fry stated that $121,800. had been paid by noncombatants since the passage of the Act of February 24, 1864, which represented a total of 406 persons. As he explained in the report:

> By section 17 of the act approved February 24, 1864, and section 10 of the act approved July 4, 1864, certain noncombatants, when drafted, may secure exemption by payment of $300. The fund derived from this source is by law appropriated 'for the benefit of sick and wounded soldiers.' This money is collected by this Bureau and deposited in the Treasury in the same manner as other commutation money; but after deposit it is at the disposal of the Medical Department of the Army for the purpose designated by law.[2]

The figure, 406, does not represent the total number of religious objectors who were drafted during the eight month's period, however, because many refused to pay commutation money.

A more accurate idea can be gained of the number of noncombatants in the Confederacy because it is known how many were exempted during the war. In the Report of Superintendent John S. Preston, of the Bureau of Conscription, to the Honorable J. C. Breckenridge, Secretary of War, in February, 1865, the total number of non-

---

[1] *Official Records*, Series 3, IV, p. 932.
[2] *Ibid.*, pp. 932–933.

combatants exempted during the conflict was given as 515.[3] This number was accounted for as follows:

| State | Age Limits | Number | Total |
|---|---|---|---|
| | 18–45 | 99 | |
| Virginia | 17–18 | ... | |
| | 45–50 | 8 | 107 |
| | | | |
| | 18–45 | 289 | |
| North Carolina | 17–18 | 31 | |
| | 45–50 | 22 | 342 |
| | | | |
| | 18–45 | 66 | |
| East Tennessee | 17–18 | ... | |
| | 45–50 | ... | 66 |
| | | | 515 |

For the Society of Friends in the North the most complete record of the effects of the draft was kept by the Philadelphia (Orthodox) Yearly Meeting. At various times throughout the war the Quarterly and Monthly Meetings were urged to preserve "lists of all their members who have been, or may hereafter be drafted, also statements of all arrests, confinements, distraint of property, or other compulsory process, suffered by any in consequence of their testimony against war."[4] On April 13, 1866, the information supplied by the subordinate meetings was summarized in the following manner:

It appears, by the Reports, that 150 members of this Yearly Meeting were Drafted during the late war, in addition to some of those reported last year.[5] Of these 38 were

---

[3] *Ibid.*, Series 4, III, p. 1103.

[4] Min. of the Meeting for Sufferings of Philadelphia (Orthodox) Yearly Meeting, 4 mo. 14, 1865, p. 252.

[5] The report referred to stated that about 100 Friends were drafted. Min. of the Meeting for Sufferings of Philadelphia Yearly Meeting, 4 mo. 14, 1864, p. 238.

released on the plea of physical disability; 1 as being the only son of a widow; 2 as being under age; one on account of informality in proceedings; one as having been a non-resident of the district he was drafted in; one was discharged without reason assigned; 16 were notified of the draft, but were never called on to report; 34 were discharged through others paying their exemption money for them; generally without their privity, or consent; 5 were released by County Officers paying for substitutes in their places; 24 paid the $300. commutation money and were released according to the provisions of the Law; 7 procured substitutes; 4 went into the army. Two of those who refused on conscientious grounds to serve in the army, or to pay a commutation, or to hire a substitute, were arrested as deserters, but prompt application to those in authority, procured a speedy release on parole. Five were arrested, forced into military clothing, and sent some to Barracks, and some to a Camp in Philadelphia. On application to the Secretary of War, they were all released after periods of confinement, varying from a few days to 5 weeks. Three were drafted and sent to Camp Curtin, near Harrisburg, but on application for them to those in authority by Friends of Philada, they were in a few days released. One was sent to the army, but after two months of trial and suffering, his release was obtained by application to the Secretary of War. Four of those who appeared before different Provost Marshalls and stated their conscientious scruples were heard with kindly consideration and were not afterward molested . . . .[6]

As a result of Friends' refusal to bear arms or to pay military taxes, their property was distrained throughout the war period, sometimes in quite large amounts. As all meetings were urged to keep records of such distraints a fairly good idea can be gained of what Friends suffered from this form of penalty. This data for the Philadelphia (Orthodox) Yearly Meeting was compiled by a special

---

[6] Min. of the Meeting for Sufferings of Philadelphia (Orthodox) Yearly Meeting, 4 mo. 13, 1866, pp. 271–272.

committee, and was presented in the following detailed form.[7]

| Friend's Name | What Meeting a member of | For what claimed | Amount Demanded | What Taken | By whom Distrained | Under what Authority |
|---|---|---|---|---|---|---|
| Thos E. Lee | Exeter Meeting | Bounty Tax 1864 | $81.00 | (Grain valued at) $87.32 | Augustus Lorah [?] | School Directors of Amity & Earl Townships, Berks Co., Pa. |
| Ellis Lee | " | " | $86.39 | $98.09 | " | School Directors of Amity Township Berks Co., Pa. |
| Francis W. Lee | " | " | $31.90 | $33.27 | " | " |
| James Lee & Sons | " | " | $50.00 | $55.00 | Elain Kline | S. Directors, Exeter Township, Berks Co., Pa. |
| Daniel Lee | " | " | Not stated | $13.56 | Augustus Lorah [?] | S. Directors, Amity Township, Berks Co., Pa. |
| Margaret Chrisman & Son. | " | " | $107.00 | $107.00 | Elain Kline | S. Directors, Exeter Township, Berks Co. |
| Robert B. Haines | Frankford Meeting | " | $229.30 | $400.00 | J. N. Fenton, Collector of Cheltenham Township Montgomery Co., Pa. | Warrant from Commissioners of Montgomery Co. Pa. |

All of the Yearly Meetings in the North showed some delinquencies in the maintenance of Quaker principles. This is known because of the answers of the subordinate meetings to the so-called "Seventh Query"[8] which read, "Are Friends clear of complying with military requisitions and of paying any fine or tax in lieu thereof?"

[7] *Ibid.*, 4 mo. 14, 1865, pp. 252–253.
[8] In some Yearly Meetings it was the Sixth Query.

The New England Yearly Meeting, for example, reported 43 enlistments up to the time of the first draft.[9] The Philadelphia (Hicksite) Yearly Meeting of 1862 said, "It is apparent from all the reports, that some of our members have not been sufficiently guarded in relation to our testimony against war, and have given encouragement to war measures, on which account much concern has been felt, and some labor has been extended." The following year it was reported that "All the Quarterly Meetings admit that some of their members have violated our testimony against bearing arms and the performance of military services."[10] And again, "All the reports but one inform that some among them have violated our testimony in relation to military requisitions and services."[11] The Philadelphia (Orthodox) Yearly Meeting of 1862 learned that " . . . all the Quarters but two report that [our testimonies] . . . against war have not been faithfully supported by a few of their members."[12]

In the two New York Yearly Meetings of Friends, throughout the entire war period, there were about 116 cases of military service, either voluntary or by draft, 53 cases of hiring substitutes or paying the commutation fee, 73 cases of complying with military requisitions, and several cases of procuring recruits and substitutes. The number who refused service on conscientious grounds is not stated but property valued at $2,217.76 was distrained for refusal to pay military fines.[13]

Further to the south the Baltimore (Hicksite) Yearly Meeting, composed of 4446 members, reported each year deficiencies in the support of their testimony against war,

---

[9] Min. of New England Yearly Meeting, 1863, p. 17.

[10] Min. of Philadelphia (Hicksite) Yearly Meeting, 1863.

[11] *Ibid.*, 1864.

[12] Min. of Philadelphia (Orthodox) Yearly Meeting, 1862, p. 233.

[13] Min. of New York (Orthodox and Hicksite) Yearly Meetings, 1861–1865.

but gave no definite figures. No figures were reported either by the Orthodox Yearly Meeting in the same city.

In the west, the Iowa Yearly Meeting of 1863[14] found that, "Friends maintain a testimony . . . with a few exceptions, against . . . bearing arms and all military services." In the two years which followed all of the Quarterly Meetings reported that some of their members had been engaged in bearing arms, and in military services, but by 1866 they were apparently free from military associations.[15] In Indiana (Orthodox) Yearly Meeting five Quarterly Meetings reported in 1862 "that one hundred of their members are engaged in bearing arms, and doing military service, and all the others report a considerable number engaged in bearing arms, and doing military service."[16] In 1863, 1864, and 1865 all of the Quarterly Meetings stated that some of their members had been engaged in bearing arms, and in 1864 one Quarterly Meeting reported that some of its members had paid commutation money, others fines in lieu of mustering, and some had paid bounty money. In 1866 mention was still made of some members bearing arms, but in 1867 no mention was made of any deficiency in this respect.[17]

This same Yearly Meeting received no reports of distraints from its membership in 1862 and 1863, but at a meeting on October 1, 1864, it received the following statement:

*Statement*

| | | |
|---|---|---|
| In Miami there was taken in property for a demand of. . . | $20.50 | $136.80 |
| In Westbranch there was taken in property for a demand of. . . . . . . . . . . . . . . . . . . . . . . . . . . . . . . . . . . | 23.50 | 186.75 |
| In Fairfield there was taken in property for a demand of. . | 44.50 | 170.50 |
| In Westfield there was taken in property for a demand of. | 25.00 | 99.62 |

[14] This was its first session as a separate yearly meeting.
[15] Min. of Iowa Yearly Meeting, 1864–1866.
[16] Min. of Indiana Yearly Meeting, 1862, p. 16.
[17] *Ibid.*, 1863–1867.

| | | |
|---|---|---|
| In Center there was taken in property for a demand of... | 20.50 | 90.10 |
| Total amount taken........................ | | $683.77 |
| Total demand............................ | $136.00 | |

There was no account of distraints in the reports of other Quarterly Meetings.[18]    In the nearby Western Yearly Meeting no distraints of property were reported in any of the war years.

An examination of various quarterly and monthly meeting records tells much the same story as the yearly meeting reports without giving additional information regarding the actual numbers involved.[19] In numerous instances practically no mention was made of the war nor of the attitude which Friends took in relation to it.[20]

In the Confederacy the North Carolina Yearly Meeting received better reports of the faithfulness of its members than did the Meetings in the North.  In 1861 the answer to the 5th query was: "Friends bear a testimony against war, except in a few instances in five of the Quarters, which are under notice."    In 1862 the answer was: "Friends bear a testimony against war, except in a few instances, in two of the Quarters, which are under notice." In 1863 the statement was merely made that "Friends bear testimony against war;" in 1864 the Meeting was advised that "Friends bear testimony against war, except one case of hiring a substitute"; and in 1865 the answer to the query was clear, except calling for a guard to pro-

---

[18] Min. of the Meeting for Sufferings of Indiana Yearly Meeting, 10 mo. 1, 1864, p. 353.

[19] Cf. New Garden Q.M. (1861–1865); White Water Q.M. (1861–1865); Salem M.M. (1861–1865); Radnor M.M. (1861–1865); Philadelphia (Race Street) M.M. (1861–1865); Purchase M.M. (1861–1865); New York M.M. (1861–1865); Westbury Q.M. (1861–1865); etc.

[20] Cf. Middletown M.M.; Bristol M.M.; Radnor (formerly Haverford) M.M.; Chester M.M.; Goshen M.M.; Amawalk M.M.; Albany M.M.; etc.

tect property, "since acknowledged to be inconsistent."[21]

The minutes of various Quarterly Meetings in North Carolina, the sessions of which were held with regularity throughout the war period, support the evidence given above although the Piney Woods Quarterly Meeting reported at the meeting of August 31, 1861, "Friends bear a faithful testimony against war except a few instances of young friends volunteering in the service, which is under notice," and the Contentnea Quarterly Meeting reported at a session held October 26, 1861, "Friends endeavor to bear a testimony against WAR . . . except three cases of exercising in military performances which are under care."[22]

An attempt has been made by one author[23] to establish more definite figures for the number of Friends in the South who were conscientiously opposed to bearing arms, although the figures are the result of an analysis of only one source—Fernando Cartland's book, *Southern Heroes*. It was found that 50 were conscripted and maltreated; 5 died from this treatment; 27 accepted non-military service; 23 escaped into hiding; and 140 paid exemption. "As far as is known only two Friends yielded and joined the army." As there are undoubtedly slight overlappings in the above figures, they are suggestive rather than authentic.

From all the available evidence, therefore, the conclusion must be drawn that there were a considerable number of Friends who engaged in military service and who in other ways failed to maintain the peace testimony of the Society to which they belonged. There has been a

[21] Min. of North Carolina Yearly Meeting, 1861–1865.

[22] The records examined included the minutes of Deep River Q.M.; Piney Woods Q.M.; Southern Q.M.; New Garden Q.M.; Contentnea Q.M.; and Cane Creek Q.M.

[23] Hirst, Margaret E. *The Quakers in Peace and War*, p. 441 (footnote).

tendency on the part of some persons to exaggerate the number of Quakers who actually fought in the war; but, on the other hand, Friends themselves have undoubtedly minimized the number of deviations from their peace testimony.    For instance, *The Friend*, under date of February 6, 1864 says:

> We know there have been exaggerated reports set afloat respecting the number of Friends who have entered the army, or in some way contributed toward carrying on the way, 'obeying patriotic impulses instead of seeking to preserve a cold consistency'; as it is above expressed; but we are glad to be able to say it is not correct that *many* Friends have thus acted in this time of trial. On the contrary such are comparatively few.

Again, the situation has been summarized by another Quaker author[24] in the following words:

> It has in recent times (1917) been asserted that the number of Friends engaged in the Civil War in proportion to the membership of the Society was greater than that represented by any other religious denomination in America. There is no historical evidence whatever to justify such a statement. The 'deviations' from the historical testimony of Friends were more numerous than one would have expected in a conservative body which made the testimony an absolutely essential feature of its faith. But even so, when all cases are counted, especially when one considers the powerful patriotic appeal and the devotion of Friends to the freedom of the slaves, the total number appears small.

Friends, especially in the North, were frequently in a dilemma during the war because some unsympathetic persons interpreted their religious opposition to the bearing of arms as political opposition to the Government.    The Society was careful, therefore, on numerous occasions to clarify its position and to reaffirm its support of the

[24] Jones, Rufus M. *The Later Periods of Quakerism*, II, pp. 736–737.

Government in all matters which did not infringe the liberty of conscience. A striking case in point is one in which the New York (Orthodox) Yearly Meeting declined to circulate among its members an address of the London Yearly Meeting because of the "unjust reflection upon our Government" and because the chance of misunderstanding was too great. The address was worded as follows:

> We have been greatly comforted by the evidence furnished to this meeting of the Christian care evinced by our dear friends in America for the faithful maintenance of this testimony [against war]. In all your care and labour,—in all your travail of spirit, be assured, dear friends, you have our sympathy and our prayers. We crave for you that you may be made *strong in the Lord and in the power of his might;* and we should unfeignedly rejoice if, with a single eye to our Lord and Master, He should open the way for you to plead effectually for peace with those on whom the awful responsibility of continuing the war more immediately devolves.

> We trust we shall not be out of our place in here acknowledging the satisfaction with which he have heard of many under the general name of 'Friends,' though not in correspondence with this Yearly Meeting, who have displayed much firmness in upholding the peaceable spirit of the Gospel, even when exposed to great difficulty and trial.

> But our sympathy is far from being limited to those under our own name. We feel for the sorrows of multitudes of our fellow Christians of other denominations, whose religious views in the subject of war do not agree with ours, and thousands of whom are now suffering the anguish of domestic bereavement or of torturing suspense and anxiety. . . .[25]

The attitude of the various religious denominations toward those of their members who maintained their conscientious convications against bearing arms was a most sympathetic one. Among the Friends, committees

---

[25] Min. of the Meeting for Sufferings of New York (Orthodox) Yearly Meeting, 8 mo. 5, 1863, p. 182.

were frequently appointed to advise those persons who might be drafted. As one instance, the Philadelphia (Orthodox) Meeting for Sufferings appointed a sub-committee to advise and assist such of their members as might be drafted for military service. This Committee gave full reports of its activities. On April 14, 1864, it reported:

> That as far as they have been able to ascertain about 100 Friends, members of this Yearly Meeting, were drafted, all of whom resided in Pennsylvania or Delaware, for many of whom the commutation money was paid by persons not members and without the consent or connivance of the parties. In a few instances only, it was paid by the drafted Friends or a substitute hired, which will doubtless claim the attention of the overseers of the Meetings where such persons belong. Some were excused on the ground of ill health or other disability. Several young men were drafted and felt conscientiously restrained from violating the Christian testimony against wars and fightings, were arrested by order of the Provost Marshalls and sent under military guard to the Rendezvous for drafted soldiers in this city; but prompt and persevering applications to the Secretary of War at Washington and some subordinate officers, in all instances procured their release, though sometimes after confinement and a considerable exercise of patience.
>
> Two Friends were closely confined in the Rendezvous in Philadelphia for 17 days and one for four weeks, but all of them were afterward permitted to go at large only reporting themselves to the officer in charge once a day and finally by order of the Secretary of War were discharged on parole to appear when called for. This was the form of discharge in nearly all the cases which came under our notice, and though not in itself absolute, yet was doubtless intended to be such. . . .
>
> In performing the duties which thus far have devolved upon us, we have often felt deeply the very serious and responsible position in which the members of our Religious

Society stand at a time like the present, and how important
it is that our movements be in the meekness of heavenly
wisdom, supported and confirmed by a consistent example;
and also that our dear young Friends for whom we are sometimes called to plead before those in authority may be encouraged very seriously to ponder their ways and standing;
and by an upright and steadfast support of all our Christian
principles and testimonies, may evince that their Religious
profession is a reality, and that their alleged scruple against
war is the result of sincere conviction.  This will make the
way much easier for them and for us. . . .

> Signed on behalf of the Committee
> Samuel Hilles
> James Emlen
> David Roberts
> Thomas Evans
> Joseph Scattergood[26]

The following report of the New England Yearly Meeting Committee, appointed early in the war to advise
drafted Friends, illustrates clearly the general leniency
of the Government towards Friends, the courteous treatment accorded members of the Society by the civil and
military authorities, and the effect which Friends apparently had on the militia laws of the New England
States.  The Committee stated:

That they [had] from time to time in pursuance of their
appointment rendered such advice and assistance in the
cases alluded to, as they were enabled to do, and which
appeared requisite.

In the State of Rhode-Island, William H. [?] Perry of
South Kingstown was drafted and appearing before the
Provost Marshall was sent to Fort Columbus on Governors
Island in New York Harbour, where he was detained a
number of weeks—and then released on parole to return

---

[26] Min. of Meeting for Sufferings of Philadelphia Yearly Meeting, 4 mo. 14,
1864, pp. 238–240.

when called for.  He was treated kindly and was not required to do any actual military duty while at the fort.  He was not well while there and after his return had a severe sickness attributable, probably at least in part, to the circumstances in which he had been placed.  From this sickness he has recovered.

Charles W. Cook of Unity, Maine . . . was also drafted and sent to the same fort.  He was detained a much shorter time than William S. [?] Perry, and was released on a parole similar to the one mentioned in that case.

In the State of Massachusetts, Edward W. Holway, was drafted and sent to the army—where, being faithful to his conscientious convictions of the unlawfulness of war he was subjected to much mental, and some physical suffering, and was about to be tried by a court martial for declining to bear arms in obedience to the commands of the officers of the regiment to which he was attached.

While he was in this State, the Colonel of the Regiment visited Boston, and was there waited upon by a member of the Committee, who laid before him, as well as he was able, the reasons why Edward W. Holway declined to bear arms.  That it was not from any disrespect to the Government, but because he believed war unlawful, and for him to take part in it would be sin, and would peril his well being in the world to come.

The colonel expressed his surprise that such sentiments were held by anyone, and thought that cowardice was the ruling motive in Edward W. Holway's refusal.  But before the close of the interview he appeared to fully appreciate the conscientious motives which ruled in the case, and said, war is indeed an awful thing, and a battle enough to make a man shudder, and that he could wish that all men were Quakers; promising to do all he could for Edward W. Holway consistent with his duty to his country, and that he would write to the officer in command of the Regiment immediately on his behalf.  While this was going on, another member of the committee went to Washington, and on his representation of the case to the Secretary of War, an order was immediately issued for his transfer to Washington, from whence he was paroled, and came home.

Henry D. Swift was drafted, and sent to Long Island in Boston Harbor, where he was kept for some time and while there was employed in the hospital, nursing the sick, to which he did not object. Two of the Committee visited him there, and procured a furlough for his release for a short time, while his case could be represented at Washington, which resulted in his being released on parole.

In the States of Massachusetts and Rhode-Island some others were drafted, who were discharged from legal causes.

In the State of New Hampshire, three of our members were drafted, and ordered to appear before the provost Marshalls, to be mustered into the army. A member of the committee accompanied one of these before the officer, and the result of the visit, was a discharge on parole in two of the three cases.

In the third case the Friend was discharged by a legal excuse, the provost marshall having been visited by a member of the committee on his behalf.

In the State of Maine about twenty five of our members were drafted. . . . A part of these were discharged by legal excuses, and all the others were paroled, without being mustered into camp.

In every case where the committee have had interviews with the officers of the Government, both civil and military, they have been uniformly treated with kindness, and respect, and their representations listened to patiently and respectfully.

It may be interesting to add that in the discussion upon a new militia bill before the Legislature of Massachusetts, the faithfulness of Friends to their testimony to the peaceable nature of the Christian religion, and the incompatability of war with its precepts, was brought before these Legislators, and it is believed had great weight with them in continuing the exemption from military requisitions of all consistent Friends, in the new law enacted at the last session.

Provision is now made for the exemption of Friends from the operation of the State militia laws in the States of Rhode-Island, Massachusetts, New Hampshire and Maine.

We believe the authorities of our Government at Washington, have appreciated the motives of Friends, in their steady adherence to the testimony of the Society against all wars and fightings, and that this appreciation has facilitated if not led to the kindly bearing of all the officers of the Government towards Friends in all their interviews with them and the discharge of such of our members who, having been drafted, have borne their testimony faithfully. . . .

|                    | John D. Lang    ) For the              |
| Newport, R. I.     | Stephen A. Chase ) Committee[27]       |
| 6 mo. 11, 1864     | Samuel Boyce    )                      |

In Western Yearly Meeting a similar committee reported under date of May 4, 1865, that "A large number of our members have been subjected to the draft, and a heavy expense on Friends thereby incurred. But we have the satisfaction to state that the burden on those drafted, has been much lessened, by the brotherly kindness and liberality of the friends."[28] From this report it is evident that many members of the Meeting did not scruple to pay the commutation fee, or at least they did not hesitate to spend money in securing their release from the draft.

Perhaps one of the most difficult tasks which these committees had was in advising young Friends as to their proper attitude towards the military authorities. Naturally the advise varied in different parts of the country and under different circumstances. In New York (Orthodox) Yearly Meeting the following suggestions were offered to members:

---

[27] Min. of the Meeting for Sufferings of New England Yearly Meeting, 6 mo. 11, 1864, pp. 305-307.

[28] Min. of the Meeting for Sufferings of Western Yearly Meeting, 5 mo. 4, 1865, p. 99.

Friends who may be exempted from Military service under the law, may properly avail themselves of such exemption; but *before* doing so, they will probably prefer to make known their conscientious objections as above expressed, where it can be done with propriety.

It is advised that some prudent and judicious Friend should accompany the person in his appearance before the Board of Enrollment.

Should a Friend be arrested and sent to a Military post for trial by a court-martial, his case should be promptly attended to by Friends of the Meeting to which he belongs; and a written statement of the circumstances, signed by some of those Friends, be forwarded without delay to the Clerk of the Representative Meeting, or to some member of it, in order that proper and timely care may be taken therein.

It is more than probable that many of our members will be subjected to trial, and perhaps to suffering, in maintaining our Christian testimony in this respect; and we feel it right to exhort all our dear friends to faithfulness therein, in order to preserve a tender and pure conscience.[29]

Special committees were also appointed to advise Friends on the subject of taxation. These committees took their task quite seriously and sometimes pondered the question a long while before reporting their convictions. One group reported:

After carefully considering the subject the committee are united in judgment that Friends cannot consistently pay any tax assessed for the specific and exclusive purpose of military service or the promotion of war, nor any debt which may have been contracted by others for such specific purpose. It would not accord with our duty as clearly enjoined by our christian discipline 'to bear a faithful testimony against war. . . .'

---

[29] Min. of the Meeting for Sufferings of New York (Orthodox) Yearly Meeting, 8 mo. 6, 1863, pp. 182–184.

The object of refusing to pay a specific war tax is to bear our testimony against war, and not to embarrass government, nor to aid our share of the public burdens which can be paid without violating our religious principles.

... In the present case it appears that the President of the United States made a 'Requisition' upon the Governor of each State for its respective quota of volunteers for military service; and it was in obedience to this 'Requisition' that measures were taken to induce a compliance with it, so as to avoid the necessity of a draft; and bounties were assessed distinctly and specifically for that purpose. The mere statement of the case seems to be an answer to the inquiry submitted to the committee; and they are of opinion that every step taken to comply with this requisition—from the volunteer down to all who influence his action—comes within the scope of the seventh query.

The committee nevertheless feel sympathy for those of our members who have entertained different views on this subject, and who have been induced, perhaps inadvertently, to act upon them; and they are united in opinion that Friends in our subordinate meetings should abstain from all disturbing comments upon the differences of the past.[30]

Although most Quaker meetings were conscientious in carrying out their obligations there were instances where they apparently evaded these obligations by passing on to others the tasks set for themselves. One example of this appears in the minutes of the Meeting for Sufferings of the Baltimore (Hicksite) Yearly Meeting.[31] It is also a good illustration of the multiplicity of committees which one often finds in the Quaker organization.

Called meeting, 12 mo. 31, 1863.

The following Minute was received from the late Quarterly Meeting—viz

[30] Extracts from the Minutes of New York (Orthodox) Yearly Meeting, 5 mo. 29, 1863, reported in *The Friend*, XXXVI, no. 45, p. 359.
[31] 12 mo. 31, 1863, p. 98.

'At Baltimore Quarterly Meeting held at Little Falls, 12 mo. 14, 1863:—

'The following communication was received from Little Falls Monthly Meeting:—to wit—

'The subject of a number of our young Friends being drafted, claiming the consideration of the meeting, it was thought best to refer it to the Quarterly Meeting for its advice and assistance.

'Which after claiming the attention of this Meeting was referred to the Meeting for Sufferings, for its consideration.

'Extracted from the Minutes of the aforesaid Meeting, by,
Caleb Stabler, Clerk'

The subject of the present tried condition of many of our members, and especially of our precious young Friends, being thus brought to the consideration of the Meeting for Sufferings; after solid deliberation, and a full interchange of sentiments, the following Committee was appointed to extend such advice and assistance as circumstances may seem by them to be required of any of our members, who may be brought into difficulty or suffering for conscience sake, or anything connected with military operations.

The Clerk was directed to send a copy of this Minute to each one of our Monthly Meetings.

The Committee appointed were

Benjamin Hallowell  Samuel Townsend
Benjamin P. Moore  Levi K. Brown
Charkley Gillingham  Richard T. Bentley
Thomas Sheppard  Gerard H. Reese

after which the Meeting adjourned.

In North Carolina Yearly Meeting seven Friends "were appointed to take into weighty consideration the subject of our suffering Friends who are in the military camp and those who may be hereafter taken there, and report to a further sitting. Also to consider the propriety of sending Delegates to wait upon the proper Legal Authorities for relief. Also to propose names to confer with the author-

ities if way should open for it."[32] Some of the subordinate
meetings took similar action, although not as frequently
as one might expect.  An illustration is that of the Contentnea Quarterly Meeting, which made a minute on April
19, 1862, to the effect that:

> Wm. Cox, Thos. Kennedy, N. T. Perkins and Mathen
> Pike are appointed to have the care and oversight of such of
> our members as may be drafted to go in to the army if aney
> should be and them such aid an instructioun as may needed
> and report to a future meeting.[33]

In addition to these committees, certain individual
members of the Society of Friends performed invaluable
services in relieving their fellow-members from military
control.  Undoubtedly, the person who did more than any
other to relieve not only Friends, but members of other
religious denominations, was John B. Crenshaw, a member
of Baltimore Yearly Meeting, but a resident of Richmond,
Virginia, throughout the war period.  His *Diary* is full of
examples of his kind deeds.  The following extracts will
serve as illustrations.

10/18/62   We paid in today the tax for five Friends and
three Dunkards.

10/20/62   J. Harris and I returned to Town and got off
young (Jesse) Gordon, . . .  When we were at the War
Office met some of the Va. Dunkards who have been
brought on here as Conscripts, some of whom already
paid Five hundred Dollars into the State Treasury under
the State Exemption Law.  When we went back to Camp
Lee, at their request, I drew up a petition to the Sec. of War
asking that those who had so paid in might be excused and
allowed to return home until the Legislature meets again, at
which time they hope to be allowed to draw the amount
from the State Treasury to pay the Confederate Treasury.

---

[32] Min. of the Meeting for Sufferings of North Carolina Yearly Meeting,
11 mo. 4, 1864.
[33] Min. of Contentnea Quarterly Meeting, 4 mo. 19, 1862, p. 81.

12/14/62   Came to Drury's Bluff where Gen. Daniel commands. Saw Stephen Hobson and Thompson and Simon D. Kemp. They have been kindly treated and not required to perform any military duty. Thompson was hoping to get exemption on account of his health and Stephen Hobson a release on the grounds of being a miller. Isaac Harvey I did not find.

2/9/63   I went in with M. H. B. this morning and got Him a passport to go home. I presented the Asst. Sec. of War a petition on behalf of Calvin Perkins, asking his release.

3/21/63   Still stormy, but I went in to Richmond to see about Thos. Kennedy and learned that he had been sent North by flag of Truce.

4/1/63   My wife and I went in to Meeting at John Whitlocks, where we met Isham Cox, who has come up to try to get some young men exempted from military services.

4/2/63   Went to Town with I. Cox to aid him in these cases. We succeeded in all of them for which I am truly thankful.

4/18/63   I was in Richmond today attending to some business. Got a release for Wm. Osborne, heard that C. H. Robinson's (Dunkard) application was refused but they offer a detail to Hospitals.

5/9/63   I went in to get an order to send Joseph Fell north and a discharge for Elvy Byrd.

2/1/65   I went with David Moffit before the Secretary of the Navy and secured the release of his son from the Confederate States Navy. [It is not known whether or not Moffit was a Friend.]

3/15/65   Got an exemption for F. Farlow.[34]

Numerous other illustrations of John B. Crenshaw's efforts on behalf of Friends are contained in the many letters which were written to him and by him during this period.

[34] The Diary for the year 1864 is lost so that no references are made to that year.

For example, Thomas S. Hallowell wrote to Crenshaw from Pikesville, Wayne County, North Carolina, on April 1, 1864, saying:

> I was conscripted about 2 weeks before the exemption act wass [sic] passed so I got the enclosed papers for my Exemption the Enroling Officer Says that he has nothing to do with me and the parties mentioned in the furlough as we were furloughed home. I ask this as a favor if thou will present my copy of exemption papers to the Secretary of War and try to get me exempted in full, also Levi H. Massy, Wm. T. Cox, Stephen R. Hallowell we all are members of the society of friends all of our life, . . .

On December 12, 1862, E. Benbow wrote to John Crenshaw from East Bend, "I have not be able to get to procure a check to send you for the money you advanced for the relief of my Brother in camp, T. H. Benbow, . . ."

Another interesting letter was written by W. T. Hales from the Camp of the 34th Regiment of North Carolina on October 23, 1864. Hales said:

> Thy note of the 19th inst. was reced with very much regret that thee had not been able to get me any relief.—as I have been between the two lines for twelve or fourteen days a knights without fire only long enough to cook my rashions and have suffered very much with cold. I was robed of all my winter clothing which leaves me in a very bad situation, . . .

Hale had only recently joined the Society of Friends, as shown by another letter of his to Crenshaw under date of October 2, 1864.

Apparently he was appealed to by friends and relatives of those who suffered for conscience' sake as well as by conscientious objectors themselves. The following letter from the father of the Hockett brothers is an example of such appeals:

> . . . As relates to the situation of Himelius M. and Jesse D. Hockett, I have had an interview with their wives, and

as to some person (without consulting the boys) going forward out of goodwill to them, and paying the $500. thereby geting [sic] a release for them on the responsibility of such individual or individuals, I think there would not be any objection raised against it being done, though not encouraged by their wives.

As to myself, knowing the situation of their minds, as I do, I am not willing to take the responsibility of doing it without their wish. Their wives are entirely opposed to leaving their homes at the present to go with their Husbands, provided the alternative should be that of sending them out of the Confederacy. If this should be done it would seem humane for the authorities to allow them the privilege of coming home first.

With due thankfulness I appreciate thy kindness in behalf of my suffering children, and remain with respect thy friend,

William Hockett[35]

Another letter to Crenshaw, dated December 4, 1864, told in quaint language of the sufferings of still another Friend. Thomas W. Johnson, who wrote the letter, said:

I received a letter from William A. Burgiss yesterday the officers was punishing him aufull he said they onley giv him six ounces of bread a day and after the first of this month they said he should onley have 3 ounces they have bucked him down and beat him sevearly and punisht him in various ways but could not make him do anything. . . .[36]

Among other Friends in the South who were active on behalf of conscientious objectors was Nereus Mendenhall. Prior to the War this Quaker had been an active agent of

---

[35] In North Carolina Yearly Meeting Collection of Crenshaw Correspondence.

[36] Many other examples might be cited of Crenshaw's activities. The Crenshaw Correspondence of the North Carolina Yearly Meeting contains a wealth of material on this subject. See also Crenshaw, Margaret E. John Bacon Crenshaw in *Quaker Biographies*, Series 2, III, pp. 180–182.

the "Underground Railroad." Together with John B. Crenshaw Mendenhall visited Jefferson Davis in an attempt to secure the release of certain Friends from Castle Thunder in Richmond. They were unsuccessful, however, in this attempt. Apparently Mendenhall was as fearless during the War as before it in supporting the peace testimony of Friends because it is stated that, " . . . he did not hesitate to maintain the principles which it professed, on the street, in the railway trains, anywhere and everywhere he would show the incompatability of all war with the spirit and teaching of Christ."[37]

It must not be presumed from what has been written that efforts to alleviate the sufferings of conscientious objectors were confined to members of the Society of Friends. There is plenty of evidence to show that members of the smaller denominations, especially members of the Mennonite and Dunker Churches, were also active. For example, Simeon Heatwole, a Mennonite of Virginia, says of Benjamin Byerly, another Mennonite who lived near Dayton, Virginia, that he "came to see us two or three times while we were in Richmond, and used all his influence to get us released. When the Exemption Act was passed, he was one to go around to raise the money to pay the fines for our release, and when the fines were paid, he with the officers came and opened the door, and he said, 'Now you can all go home' ".[38] Or, as another instance, "Brother Sayler [D. P. Sayler] was one of the church's strong representatives during the [Civil] War, in defense of her peace principles, and was frequently called up before the war department to give an explanation of those endearing principles. By his extraordinary power he was

---

[37] *Quaker Biographies*, Series 2, V, pp. 273–279.

[38] Sanger, Samuel F. and Hays, Daniel. *The Olive Branch*, p. 111.

[39] *Brethren's Almanac*, 1898. Also quoted in *Ibid.*, p. 133.

the means of the release of some of our Brethren from a life of war."[39]

In addition to the various committees and individuals who labored on behalf of conscientious objectors, Quaker periodicals also performed a valuable service in helping to reunite families separated by the war, or in assisting those who escaped from the Confederate Army to find relatives and friends in the North. The notices which follow are typical.

Information Wanted.

Mitchel M. Rogers, who was a conscript in the rebel army, in North Carolina, and has escaped to Ohio, is anxious to find his wife, Amy Rogers, and their six children, who, he supposes, have come North, and are in one of the Western States. Information of them will be gratefully received if addressed to Jonathan Bailey, Wilmington, Clinton County, Ohio.[40]

Information Wanted.

Of Richard Jones, who was forced into the Rebel army against his will; he was living at the time in Guilford county, North Carolina, and left a wife and two small children in a destitute condition, wholly dependent on him for their daily bread; but by the aid of a few friends, she was enabled to get to the State of Indiana, where she hoped to be able to support herself and children, and hear from her husband. When he was last heard from he had deserted the Rebel service, and is supposed to be somewhere in the Free States, and is not aware of his family's escape to the North. Any person having any knowledge of his whereabouts, will confer a blessing upon the distressed and anxious wife, who will feel herself under obligations to those who may aid her in this extremity, by addressing

William Clampitt,<br>Westfield, Hamilton county, Ind.[41]

---

[40] *Friends' Review*, XVIII, no. 20, p. 313.
[41] *Friends' Review*, XVIII, no. 8, p. 121.

The attitude of the various peace denominations to-wards those of their members who transgressed their fundamental peace testimony was, on the whole, a very lenient one.  In fact, all of them, with the exception of the Society of Friends, considered that payment of the commutation fee or even the hiring of substitutes did not violate their principles.  The greatest stress was laid on the sinfulness of shedding blood.  As one Mennonite historian explains:[42]

> A few of the younger brethren went into the army with the first volunteers;[43] others hid themselves away in the mountains and timbered sections of the country and made frequent visits to their families under cover of night; while others—along with such as were drafted into the service later in the fall of 1861, were taken into the army under protest—with the understanding among themselves and their families at home, that neither of them would strike a blow or fire a gun.

The author proceeded to tell how in action near Winchester and before Harper's Ferry, some refusing to fight, were reported to their officers and threatened with court martials.  However, they were detailed as cooks, teamsters, and to tend the sick and wounded.  During the general draft of 1862, to answer to which "was looked upon by the Church as equivalent to volunteering for military service," some of the younger brethren responded and went into the ranks.  Bishop Coffman, however, took a stand against the draft and preached his convictions from the pulpit.  For this he was forced to flee temporarily to the brethren in Maryland and Pennsylvania.[44]  This

[42] L. J. Heatwole in Hartzler, J. S. and Kauffman, Daniel. *Mennonite Church History*, p. 207.

[43] Other authorities claim that there was only one known case of volunteering in the South.  See Sanger and Hays, *The Olive Branch*, p. 84, and Zigler, D. H. *History of the Brethren in Va.*, p. 97.

[44] Hartzler and Kauffman, *op. cit.*, pp. 207–208.

same author stated[45] that he was witness of an occasion when a volunteer in the army made public confession before his home congregation, showing that service of a military nature was not condoned.

Another author[46] explained the situation in the Mennonite Church in the South somewhat differently. He said:

> Just before the time the war began the Mennonite Church decided that if any one of the members would voluntarily go to war they would voluntarily go out of the Church, without a church trial or anything of the kind. It was a dangerous thing to have a church trial. . . . Only two brothers, Shenk by name, voluntarily went into the war. I knew them both. One of them was wounded and taken prisoner and died in prison. The other one came home but never came back into the Church.

In the Church of the Brethren one historian wrote, " 'I remember only one [person] who went into the army, as a volunteer, and he, poor fellow, never returned.' "[47]

Another Brethren historian said:

> In the spring of 1861, when volunteers were called, derision was heaped upon them. They were branded with a lack of patriotism and with cowardice. These were borne with a true Christian spirit. But one brother is known to have yielded to the military spirit of the time.

In referring to the Virginia State draft in July, 1861, he says:

> Some secured substitutes among those who were willing to go to the army and were not included in the draft, paying for their services from $800. to $1500. each. Others were carried off to the army. A few were literally bound and

---

[45] In a letter to the author, from Dale Enterprise, Va., Nov. 5, 1928.
[46] Hartman, Peter S. in *Civil War Reminiscences*, p. 8.
[47] S. F. Sanger in Sanger and Hays, *op. cit.*, p. 84.

hauled away from their homes. While there they were obedient to every command, save to shoot down their fellow
man.[48]

There is little question that most of these sects paid the
commutation tax whenever they could. As one resident
of Virginia during the conflict wrote,[49] "'Times, my dear
brethren, are truly dark with dangers, and uncertain. . . .
Our brethren have much to pay, so that it will be a considerable burden on all—those that are able have paid
from $800. to $1,500. for substitutes, and now to help those
that are not able to pay the $500. fine to get them free is
hard. It may wean us off from the worldly treasure.'"
This same person mentions in his memorandum book
that he paid $500. for each of 18 persons, making up the
deficiency in the amount himself, or calling on other
members of the church at large to do so.[50]

Members of the Amana Society also hired substitutes
when recruits were called for in Iowa County, and, when
drafted, they did not scruple to pay the commutation tax.[51]
The Community realized evidently that its attitude was
inconsistent, because one of its principal leaders, Christian
Metz, in a letter to the Brethren at Ebenezer, felt called

[48] Zigler, David H. *A History of the Brethren in Virginia*, pp. 97–98.

[49] John Kline in a letter from Bowman's Mill, Rockingham County, Va., July
2, 1862, quoted in Sanger, Samuel F. and Hays, Daniel. *op. cit.*, p. 224.

[50] Zigler, David H. *op. cit.*, p. 125.

[51] Noe, Charles F., in a letter to the author, from Amana, Iowa, dated
August 22, 1928, says, ". . . as far as known to me all of our members were
exempted by the payment of a fee provided for by law." Wick, B. L., in a letter
from Cedar Rapids, Iowa, dated June 22, 1927, says, "These people (the
Inspirationists) took advantage of the laws as passed by paying $300. to the war
department for hospital and other expenses." George Hinemann, in a letter
from South Amana, dated August 3, 1928, says, "I find in the records of the
Society at the time of the Civil War, that the Congress of the United States . . .
enacted a law to pay the Sum of Three hundred Dollars for each of such noncombatant members, which was paid, besides other donations for Hospital
Services, &c." See also Shambaugh, B. M. H. *op. cit.*, p. 164 and Perkins, W. R.
and Wick, B. L. *op. cit.*, p. 61.

upon to excuse the payment of the tax in the following words, " 'Since war is contrary to our calling and faith we know of no other way out than to pay the $300. prescribed by the law in order to show our patriotic attitude as citizens and supporters of the Union.' "[52]

Undoubtedly the Amana Society aided the Union Army throughout the war with its contributions of clothes and money. In another letter to those who were still in charge of the New York property, Christian Metz says, " 'We sent a circular letter to this and the other Communities that we considered it our duty that every member, household, or family should contribute a gift or offering each one according to his means, . . . . The Brethren had indeed already sent $200. to the Governor; but I believe that this is or will be even more acceptable, for all these contributions consist of good warm clothing.' "[53] Such contributions were repeated and amounted to thousands of dollars before the close of the war.[54]

There is no mention in the records of the Amana Society of the exact number who were drafted during the war and who paid the commutation tax of $300. but, judging from the fact that the total population of the Community in 1860 was only about 1200, the number must have been small.

The Society of Friends, as we have already seen, allowed its individual members to follow the dictates of conscience, but officially it refrained from all forms of military service

---

[52] Shambaugh, B. M. H. *op. cit.*, p. 164. Perkins, W. R. and Wick, B. L. *op. cit.*, in a footnote on p. 61 say, "This purchase of substitutes for those who were drafted has afforded the Society regret, and it has seemed to the members that it was perhaps inconsistent."

[53] Shambaugh, B. M. H. *op. cit.*, p. 165.

[54] Ely, Richard T. in an article entitled *Amana: A Study of Religious Communism* in *Harper's Monthly Magazine*, CV, pp. 659–668, places the total contributions at $20,000.

and from payment of military requisitions.[55] Its attitude toward those of its members who transgressed Quaker principles during the war, but who wished to return to the Society at its close, was almost uniformly liberal and forgiving. A great deal depended, however, on the attitude of the member wishing to be restored to the privileges of the Society. Many Friends, who took an active part in the war, made no attempt to ask for forgiveness, while others wished to remain members of the Society of Friends but considered that their actions, in aiding the military forces of the country were entirely proper.

Those Friends who entered the military forces and later justified their actions on patriotic or other grounds were generally "disowned" by their local Meeting. Several examples follow:

> Robert B. Twining a member of our society has so far deviated from the peaceable principles of the gospel as professed by us as to join in military services, for which departure he has been laboured with for his restoration, but not being in a state of mind to condemn his courses we testify that he is no longer a member amongst us until he may be favored to come more under the reign of the Prince of peace which is our desire for him.
>
> signed on behalf of Little Falls Mo. Meeting<br>held the 8th of 7th mo. 1862<br>Wm. C. Haviland, clerk.[56]

The Friends appointed to prepare a testimony of disownment against Levi Haines produced one which was read approved and signed and the same committee are continued to furnish him with a copy thereof, inform him of his right of appeal and report to next meeting.

The testimony is as follows:

---

[55] At least one exception to this was the case of the Salem Monthly Meeting of Friends which borrowed an amount sufficient to pay the exemption money of several of its members. See Min. of Salem Monthly Meeting, 1864, p. 14.

[56] Min. of Little Falls Monthly Meeting (Fallston, Md.) 7 mo. 8, 1862.

# CONSCIENTIOUS OBJECTORS

Levi Haines having had a birth and education in the society of Friends, and having so far deviated from our ancient testimony against war as to volunteer in the United States service and on being treated with, justifies his conduct. We therefore disown him from membership.

James E. Price having voluntarily entered military service, for which he has been treated with, but without desired effect, this Meeting therefore discontinues him as a member of our Society, until he returns to the satisfaction of Friends, which is our desire. Which was approved and the Committee was continued to furnish him with a copy of this minute and of his right of appeal.[57]

Wilmington Preparative Meeting informs that Thomas Fell, long a resident of the state of Georgia, remote from any settlement of Friends, has become entirely estranged from Friends, and has violated our testimony by serving as a soldier in the late war, and desires his name to be stricken from our list of members without further treatment. To communicate with him if way opens, and if they find no cause for delay prepare testimony in his case, Joseph Chandler and T. Clarkson Taylor were appointed.

At the next monthly meeting the above committee reported recommending disownment, which was approved by the meeting.[58]

At first Friends were in doubt as to their proper course of procedure regarding former soldiers who wished to return to their affiliation with the organized church. The conclusions reached by the Baltimore Yearly Meeting of 1865 summarize, however, the attitude finally taken by all of the Yearly Meetings.

The Committee appointed to consider the question brought up by the Baltimore Quarterly Meeting, in relation

[57] Min. of Gunpowder Monthly Meeting (near Cockeysville, Md.) 10 mo. 5 1864.

[58] Min. of Wilmington (Del.) Monthly Meeting, 11 mo. 27, 1868.

to the violation of our testimony against war and military services, report: that, after serious and deliberate consideration, we have agreed to submit to the Meeting, the following views on this important and interesting subject.

. . . . . . . . . . . . .

During the dreadful civil war, through which the nation has just passed, the members of our Society have been subjected to a severe test of these peaceable principles, and when we consider that many among us are members by birthright, and have not passed through the furnace of spiritual baptism, it is not surprising that they should be carried away by the current of popular enthusiasm. . . .

In consideration of the extraordinary circumstances in which Friends have been placed, we recommend, that in regard to past offenses in the violation of our testimonies against war and military services, a lenient course should be pursued. We therefore propose, that the Yearly Meeting direct Monthly Meetings to appoint committees of judicious Friends, to whom voluntary acknowledgments may be made, and when such verbal acknowledgments are satisfactory to the committee, they may be accepted without reporting the names of the individuals to the Monthly Meeting.

Voluntary acknowledgments may also be made in the Monthly Meeting, and accepted, if satisfactory, without recording the names of the parties.

In cases where the labors of the committee are ineffectual, the names of the delinquents shall be reported to the Monthly Meeting.

In regard to the purchase and holding of Government bonds, and the payment of certain taxes, by some called war taxes, there appears to be a difference of sentiment among Friends, and we recommend that each individual be left, in these matters, to follow his own religious convictions, trusting that the dictates of an enlightened conscience may be observed, and that Friends will be charitable in judging the conduct of others. . . .[59]

---

[59] Min. of Baltimore (Lombard St.) Yearly Meeting, 1865, pp. 33–34.

The records show that many Friends availed themselves of this liberal policy. For instance, the New York Monthly Meeting, in December 1865, took up the case of Joseph B. Leggett who voluntarily joined the Army, but resigned his commission and wished to be retained as a member of the Society. His request was granted.[60] In another case twelve members addressed their local meeting in the following words:

> The undersigned members of this meeting having in the late troubles through which our Country has passed been induced to take up arms in defense thereof contrary to our testimony in regard to war and having been favoured to return home, in gratitude therefor and love to the testimony of our Society we feel bound to acknowledge our departure therefrom and hope Friends will pass it by and accept this and retain us in membership.
>
> The above voluntary acknowledgment from the young men of our Monthly Meeting having been read and considered, was accepted and they retained in membership.[61]

In still other instances 31 and 71 persons respectively applied successfully to their Monthly Meeting for reinstatement.[62]

Some Friends who took an active part in the military service were somewhat at a loss to justify their actions when they wished to return to membership in their meetings at the end of the war. However, in most cases their explanations, even though apparently inconsistent, were sufficient to reinstate them in the Society.

One such case was that of Wilmer Atkinson, founder of the *Farm Journal*. He explained that he joined a volunteer regiment called by Governor Curtin of Pennsylvania at

---

[60] Min. of New York (Hicksite) Monthly Meeting, 12 mo. 6, 1865.

[61] Min. of Chester (Pa.) Monthly Meeting, 3 mo. 19, 1866.

[62] Min. of Wilmington (Del.) Monthly Meeting, for 1865–1868, and Min. of Horsham Monthly Meeting, 11 mo. 28, 1866.

the time of the Battle of Antietam.[63] He found in the ranks
his brother, James, and two of this cousins—all members
of the Society of Friends.  In 1864 he was drafted, but
employed a substitute at a cost of six hundred dollars.
Later in the same year he enlisted in the regular army,
after helping to organize "a squad of Upper Dublin farm
boys full of martial ardor."[64]   In explanation of his
participation in the military ranks Wilmer Atkinson said:

> I am deeply impressed with the truths of this testimony
> [of the Society of Friends] against war, and yet there are
> times when it seems necessary to engage in a forceful defense
> of sacred rights, when such rights are imperilled—as they
> were from 1861 to 1865 by those who would extend the
> system of human slavery throughout all the nation. . . . As
> to the part taken by me in the Civil War, I may say that I
> regret that I was compelled to act contrary to the Friends'
> Book of Discipline. . . . The most I can say in the way of
> apology and in extenuation is that I will never go to war
> again.[65]

Apparently an explanation of this kind was satisfactory
for the Meeting to which Wilmer Atkinson belonged because there is no record of his disownment.

Another Friend recognized that:

> There was something anomalous in the action of these
> Quaker knight-errants in the line of duty.  Ignoring their
> deviation from a fundamental principle of Friends, opposi-
> tion to war, they in instances became sticklers for the
> minor tenets of their religion, one of these in reference to the
> taking of oaths.  Swearing in soldiers to the service is a rule
> demanded by the articles of war, yet when the writer of
> this, with a group of fellow believers, asked to have these
> rules suspended, the request was granted and they were

---

[63] *Wilmer Atkinson, An Autobiography*, p. 88.
[64] *Ibid.*, p. 102.

[65] *Ibid.*, pp. 107–108.

affirmed to do their duty at shooting and killing their fellow men![66]

The attitude of other "deviators" is explained by another Friend by the name of Charles K. Whipple. He says:

Whether the temptations of this time have been absolutely unconquerable or not, some of the Progressive Friends, as well as the old-fashioned *stationery* Friends—some who called themselves Peace men, and some who called themselves Non-Resistants—have been drawn into voluntary coöperation with the existing war. And all of us have found ourselves in such unwonted straits, so beset by antagonistic evils, and so urged by the evident necessity of immediate and decisive action, that we have joyfully welcomed that which seemed to promise us deliverance from slavery, even though it wore the hideous aspect of war. . . . Now, as heretofore, they that take the sword are likely to perish by the sword, and are sure to undergo deterioration and corruption in the process of using it. Now, as heretofore, the overcoming of evil with evil is not only a forbidden method, but a method pernicious to him who adopts it. . . . But the man who is at once conscientious and enlightened will see immediately, . . . , that the army is not his place; that if he remains there he must *mutiny*, either by using his arms in defence of liberty and justice against military authority, or by refusing to obey the unjust mandate. In the latter case he will fall back upon non-resistance principles, choose to suffer wrong rather than do wrong, find his old faith confirmed by his new experience, and see more plainly than ever the folly of expecting Satan to cast out Satan.[67]

The following quotation from the minutes of the Meeting for Sufferings of the Philadelphia (Orthodox) Yearly

---

[66] Kenderdine, Thaddeus S. "Friends in the War of the Rebellion," in the *Friends' Intelligencer*, LXVI, no. 29, pp. 459–460.

[67] Min. of the Yearly Meeting of Progressive Friends, 1862, pp. 20–21.

Meeting is given as an appropriate conclusion to this chapter because it embodies in Friendly language a restatement of the principles underlying all conscientious objection to war, the difficulties involved in maintaining these principles during a war, the partial recognition of the scruples of religious objectors by those in authority during the Civil War, and the hope for more peaceful settlements of future difficulties among men.

To the Meeting for Sufferings.

The Committee to advise and assist such of our members as might be drafted for service in the army of the United States: Report;

That numerous applications have been made to them, all of which have been attended to; and such counsel and aid given to the parties as their respective cases appeared to require.

Three Friends were taken from their homes, in the interior of Pennsylvania, and sent to Camp Curtin at Harrisburg; from whence they wrote to the Committee, informing of their trying situation. Application was promptly made to the proper Officers in Philadelphia, and a letter procured from one of them to the Military Commander at the Camp, recommending the cases to his favorable attention. Two of the Committee went with this to Harrisburg; and had an interview with the officer in charge, who treated them kindly, and granted permission to the three young men to return to their homes until called for; since which they have not been disturbed.—

In two other cases military passes have been granted to drafted Friends; releasing them from the rendezvous, and permitting their return home; and these have been renewed on the application of the Committee; evincing a Friendly feeling toward those who are conscientiously engaged, under a sense of religious duty to uphold the christian testimony to peace.

One young man, when before the Provost Marshall, in his anxiety to escape being sent to the field, inadvertently expressed his willingness to serve in the Army Hospitals. He was soon sent to Camp, where he was expected to drill, and to do other acts which were trying to his feelings; and the more so, because he felt that he had compromised the testimony of Truth by choosing Hospital duty; and thus had deprived himself of the inward strength and support which are the accompaniments of faithfulness.

When assigned to a Hospital, he found the associations and examples extremely repugnant to his moral and religious feelings, and in several letters, deplored the mistake he had made, and the sad situation into which he had introduced himself. Being taken sick, his feelings were more fully awakened, and in another letter, he entreated Friends to intercede for his release, that he might not end his days amid scenes of such wickedness. He was favored to recover, was discharged, and restored to his Father's family, deeply impressed with his error, and more than ever attached to the principles of Friends. His experience, we think, furnishes evidence of the great importance of steadily and unflinchingly adhering to religious principles, without compromise.

The 17th Section of the 'Amandatory enrolment Act' approved the 24th of 2nd month 1864 provides 'that members of religious denominations, who shall by oath or affirmation declare that they are conscientiously opposed to the bearing of arms, and who are prohibited from doing so by the rules and articles of faith and practice of said religious denominations, shall when drafted into the military service, be considered non-combatants, and shall be assigned by the Secretary of War to duty in the hospitals, or to the care of freedmen, or shall pay the sum of three hundred dollars to such person as the Secretary of War shall designate to receive it, to be applied to the benefit of the sick and wounded soldiers: Provided, That no person shall be entitled to the provisions of this section unless his declaration of conscientious scruples against bearing arms shall be supported by satisfactory evidence that his deportment has been uniformly consistent with such declaration.'

This, we believe, is the first recognition in the Statutes of the United States, of a religious scruple against war, and, coming in the midst of so mighty and desperate a struggle as that then pending, it may well be considered as a most important movement in favor of the Christian principle of 'Peace on earth and good-will toward men'.

There can be no doubt that it had its origin in feelings of kind consideration for the members of our Religious Society, and of any other which may hold the same views of the peaceable nature of the gospel: and it demands our grateful acknowledgment to the government. It should also be an incentive to Friends, to maintain with integrity their religious testimony; for if those who preceded us had balked or betrayed it, there is no probability that this advance would have been obtained.

That it is a relief to be placed on the list of non-combatants is obvious; inasmuch as it releases from liability to be sent into the battle-field; but the law does not afford a mode of escape from military duty which our discipline acknowledges as consistent with the religious principles of Friends.

Believing that liberty of conscience is the gift of the Creator to man, Friends have ever refused to purchase the free exercise of it, by the payment of any pecuniary or other commutation, to any human authority.

From no other class of citizens, is the payment of $300, the service in hospitals, or among the Freedmen, required; and it is obviously in consequence of their conscientious scuple against war that these are demanded of Friends; and the payment of the money, or the performance of the service, would be an acknowledgment that human authority may abridge and control the Christian's liberty of conscience, which our Society has ever denied.

The money, moreover, is only applicable to military purposes; and therefore paying it, is violating our Christian testimony. The long established Discipline of Friends prohibits such payment; declaring it to be 'the judgment of the Yearly Meeting that,' if any of its members do, either openly or by connivance, pay any fine, penalty or tax in lieu of personal service for carrying on war 'and are not brought to an acknowledgment of their error, Monthly Meetings should proceed to testify against them.' This rule was confirmed and explained, a few years afterwards by another, which says: 'It is the sense and judgment of this meeting that it is inconsistent with our religious testimony and principles for any Friends to pay a fine or tax levied on them on account of their refusal to serve in the militia, although such fine or imposition may be applied toward defraying the expenses of *civil* government;' and it directs the same course to be pursued by monthly meetings, as in the former case, toward such as violate it.

The Committee have been weightily impressed with the seriousness of making a solemn affirmation of conscientious scruple against bearing arms or being concerned in war, as the law we have quoted calls for; and have much desired that it may not be lightly done by any of our members; but that such as are required to do it, in order to be placed on the list of non-combatants, may be encouraged closely to examine themselves, and be satisfied that they do it from sincere conviction, and not merely from a desire to escape suffering, or to make their way easier.

In endeavoring to discharge the duties of their appointment; while the committee have been much aided and cheered by the kind consideration shown by the officers of the government; they have been pained to find that some of our members have compromised our peace principles by paying the penalty imposed; thus lowering our profession of religious scruple in the estimation of those in authority, and greatly adding to the embarrassment and difficulty of such members as could not, for conscience sake comply with the demand.

Another source of trial and discouragement to us has been that some members have subscribed to funds raised for the payment of bounties to Soldiers, and others have paid taxes levied and applied expressly for the same object; both which are clearly violations of our Christian testimony and discipline, and have tended to discourage and weaken the hands of faithful Friends, as well as to lessen the weight and influence of the Society when appealing to government for the relief of our drafted members.

If those who thus aid in hiring men to fight were transported to the field of battle, and could witness the angry passion engendered, see the soldier who was tempted to enlist, and hired for his work, in part by their money, dealing destruction around him, wounding, maiming, and killing men who are strangers to him; hear the piercing cries and groans of the poor sufferers, and perhaps behold the man himself sent from the murderous employ to his final reckoning; and witness the grief of the bereaved widows and the destitute orphans, in their desolate homes; surely they could not but lament that they had incurred the responsibility of helping forward the dreadful business, with its awful consequences. Distance from the scene of action does not lessen their accountability.

The Committee impressed with a lively sense of the great value and importance of the testimony to universal peace, as an integral part of the Gospel dispensation: and, convinced that we can only hope to see it spread in the world, by individual faithfulness, and consistency; affectionately desire that these views may claim the serious attention of Friends, and that under the influence of Divine love, we may, as brethren of the same household of Faith, feel for, and with, each other; and endeavor as well by example as precept to strengthen, encourage, and help one another, in the upright support of our religious profession.

.   .   .   .   .   .   .   .   .   .   .   .   .   .   .   .

Signed on behalf and by direction of the Committee.

Thomas Evans
Morris Cope
Aaron Sharpless
David Roberts
John E. Sheppard

Philada 4th mo. 13, 1865

# Chapter VII

## The Civil War and the World War— A Comparison in Conscientious Objection

TO MOST persons living at the present time the expression *conscientious objector* is associated with the World War and not with any struggles of the past. Many of those who suffered or conscience' sake in the world conflict doubtless did not realize how many had suffered before them in a similar cause. Nevertheless, as with war, objection to compulsory military service is an old problem, not a new one; a problem which must be faced by every government which resorts to military conscription; a problem which is still unsolved.

Although the question of conscientious objection to combatant service existed for the United States in both the Civil and World Wars there are obvious differences to be recognized in making comparisons or in drawing conclusions. In the first place, the setting for the two struggles was utterly different  One, in the nineteenth century, was fifty years prior to the other in the twentieth century. One was a localized, civil war, the other was a vast international conflict calling for cooperation among nations and peoples. The first was practically confined to the territory of the United States, the second was fought on the continents of Europe, Asia, and Africa. In the second place, the causes of the wars were different. The Civil War was caused primarily by slavery and by the divergent political, economic, social, and industrial ideals of Americans, North and South. The causes of the World War were more involved, but slavery was not one of them. Finally, the late entrance of the United States into the World War must be taken into consideration. There were several years of actual fighting in which Americans had the chance to view the war from a distance; to discuss the merits and objectives of the combatants as far as the censorship and propaganda of the belligerents would allow. There was also the chance to profit by the examples of the warring nations. The mobilization of the American Army, the drafting of the conscription law, and the provision for conscientious objectors are but examples of the influence which the other countries undoubtedly had on the United States prior to its participation in the war. In spite of these and other differences between the two wars a brief comparison of the problem of conscientious objection is possible, at least a comparison of those phases which have been discussed in the preceding chapters of this book.

Considering the fact that fifty years elapsed between the two conflicts it is not surprising to learn that differences arose in the type of objector. In the World War the so-called religious objector again predominated but there were also a number who based their objections to military service on moral, economic, or political rather than on religious grounds and who were unaffiliated with any church. Various attempts have been made to classify these different types. In an executive order of President Wilson, dated March 20, 1918, only two groups were recognized: (1) those certified by their local draft boards as members of a religious sect, and (2) those who were not so certified.[1] A more specific classification was that of Major Walter Guest Kellogg, a member of the Board of Examiners, appointed by the War Department during 1918. He divided objectors into three groups: (1) those who be-

---

[1] U. S. War Department. *Statement concerning the treatment of conscientious objectors in the army*, p. 18.

longed to a well-recognized religious sect, (2) those who based their convictions on the Bible yet belonged to no church, and (3) political objectors, such as Socialists.[2] A somewhat similar grouping was made by Lieutenant Mark A. May, Professor of Psychology at Syracuse University, formerly a member of the Division of Psychology, Surgeon General's Office. He classified objectors as (1) religious literalists, (2) religious idealists, and (3) the socialist type.[3]

Perhaps a better idea of the type of objector can be gained by reading the recorded objections to military service of about five hundred men in five of the military camps. To 125 of them war was forbidden in the Scriptures in general; to 120 it was forbidden by conscience; to 115 by church and creed; to 95 by Christ specifically; to 60 by the Commandment; to 21 war was wrong in and of itself; to 16 war promoted evil; and 30 had objections of some other type.[4]

Just as there were a greater number of types of individual objectors in the World War there were also a greater number of religious denominations represented. In addition to the already familiar Society of Friends, Mennonite Church, Church of the German Baptist Brethren, and Christadelphians there were also the Plymouth Brethren, The International Bible Students Association or Russellites, Seventh Day Adventists, Church of God and Saints of Christ, Disciples of Christ, Church of Christ, Church of Daniel's Band, Church of the Living God, Pentecostal Church of the Nazarene, Church of the True Light, Brethren in Christ, Church of the First Born, Israelites of the House of David, Church of the Holiness, Koreshan Unity, International Apostolic Holiness Church,

---

[2] Kellogg, Walter Guest. *The Conscientious Objector*, pp. 28–29.
[3] Thomas, Norman M. *The Conscientious Objector in America*, p. 19.
[4] Kellogg, Walter G. *op. cit.*, Appendix VI, p. 130.

Metropolitans, Molokans, Moravians, Doukhobours, Christians, Holy Rollers, and Zionists.[5]  It is quite possible that there were others not included in the above long list.

Accurate figures of the number of members in each of the above sects who were conscientious objectors are not available, but a table, compiled by Lieutenant May, based on the reports from twelve army camps, shows a surprising preponderance of Mennonites.  The complete table follows:[6]

| | |
|---|---|
| Mennonites | 554 |
| Friends | 80 |
| International Bible Students | 60 |
| Israelites of the House of David | 39 |
| Dunkards | 37 |
| Church of Christ | 31 |
| Church of God, etc. (colored) | 20 |
| Seventh Day Adventists | 20 |
| Pentecostal Assembly | 13 |
| All other denominations | 206 |
| | 1060 |

In addition to the churches there were other organizations which took a distinct interest in conscientious objectors; particularly the Fellowship of Reconciliation, the National Civil Liberties Union, the Bureau of Legal Advice, the American Union Against Militarism, the Collegiate Anti-Militarism League, the American Friends' Service Committee, the League for Democratic Control,

[5] *Ibid.*, p. 33; American Civil Liberties Union. *The Facts about Conscientious Objectors in the United States*, p. 30; and Meyer, Ernest L. *Hey! Yellowbacks!*, p. 83.

[6] Kellogg, Walter G. *op. cit.*, Appendix IV, pp. 128–129.

Young Democracy, the American Liberty Defense League, and the Young Peoples Socialist League.[7]

When the United States declared war on Germany, April 6, 1917, the status of conscientious objectors was much the same as it had been prior to the Civil War. By the constitutions of at least twenty-one states persons having conscientious scruples against bearing arms were exempt from militia duty, usually upon the payment of a monetary equivalent.

It soon became evident that conscription was to be the policy of the American Government in raising its military forces. Several organizations, therefore, such as the American Union Against Militarism, the Fellowship of Reconciliation, and individual members of the Society of Friends took immediate steps to secure exemption for objectors. Secretary of War, Baker, was interviewed by a committee composed of Jane Addams, Lillian Wald, and Norman Thomas. Efforts to interview President Wilson were unsuccessful but he was appealed to in writing. The Military Affairs Committees of the House and Senate were appealed to, and a subcommittee in the Senate even held a special hearing on the subject. Nothing definite, however, came of these appeals.[8]

In the meantime the Selective Service Act was passed on May 18, 1917. In Section 4 it was stated that:

... nothing in this act shall be construed to require or compel any person to serve in any of the forces herein provided for who is found to be a member of any well recognized religious sect or organization at present organized and existing and whose existing creed or principles forbid its members to participate in war in any form and whose religious convictions are against war or participa-

---

[7] Thomas, Norman M. *op. cit.*, pp. 70–72, and American Civil Liberties Union, *op. cit.*, p. 32.

[8] Thomas, Norman M. *op. cit.*, pp. 74–77.

tion therein in accordance with the creed or principles of said religious organizations, but no person so exempted shall be exempted from service in any capacity that the President shall declare to be noncombatant . . .[9]

This exemption clause was similar to the provision in the Federal Act of February 24, 1864, in that it only recognized *religious* objectors but dissimilar in that it did not permit money to be paid in lieu of personal service. Both acts provided for noncombatant service as an alternative to actual military service. A defect in the 1917 law which soon became apparent was the lack of any provision for deciding which religious sects should be recognized as having conscientious scruples. The determination of these sects was left entirely in the hands of the 156 district enrollment boards. Consequently sects recognized by one board were not necessarily recognized by another, nor were the Rules and Regulations promulgated June 30th, under authority of the Selective Service Act, of any real assistance.[10] These rules merely called the board's attention to:

Any person who is found by such local board to be a member of any well-recognized religious sect or organization organized and existing May 18, 1917, and whose then existing creed or principles forbid its members to participate in war in any form, and whose religious convictions are against war or participation therein in accordance with the creed or principles of said religious organization.

. . . . . . . . . . . . . . . . . .

In case any such person substantiates [by affidavit], in the opinion of the local board, his claim, such local board shall issue a certificate stating that such person shall not be required or compelled to serve in any capacity except in

[9] *U. S. Statutes at Large*, XL, p. 78 (65 Cong., Sess. 1, chap. 15), and U. S. War Department, *op. cit.*, p. 14.
[10] American Civil Liberties Union, *op. cit.*, p. 7.

some capacity declared by the President to be noncombatant.[11]

During the passage of the Selective Service Act through Congress attempts had been made to liberalize the provisions applying to objectors. Robert M. LaFollette, of Wisconsin, introduced an appropriate amendment in the Senate and Representative Keating, of Colorado, did the same in the House, but their efforts were unavailing. Naturally this was a disappointment to the persons who were working in the interest of conscientious objectors. As one of them expressed it:[12]

Some of the very small group who were working for exemption laws were bitterly disappointed at this cavalier treatment given to their cause. Probably their disappointment was unreasonable. The most that could have been hoped for was that a good administrative system would be worked out on the basis of experience for dealing with certain classes of objectors. Even had there been power to obtain a more liberal law before the full hysteria of the war psychology was upon us it is probable that its more generous provisions would have been ignored or evaded as was the case in England.

Among conscientious objectors the question soon arose as to whether it would be proper to register under the terms of the Selective Service Act. Almost without exception the organizations which were interested in their welfare recommended such registration. The few who refused to register were prosecuted in the civil courts and were subjected to varying sentences in civil prisons. As in the Civil War, the great majority reported to their local draft boards and later to their specified cantonments, when called upon to do so. A few complied with all provisions of the law up to the point of entraining for camp, notifying

[11] U. S. War Department, *op. cit.*, p. 35.
[12] Thomas, Norman M. *op. cit.*, p. 78.

their local boards in the meantime that they would go only under compulsion. As a rule these men were treated by the Government not as conscientious objectors but as technical deserters.[13] Various attitudes were taken by objectors regarding the physical examination required of all drafted men. Some refused to take it while others took it under protest. Those who refused to take it were either prosecuted in the Federal courts or were merely reported as liable for service by the draft boards.[14]

If the local boards believed in the sincerity and credentials of the objector and if he was physically fitted for service he was given a certificate exempting him from combatant service, but he was required to report at a concentration camp in common with other drafted men. When he reported at the camp he usually restated his conscientious objection to military service and showed his certificate from the local board.

As the Selective Service Act did not provide for the handling of these men in camp a series of executive orders was necessary for the guidance of camp officials. One of the first orders was dated September 13, 1917. It read:

> . . . Pending final instruction . . . , the Secretary of War directs that this class [of conscientious objectors] be segregated, but not subjected to any punishment for refusal to perform duty, and that timely reports as to the numbers received at your cantonment be forwarded for his information, with such remark and recommendation by you as will enable the Department to consider the non-general question in all its phases.[15]

This order was the only announced policy of the Government toward conscientious objectors from September, 1917, to March, 1918.

---

[13] American Civil Liberties Union, *op. cit.*, pp. 13–15.

[14] *Ibid.*, p. 16.

[15] *Ibid.*, p. 17

Various confidential orders were issued by the War Department, however, to take care of particular situations as they arose. One of the earliest questions which had to be solved was what to do with Mennonite objectors who refused to wear uniforms. The War Department wisely ordered that such individuals be not compelled to wear uniform "as question of raiment is one of the tenets of their faith."[16] Mennonites were not the only ones, however, who refused to wear military uniform.

A later confidential order of October 10th redirected (1) that conscientious objectors be segregated and placed under instructors "who shall be specially selected with a view of insuring that these men will be handled with tact and consideration and that their questions will be answered fully and frankly";(2) that the men will not be treated as violating military laws "thereby subjecting themselves to the penalties of the Articles of War, but their attitude in this respect will be quietly ignored and they will be treated with kindly consideration"; (3) that report shall be made of what happens in cases of conscientious objection; and (4) that "under no circumstances are the instructions contained in the foregoing to be given to the newspapers."[17] Under another significant order of December 19, 1917, the term *conscientious objector* was expanded to include those having "personal scruples against war," such persons to be treated in all respects as other [religious] conscientious objectors. Under still later orders of March 6 and March 11, 1918, it was ordered that a psychological, and, where necessary, a psychiatric, examination be made of all conscientious objectors and a report thereon furnished to the Secretary of War; also that nothing in previous orders should be construed "as

---

[16] U. S. War Department, *op. cit.*, p. 36. This order was dated September 25, 1917.

[17] *Ibid.*, p. 37.

requiring the mingling in one group of different classes of conscientious objectors, who, for the good of the service, may be kept apart."[18]

All of these orders reflect a just attitude on the part of the War Department. However, as in the Civil War, these uniform orders were not uniformly interpreted and carried out by different commanding officers which meant that there was considerable variety in the treatment accorded objectors in different camps.

On March 20, 1918, President Wilson issued an executive order defining noncombatant service and clarifying the Government's future policy toward conscientious objectors. In summary, the order declared service in the Medical Corps, Quartermaster Corps, and Engineering Service to be noncombatant; objectors were to be classified for convenience into two groups—those certified by their local boards as being members of a religious sect the tenets of which were opposed to war and those who were not so certified; men in these two classes were to be offered noncombatant service and assignments were to be made to the extent they were able to accept such service without violation of "the religious or other conscientious scruples by them in good faith entertained"; monthly reports were to be made on all those who might not be willing to accept noncombatant service, with reasons therefor; and, pending directions from the Secretary of War, "all such persons not accepting assignment to noncombatant service shall be segregated as far as practicable and placed under the command of a specially qualified officer of tact and judgment, who will be instructed to impose no punitive hardship of any kind upon them, but not allow their objections to be made the basis of any favor or consideration beyond exemption from actual military service which is not extended to any other soldier in the service

---

[18] *Ibid.*, p. 17.

of the United States"; uniformity of penalties in sentences of courts-martial were recommended and confinement in United States Disciplinary Barracks rather than in penitentiaries (except in cases of actual desertion) was prescribed; and finally, a revision of sentences of courts-martial imposed prior to this order was ordered with a view to their remedy by the President if found to be at variance therewith.[19] The last part of this order was especially significant because a considerable number of death sentences had already been imposed by courts-martial.

In the meantime the organizations and individuals acting on behalf of conscientious objectors were active. A conference of most of these organizations, held in New York City on January 8, 1918, adopted a memorandum of recommendations for the War Department. This Memorandum reminds one of the *memorials* of the Society of Friends and of other religious bodies at the time of the Civil War, except that it was much more specific in its recommendations than were most of the Civil War petitions. It began:

> We are appreciative of the liberal spirit of the War Department in dealing with a problem made difficult by the narrow and arbitrary definition of conscience in the Selective Service Act. We recognize that the Department cannot change the law, and that at present it is inopportune to suggest amendments, providing a more liberal basis of recognition of conscience. It is rather as a practical problem on which we offer these recommendations, believing that it is the desire of the War Department to avoid the injustices which would make a controversial issue of liberty of conscience.

There then follow nine specific recommendations.

(1) 'No distinction should be made between conscientious objectors once the authorities are convinced of the

---

[19] *Ibid.*, pp. 18, 19, and 39.

genuineness of an objector's stand'—whether or not he holds Form 174 (exemption certificate of local board).

(2) In order to determine the genuineness of the stand taken by those who do not hold exemption certificates a committee of three in each military post should be appointed to examine and pass on all such cases, with the right of appeal to the Secretary of War.

(3) 'Conscientious objectors should be defined as men who take the stand that it is morally wrong for them to participate in this war.' The following measures were suggested as means of securing proof of moral conviction: (a) Obtain record of membership before the war in a religious society the tenets of which were opposed to war, (b) inquiries by letter through local boards with affidavits of responsible citizens, and (c) personal examination.

(4) All men in camp who claim to be conscientious objectors should be disposed of at once through these committees.

(5) Review by the Secretary of War of all court-martial cases.

(6) Treatment of those who refused to entrain for camp but who made no effort to escape detection should be the same as other conscientious objectors.

(7) In determining the form of noncombatant service to be provided for conscientious objectors men should first be offered noncombatant service with fighting units, second, noncombatant service in hospitals in the United States or abroad, and finally, work with the Friends' Reconstruction Unit in France or government work not directly connected with carrying on the war.

(8) For men who refuse all service, and who will presumably be court-martialed and imprisoned, specific detention camps should be provided if the numbers justify it; sentences for refusal to perform any service should be made uniform and in no event to exceed the duration of the war; and no man should be court-martialed and sentenced more than once for what is in fact the same offense.

(9) It is suggested that the Department make public announcement of its policy in the matter.[20]

A portion of these recommendations were later embodied in the orders of the War Department, but it is not known what effect the memorandum as a whole had upon the policy of the Government.

A significant difference between the Civil War and the World War was the greater unity of action on the part of the noncombatant sects.  In the Civil War most religious organizations were divided by the actual line of battle, besides being hampered by a lack of rapid communication.  In the World War greater ease of communication and a natural growth in unity, particularly in the Society of Friends, led to significant results.  As an illustration, the three largest bodies of Friends in America—the Five Years' Meeting, the Friends' General Conference, and the Philadelphia (Orthodox) Yearly Meeting—began united action as early as April 30, 1917, when a group of their representatives met in Philadelphia to organize an American Friends' Service Committee.[21]  The immediate objects of this Committee were to aid English Friends in their relief work in the devastated regions of France and to offer to Friends in America (and to those in sympathy with them) an opportunity for service during the war.[22]  This Committee, together with such individuals as William B.  Harvey, the Secretary of the Exemption Committee of Philadelphia (Orthodox) Meeting for Sufferings, was instrumental in giving advice and comfort to conscientious objectors in the camps, in working out satisfactory relationships with the Civilian Branch of the American Red

---

[20] American Civil Liberties Union, *op. cit.*, pp. 25–27.

[21] Jones, Lester M. *Quakers in Action*, chap. 4.

[22] Bulletin #60 of the American Friends' Service Committee and Jones, Rufus M. *A Service of Love in War Time.*

Cross, and in having the so-called Furlough Law applied to conscientious objectors.

Apart from the Selective Service Act there was only one act of Congress passed during the war which had a direct bearing on conscientious objectors. This was the Furlough Law of March 16, 1918. As originally passed the law provided for the furloughs of enlisted men to engage in civil occupations upon voluntary application and under regulations of the Secretary of War.[23] As later interpreted, however, by the Acting Judge Advocate General on May 31, 1918, it was made applicable to conscientious objectors, and provided a successful alternative to noncombatant service for many of them. In some respects the furlough of drafted objectors in the World War was similar to the parole of Northern objectors in the Civil War, but from the standpoint of the National Government, the furlough of men for specific employment was far more effective than the "parole until called for" of the Civil War. Although this assignment to civil employment was a satisfactory alternative for some objectors, it was nevertheless a compromise, and was therefore not acceptable to the so-called *absolutists*, or those who refused to cooperate in any way with the military authorities.

An important step was taken by the War Department on July 30, 1918, when it provided for a special Board of Inquiry composed of Major Richard C. Stoddard, judge advocate and chairman, Judge Julian W. Mack, of the Federal Circuit Court, and Dean Harlan F. Stone, of the Columbia Law School. Major Stoddard was succeeded about August 15th by Major Walter G. Kellogg, judge advocate. It was the duty of this board to examine all men in the military contonments professing conscientious scruples against warfare, except those under charges or

<hr/>

[23] *U. S. Statutes at Large*, XL, p. 450 (65 Cong., Sess. 1, chap. 23), and U. S. War Department, *op. cit.*, p. 19.

being tried by court-martial; to recommend for assignment to noncombatant service or to furloughs the men so examined; and to set forth rules regulating furloughs and their termination.[24] This step on the part of the Government, which made for greater uniformity of treatment, had no parallel in the Civil War.

Apparently the unequal treatment of conscientious objectors in different camps came to the notice of the War Department, even after the Board of Inquiry began to function, because on October 2nd the Secretary directed that an order be issued, calling attention to the various provisions already made for these individuals, and stating further:

> It is not intended or desired that they be pampered or accorded special privileges in any respect not covered by existing instructions; on the other hand, they should not be treated, as in a few cases they have been, as men already convicted or cowardice and deceit. It is the experience of the Department that a tactful attitude toward these men has in many cases resulted in their acceptance, either of noncombatant, or in many cases combatant service, whereas a hectoring and abusive attitude has had an opposite effect.[25]

The remaining orders of the War Department, issued around the time of the armistice, dealt chiefly with farm furlough regulations and with the enlargement of the Board of Inquiry.

Before discussing the attitude of certain civil and military authorities in the World War it may be of interest to review briefly the procedure usually adopted by the Government in handling a conscientious objector. As in the Civil War the individual first came to the attention of the authorities after he was drafted. The typical ob-

---

[24] *Ibid.*, pp. 21–22.
[25] *Ibid.*, p. 22.

jector first presented his reasons for refusing combatant service to his local draft board. Upon proper presentation of facts and if judged sincere he was certified as a conscientious objector by the local board. Upon call he then reported at a specified cantonment with other drafted men. Pending a hearing by the special Board of Inquiry, the individual objector was segregated with other objectors but was not required to do work of a military nature. The Board of Inquiry, which traveled from camp to camp, examined informally the objector and judged of his sincerity. Those adjudged insincere were required to perform military service in default of which they were court-martialed and remanded to the Disciplinary Barracks at Fort Leavenworth. Those adjudged sincere were encouraged to enter noncombatant service. If, however, such service was refused they were usually furloughed to farms, to the Friends' Reconstruction Unit, or to other forms of service under the jurisdiction of a civilian commission. Where such furloughs were granted each objector was paid an ordinary wage for his type of work, but he was only allowed to retain the equivalent of a private's wage, any surplus going to the American Red Cross. As a matter of fact many of the men voluntarily turned over their entire wage to the Red Cross.

In the World War as in the Civil War the highest civil and military authorities maintained for the most part a generous attitude towards the small group of conscientious objectors. It was usually ordinary civilians or military officers of lower rank and enlisted privates who showed the greatest animosity toward, and misunderstanding of, objectors to military service.

President Wilson's personal attitude is difficult to judge. Like Jefferson Davis and unlike Abraham Lincoln he was either too busy or too little interested in the question of conscience to attend to the problem personally. It was understood that both he and Secretary Baker were at least conversant with the situation in England prior to the spring of 1917. It was even understood by some individuals that he expressed to certain English visitors "his dislike of the English brutality to conscientious objectors."[26] However, the efforts of American committees to interview him on the subject were unavailing, nor did he give any formal answer to the communications addressed to him. In one of his private letters he explained that the Military Affairs Committee felt that the exemption of individual objectors was not feasible "for fear that the unconscientious would escape" but this may not have been a true expression of his own personal feelings. He may even have thought "that as Commander-in-Chief of the army and navy he would be able to mitigate the force of coercive measures against genuine objectors."[27] In any case his attitude was a negative rather than a positive one. What initiative, if any, he took with reference to objectors is unknown.

The attitude of Secretary Baker is much better known. Throughout the war he showed a liberality and fairness comparable with that of Secretary Stanton. However, he was slow in deciding on proper policies, and when decided, was too often timid in carrying them out. As Norman Thomas, familiar with his attitude, expressed it:

Mr. Baker convinced himself that he was more liberal in his treatment of conscientious objectors than the general opinion of the army or of civilians thought proper. That may have been true of the earlier stages of his dealing with the problem; it was less certainly true of later stages. What he did not understand was that a bolder course would have informed and guided public opinion. His timidity declined the issue.[28]

---

[26] Thomas, Norman M. *op. cit.*, p. 74.
[27] *Ibid.*, p. 76.
[28] *Ibid.*, p. 253.

Although the Secretary was usually wise in his handling of objectors he occasionally issued an order which was subject to misinterpretation. An order of this type was one dated April 28, 1918, in which he directed that any man classed as a conscientious objector (a) whose attitude in camp was sullen and defiant, (b) whose sincerity was questioned, or (c) who was active in propaganda, should be pomptly brought to trial by court-martial.[29] It was very easy for unsympathetic camp commanders to interpret this sweeping order too broadly.

The person in the War Department to whom most of the problems of conscience were referred was F. P. Keppel, Third Assistant Secretary, and former Dean of Columbia College. Assistant Secretary Keppel of the World War and Assistant Secretary Campbell of the Civil War had much in common. They both held somewhat similar positions and both brought to bear on a difficult problem an insight and fairmindedness that was highly commendable. Again quoting from Norman Thomas we learn that:

> He had a truer understanding of the problem than his chief and more real tolerance. He personally rectified many wrongs when they were brought to his attention. But he lacked the effective support of his chief and of the military who were inclined to resent many of his modern ideas with regard not only to conscientious objectors but also to other matters of personnel.[30]

Keppel himself believed that the difficulty of dealing with the situation was one of practical procedure rather than one of policy; for example, the sincere had to be differentiated from the insincere and objectors had to be disposed of in such a way as to conserve the man-power of the nation.[31] In a public report of his on September 28, 1918, he ends with the following significant words:

---

[29] U. S. War Department, *op. cit.*, p. 19.
[30] Thomas, Norman M. *op. cit.*, p. 254.
[31] U. S. War Department, *op. cit.*, p. 47.

There is unquestionably strong sentiment in many quarters against the granting of immunity from military service to any group in our population however small. But many objectors are not without the courage of their convictions. They would resist compulsion to the end. We might imprison or shoot them. But Prussian practices such as these would hardly appeal in a Democracy. On the other hand, a method which conserves the man power of the Nation, and accords to furloughed objectors a lot that is endurable and serviceable, but in no sense pampered, will, it is believed, commend itself to the common sense and practicability of the American people.[32]

As the Congressmen who passed the Selective Service Act of 1917 gave less attention to the question of conscience than did the legislators of the Civil War period there is less opportunity to gauge their attitude on the subject. "By actual count, the House spent as many minutes in discussion of *the wording* of exemption of ministers of the gospel as on the whole subject of conscientious objection."[33] Those who expressed the greatest interest in objectors were Senator Robert M. LaFollette of Wisconsin, and Representatives Keating of Colorado and Hayden of Arizona. The two former introduced amendments to the Selective Service Act for the purpose of liberalizing the clauses relating to conscientious objectors and the latter explained the viewpoint of objectors in a speech of August 7, 1917.[34]

The attitude of state governors and of the other state officials is even harder to judge than it was during the Civil War, because, unlike the Federal Militia Act of 1862, the Selective Service Act of 1917 was executed through Federal agencies, and the draft was never under state control.

---

[32] *Ibid.*, p. 48.
[33] Thomas, Norman M. *op. cit.*, p. 78.
[34] *Ibid.*, pp. 77–78, and American Civil Liberties Union, *op. cit.*, p. 25.

Conscientious objection, by its very definition, means opposition to military authority. It is not surprising, therefore, to find in the World War as in the Civil War some military authorities not only unsympathetic but actually hostile toward objectors. Fortunately the United States Army contained plenty of individuals of broad vision and tact, so that, viewed as a whole, the attitude of the military authorities was a fair one, especially when it is considered that public opinion in general was so unsympathetic with the small group of those who objected to the bearing of arms.

At the very top of the military regime in the United States (aside from President Wilson as Commander-in-Chief) was General John J. Pershing. His personal feelings about objectors is unknown, but in one notable case, he favored the transfer of an objector to noncombatant service. The case in point was that of Richard L. Stierheim.

'Richard L. Stierhiem was drafted and sent over-seas before the government had provided any means of relief for the conscientious objector. In France he refused to perform military service and deserted. He was tried by court-martial, convicted, and sentenced to death. While awaiting execution of sentence, on November 3, 1918, as reported by the commanding general, he volunteered to go out into No Man's Land at the imminent peril of his life to rescue the wounded. He rescued six wounded men, unassisted, under machine-gun fire. He then volunteered to go into No Man's Land to bury the dead, and for nine successive days he continued to render service of this character, exposing himself unhesitatingly to imminent peril of death in the aid and succor of wounded men. General Pershing forwarded his record to the Judge Advocate General with the recommendation that his sentence be remitted and that he be assigned to duty in the noncombatant service.'[35]

---

[35] Quotation from Dean Harlan F. Stone in Thomas, Norman M. *op. cit.*, pp. 141-142. See also Kellogg, Walter G. *op. cit.*, pp. 108-110.

So far as is known this is the only instance of a conscientious objector being forced into the actual fighting area. In this respect the World War differed considerably from the Civil War when numerous objectors were forced into the zone of battle, especially in the South.

Objectors mostly came under the influence of the military authorities in the cantonments and disciplinary barracks. As might have been expected their treatment varied as greatly as did the treatment of conscientious objectors in the Civil War. The mildness or severity of their treatment depended very largely on the camp or prison in which they happened to be placed. At Camp Funston, for example, under the command of Major General Leonard Wood, objectors were treated with such severity that, after an official investigation, it was recommended that five officers be summarily dismissed from the service.[36] At another camp the sanitary regulations were so malicious as to call forth a severe condemnation from the Inspector of the Army.[37] On the other hand, objectors at Camp Upton were treated with greater respect, possibly because of the fairmindedness of the commanding general, J. Franklin Bell.

One of the best examples of severity on the part of the military authorities is found in the following list of original court-martial sentences of 503 objectors.[38]

*Original Sentences of Courts*

| | | | |
|---|---|---|---|
| Death | 17 | 2 years | 3 |
| Life | 142 | 50 " | 3 |
| 10 years | 89 | 8 " | 1 |
| 20 " | 73 | 11 " | 1 |
| 25 " | 57 | 12 " | 1 |

[36] Moomaw, D. C. *Christianity versus War*, pp. 312–316, and Thomas, Norman M., *op. cit.*, pp. 161–162.

[37] Meyer, Ernest L. *Hey! Yellowbacks!*, pp. 27–80, and Thomas, Norman M., *op. cit.*, p. 93.

[38] U. S. War Department, *op. cit.*, p. 51.

| | | | | |
|---|---|---|---|---|
| 15 " | ..................... 47 | 13 " | ..................... | 1 |
| 5 " | ..................... 29 | 18 " | ..................... | 1 |
| 30 " | ..................... 19 | 28 " | ..................... | 1 |
| 3 " | ..................... 5 | 45 " | ..................... | 1 |
| 1 " | ..................... 4 | 99 " | ..................... | 1 |
| 40 " | ..................... 4 | | | |
| Less than one year | ............. 3 | | | 503 |

It is interesting to compare the above list with the following statement of sentences as finally approved after review by reviewing authorities and by the Judge Advocate General's Office. It is further interesting to note that in both the Civil and World Wars conscientious objectors were sentenced to death, but in neither war were the sentences carried out.[39]

*Sentences as Finally Executed*

| | | | | |
|---|---|---|---|---|
| 25 years | ..................... 166 | 35 years | ..................... | 1 |
| 10 " | ..................... 94 | 8 " | ..................... | 1 |
| 15 " | ..................... 65 | 11 " | ..................... | 1 |
| 20 " | ..................... 49 | 12 " | ..................... | 1 |
| 5 " | ..................... 32 | 13 " | ..................... | 1 |
| 30 " | ..................... 18 | 18 " | ..................... | 1 |
| 3 " | ..................... 8 | 28 " | ..................... | 1 |
| 1 " | ..................... 4 | Sentence disapproved and accused | | |
| Less than one year | ............. 2 | released | ............... | 53 |
| 2 years | ..................... 2 | Sentence suspended | ........... | 1 |
| 50 " | ..................... 2 | | | |
| | | | | 503 |

In most cases of conscience the individual undoubtedly suffered mentally more than physically. The alienation, or at least misunderstanding, of family, friends, and associates; the difficulty of maintaining a consistent attitude and of convincing the authorities of one's sincerity; the taunts and reproaches of soldiers; the social segregation in camps; and the uncertainty of treatment all played a part in the mental suffering of many objectors. One case of suicide is recorded, that of Ernest Gellert at Fort Hancock,

[39] *Ibid.*, p. 51.

New Jersey, in which the mental strain was clearly manifest. Beside his body he left the following note:

> I fear I have not succeeded in convincing the authorities of the sincerity of my scruples against participation in the war. I feel that only by my death shall I be able to save others from the mental tortures I have gone through. If I succeed I give my life willingly.[40]

As the numerous trials and experiences of American objectors in camp, before military courts and the Court of Inquiry, in prison, on farm furloughs, or in service with the Friends' Reconstruction Unit have already been the subject of other books, such stories will not be repeated here.[41]  The following statement is quoted, however, to show the kinds of treatment some objectors received at the hands of the military authorities, together with the action of the War Department in cases actually brought to its attention. As the statement applies almost equally well to the Civil War it would appear as if the military machine had undergone but little change in the course of fifty years.

As would be expected, a number of cases of brutal treatment of objectors, either by officers or enlisted men, were reported. All were called to the attention of the War Department, and in most cases satisfactorily and promptly attended to. Everything considered, the number of such cases was surprisingly small (perhaps 40 altogether up to April 1, 1918). They consisted of forcing on the uniform, forcible feeding of hunger-strikers, forcible labor, exposure to cold, deprivation of food, beating, attempted terroriza-

---

[40] American Civil Liberties Union, *op. cit.*, p. 20, and Thomas, Norman M. *op. cit.*, pp. 145–146.

[41] E.g. Jones, Lester M. *Quakers in Action*; Jones, Rufus M. *A Service of Love in War time*; Stephens, D. Owen. *With Quakers in France*; Meyer, Ernest L. *Hey! Yellowbacks!*; Moomaw, D. C. *Christianity versus War*; Thomas, Norman M. *The Conscientious Objector in America*; and the American Civil Liberties Union. *The Facts about Conscientious Objectors in the United States.*

tion by weapons, and hazing by soldier mobs. Of course, taunts, epithets and threats of violence have been the common lot of objectors everywhere they come in contact with bodies of soldiers. Threats by officers of court-martial and long imprisonment have also been frequent. On the other hand, most of the regular officers and a very large proportion of the soldiers have shown a human regard for objectors. . . . The brutalities occurred chiefly at army posts and regular army or militia camps where drafted men were a novelty—particularly those who took the position of the conscientious objector. In several cases the officers and men guilty of brutality were severely disciplined.[42]

One is apt to gain the impression that conscientious objection in the World War was a greater problem proportionately than it had been in the Civil War. If anything the reverse is true. Fortunately more figures are available for the World War than were available for the earlier struggle so that one is left in no doubt as to the size of the problem, at least from a military point of view.

From the second report of the Provost Marshal General which covers the whole period of the administration of the selective service law . . . and further subsequent data furnished by the boards but not included in the second report . . . it appears that there were 64,693 claims made for noncombatant classification, of which 56,830 were recognized by the boards. Of these, 29,679 were classified in class I and found physically fit for general military service of whom 20,873 were inducted into the service from the beginning of mobilization to the termination thereof on November 11, 1918.

No statistics are available as to the number of religious or other conscientious objectors who made no claims before the local boards or whose claims were rejected by the boards and who were inducted, but there was undoubtedly a substantial number of such objectors inducted into the army.

[42] American Civil Liberties Union, *op. cit.*, p. 20.

So far as statistics are available it appears that about 4,000 men inducted into the military service made any claim in camp, either by presentation of a certificate or otherwise, for exemption from combatant service or from all military service. It would therefore appear that more than 80 per cent of religious objectors whose claims were recognized by the local boards and who were furnished with noncombatant certificates changed their minds before or shortly after reaching camp and failed to claim the advantage of exemption from combatant service. Undoubtedly this was due in large measure to the character of treatment prescribed by the order of the Secretary of War of October 10, 1917.[43]

It follows, therefore, that the ratio of men professing conscientious objection in the camps to the total inductions into the army was as 3,989 to 2,810,296, or .0014%. Of these 3,989 the following classification was made:[44]

Those who originally accepted, or were assigned to, noncombatant service........................ 1,300
Those who were furloughed to agriculture.......... 1,200
Those furloughed to the Friends' Reconstruction Unit    99
Class I remaining in camp after the armistice........ 715
Class II remaining in camp after the armistice....... 225
General court-martial prisoners.................... 450

3,989

The two groups designated as Class 1 and Class 2 in the table above referred to those found by the Board of Inquiry to be (1) sincere religious objectors and recommended for farm or industrial furlough and (2) those found to be sincere conscientious objectors as to combatant, but not sincere as to noncombatant service, and

[43] U. S. War Department, *op. cit.*, pp. 15–16.
[44] *Ibid.*, p. 25.

who were therefore recommended to be assigned to non-combatant service.

. . . . . . . . . . . . . . . . . . . . . . . .

From all that has been said in this and preceding chapters the conclusion is inevitable that only those persons whose scruples against war are deeply rooted can hold out against military authority. In the Civil War and World War the individuals who lacked the courage of their convictions were inevitably absorbed by the powerful military machine. No one is wise enough to estimate the effect which these courageous consciences of the past have had on the power of war. Too often the objector's stand has not been taken against the military system until war was a grim reality. Always the objector has been a member of a small minority, a lonely person struggling apparently against tremendous forces. Through his loneliness, however, he has learned to think, and to act independently. From certain standpoints his struggle has been a negative one because he has objected to a military system which the majority has accepted, or at least tolerated. Perhaps from being an objector to a system which he cannot condone he can become a projector of his own ideas regarding the stupidity of war. Perhaps the time is not far distant when most people will learn to "live in the virtue of that life and power" which will take away the occasion for wars.

Full long our feet the flowery ways
   Of peace have trod,
Content with creed and garb and phrase:
A harder path in earlier days
   Led up to God.


But now the cross our worthies bore
   On us is laid;
Profession's quiet sleep is o'er,
And in the scale of truth once more
   Our faith is weighed.


This day the fearful reckoning comes
   To each and all;
We hear amidst our peaceful homes
The summons of the conscript drums,
   The bugle's call.


Our path is plain; the war-net draws
   Round us in vain,
While, faithful to the Higher Cause,
We keep our fealty to the laws
   Through patient pain.


The levelled gun, the battle-brand
   We may not take:
But, calmly loyal, we can stand
And suffer with our suffering land
   For conscience' sake.


Why ask for ease where all is pain?
   Shall we alone
Be left to add our gain to gain,
When over Armageddon's plain
   The trump is blown?

Who murmurs that in these dark days
  His lot is cast?
God's hand within the shadow lays
The stones whereon his gates of praise
  Shall rise at last.

—JOHN G. WHITTIER

(From the Anniversary Poem, read at the
Annual Meeting of the Friends' Yearly Meeting
School, Newport, Rhode Island, June 15, 1863.)

# Bibliography

## PRIMARY SOURCES

(1) *Manuscript Material*

(a) *Meeting Records* (1861–1865)

Minutes of the following Yearly Meetings: Baltimore (Hicksite), Baltimore (Orthodox), Indiana (Orthodox), New York (Hicksite), New York (Orthodox), North Carolina (Orthodox), and Philadelphia (Orthodox).

Minutes of the following Half-Year Meetings: Virginia.

Minutes of the following Meetings for Sufferings: Baltimore (Hicksite), Indiana (Orthodox), New England (Orthodox), New York (Hicksite), New York (Orthodox), North Carolina (Orthodox), Philadelphia (Orthodox), and Western (Orthodox).

Minutes of the following Quarterly Meetings: Cane Creek, Centre (Baltimore Yearly Meeting), Contentnea, Deep River, New Garden (Indiana Yearly Meeting), New Garden (North Carolina Yearly Meeting), Piney Woods, Southern (North Carolina Yearly Meeting), and White Water.

Minutes of the following Monthly Meetings: Goose Creek, Hopewell, New Bedford, New York (Hicksite), New York (Orthodox), Providence, Radnor, and Salem.

Miscellaneous: Philadelphia (Hicksite) Yearly Meeting.

(b) *Personal Collections*.

Crenshaw, Margaret E. *Diary of John B. Crenshaw.*

North Carolina Yearly Meeting Collection of the Correspondence of John B. Crenshaw.

Manuscript Notes of Thomas Atkinson Jenkins. (This material has reference to the attitude toward war during the nineteenth century of the following Monthly Meetings of the Hicksite Branch of the Society of Friends):

Alexandria      Goose Creek      Millville

5

| Albany | Goshen | New York |
|---|---|---|
| Amawalk | Greenwich | Pilesgrove |
| Baltimore | Gunpowder | Philadelphia |
| Bristol | Horsham | (Race Street) |
| Chester (Pa.) | Little Falls | Purchase |
| Chester (N.J.) | Little Britain | Radnor |
| Center (Del.) | London Grove | Wilmington |
| Fairfax | Middletown | Wrightstown |

(c) *Government Documents.*

Records in the Adjutant General's Office, War Department, Washington, D. C.

Stanton, Edwin M., Papers. Vols. XI–XXV.
Manuscript Division, Library of Congress, Washington. 1920

Holt, Joseph, Papers. Vols. XLI–XLVI.
Manuscript Division, Library of Congress, Washington. 1917.

(d) *Correspondence.*

(2) *Printed Material*

(a) *Official Documents*

(1) *United States Government*

*Christadelphians.* Census of Religious Bodies, 1926.
Department of Commerce—Bureau of Census.
Washington, D.C.: Gov't Print. Office, 1926.

*Congressional Globe, The* Vols. XLII–XLIV.
Washington, D.C.: Gov't Print. Office, v.d.

*Executive Documents, House of Representatives, 38th Congress.*
Washington, D.C.: Gov't Print. Office, 1865.

*General Orders of the War Department and of the Provost Marshal General.*
Washington, D.C.: Gov't Print. Office, 1863–65.

*Journal of the Congress of the Confederate States of America, 1861–1865.* Senate Documents #234, 58th Congress, 2nd Session.
Vols. I–IV, Journal of the Senate.
Vols. V–VII, Journal of the House.

*Report to the Secretary of War by the Provost Marshal General of the Operations of the Bureau of the Provost Marshal General of the United States, from the commencement of the Business of the Bureau, March 17, 1863, to March 17, 1866.*
Washington, D.C.: Gov't Print. Office, 1866.

*Report of the Secretary of War and Postmaster General, 38th Congress, 1st Session, Vol. V.*
Washington, D.C.: Gov't Print. Office, 1865.

Richardson, James D. *A Compilation of the Messages and Papers of the Presidents (1789–1897), Vol. VI.*
House Miscellaneous Documents, 53rd Congress, 2nd Session, Vol. XXXVII, Pt. 6. Washington, D.C., 1893.

Richardson, James D. *A Compilation of the Messages and Papers of the Confederacy, including the Diplomatic Correspondence (1861–1865), 2 Vols.*
Nashville: U. S. Publishing Co., 1905.

*Statistics of the United States in 1860, Compiled from the Original Returns and being the final Exhibit of the Eighth Census under the Direction of the Secretary of the Interior.*
Washington, D.C.: Gov't Print. Office, 1866.

*Statutes at Large of the Confederate States of America.* 2 Vols.
Richmond, Va.: J. M. Matthews (Editor), 1862–64.

*Statutes at Large, Treaties, and Proclamations of the United States of America.* Vols. XII, XIII, XIV, XL.
Boston: Little, Brown & Co., 1865.

Thorpe, Francis N. *The Federal and State Constitutions, Colonial Charters, and other Organic Laws of the States, etc.*
Washington, D.C.: 1909.

U.S. War Department: *Statement concerning the treatment of conscientious objectors in the army. Prepared and pub. by direction of the secretary of war, June 18, 1919.*
Washington: Gov't Print. Office, 1919.

U. S. War Department—*Circulars from Provost Marshall General's Office.*
1863–65.
*War of the Rebellion: Compilation of official records of the Union and Confederate Armies.* 128 serial volumes. (Referred to in this study as *Official Records*). Washington, D.C.: 1880–1902.

(2) *State Governments*

*Iowa, State of, House Journal of,* 1862.
*Journal of the House of Delegates of the State of Virginia for the Session of 1861–62.*
Richmond, Va.: William F. Ritchie.
*North Carolina, Public Laws of the State of.*
Raleigh, N.C., v.d.
Shambaugh, Benjamin F. *Messages and Proclamations of the Governors of Iowa.* Vol. II. Pub. by the State Historical Society of Iowa. Iowa City: 1903.
*Virginia, Acts of the General Assembly of, for the years 1861–62.*
Richmond, Va.: William F. Ritchie.

(3) *Religious Denominations*

*An Account of the Sufferings of Friends of North Carolina Yearly Meeting, in Support of Their Testimony Against War, from 1861 to 1865.* (Pub. by order of the Representatives of North Carolina Yearly Meeting of Friends).
Baltimore: William K. Boyle, 1868.
Barclay, Robert. *The Inner Life of the Religious Societies of the Commonwealth.*
London: Hodder & Stoughton, 1876.
*Exiles in Virginia, with observations on the conduct of the Society of Friends during the Revolutionary War, comprising the official papers of the government relating to that period.*
Philadelphia: Pub. for the Subscribers, 1848.
*Memorial of the Religious Society of Friends to the Legislature of Virginia on the Militia Laws with a Letter*

*from Benjamin Bates (Bearer of the Memorial) to a Member of the Legislature.*
> New Bedford: Printed for A. Sherman, Jr., 1813.

Simon, Menno. *A Foundation and Plain Instruction of the Saving Doctrine of our Lord Jesus Christ* (Trans.).
> Lancaster: Barr, 1869.

Yearly Meetings of the Society of Friends, Minutes of (1861–65): Baltimore (Lombard Street); Indiana (Richmond); Indiana (Waynesville); Iowa; New England; North Carolina; Philadelphia (Race Street); Philadelphia (Arch Street).

Yearly Meeting of Progressive Friends, Minutes of Longwood, Chester County, Pennsylvania. (1862–65)

(b) *Newspapers and Periodicals*

*Atlantic Monthly, The.* Vols. VII–XV.
> Boston: Ticknor & Fields, 1861–65.

*Friend, The, a Religious and Literary Journal.* Vols. XXXIV–XXXVIII; LXVIII; LXXXI.
> Philadelphia: William H. Pile, 1861–65.

*Friends' Historical Society of Philadelphia, Bulletin of.* Vols. IV and VII.
> Philadelphia: Ferris & Leach, 1906–26.

*Friends' Historical Society, Journal of the.*
> London: Friends' Bookshop, 1903–27.

*Friends' Intelligencer.* Vols. XVII–XXI; LXVI.
> Philadelphia: Edited & Published by an Association of Friends, 1861–65.

*Friends' Review, a Religious, Literary and Miscellaneous Journal.*
> Philadelphia: Joseph Potts, 1864–65.

*Harper's New Monthly Magazine,* Vols. XXIV–XXX; CV.
> 1861–65.

*Harper's Weekly,* Vols. VI–IX.
> 1862–65.

*Living Age,* Vols. LXXII–LXXXII.
> 1861–65.

*Niles' Weekly Register,* Vol. IX.  1815–16.

*North American Review, The*, Vols. XCIII–CI.
1861–65.

*The Peacemaker*, Vol. XXII.
Parkesburg, Pa.: Universal Peace Union.

*Southern Friend, The—A Religious, Literary and Agricultural Journal*, Vol. I.
Richmond, Va.: John B. Crenshaw, 1864–66.

(c) *Pamphlets*

American Civil Liberties Union. *The Facts about Conscientious Objectors in the United States (Under the Selective Service Act of May 18, 1917)*.
New York and Washington: National Civil Liberties Bureau, 1918.

Civil War Pamphlets—Miscellaneous. In University of Pennsylvania Library, Philadelphia.

*Draft, The; or Conscription Reviewed for the People*.
Providence, R.I.: For the author, 1863.

Fry, James B. *New York and the Conscription of 1863*.
New York and London: Putnam, 1885.

Gilmore, Governor J. A. *The Conscription in New Hampshire*.
Concord, N.H.: Fogg, Hadley & Co., 1863.

Hillhouse, Thomas. *The Conscription Act Vindicated*.
Albany: Weed, Parsons & Co., 1863.

Secession Pamphlets—Miscellaneous. In University of Pennsylvania Library, Philadelphia.

*Southern Historical Society Papers*, Vols. I–X, XIII, XV–XXI, XXIII, XXV–XXVI, XXXIV, XXXVI–XXXVII.

(3) *Personalia*

Atkinson, Wilmer. *Wilmer Atkinson, An Autobiography*.
Philadelphia: Wilmer Atkinson Co., 1920.

Ballou, Adin. *Autobiography of Adin Ballou (1803–1890)*.
Lowell, Mass.: Thompson & Hill, 1896.

*Coffin, Levi, Reminiscences of*
London and Cincinnati: Western Tract Soc., 1876

Davis, Jefferson. *The Rise and Fall of the Confederate Government.* 2 vols.

> New York: D. Appleton & Co., 1881.

*Elkinton, Joseph S., Selections from the Diary and Correspondence of.*

> Philadelphia: Leeds & Biddle Co., 1913.

Foster, Ethan. *The Conscript Quakers, being a narrative of the distress and relief of four young men from the draft for the year 1863.*

> Cambridge: Riverside Press, 1883.

*Fox, George, Journal of,* 2 vols.

> Cambridge Univ.: England, 1925.

*Gurney, Eliza Paul, Memoir and Correspondence of.*

> Philadelphia: J. B. Lippincott & Co., 1884.

Hamilton, J. G. deRoulhac. *Papers of Thomas Ruffin,* Vol. III, Publications of the North Carolina Historical Commission.

> Raleigh: Edwards & Broughton Printing Co., 1920.

Hamilton, J. G. deRoulhac. *The Correspondence of Jonathan Worth,* Vol. I., Publications of the North Carolina Historical Commission.

> Raleigh: Edwards & Broughton Printing Co., 1909.

Hartman, Peter S. *Civil War Reminiscences* in *The Eastern Mennonite School Journal,* Vol. VI, no. 2 (February, 1928).

> Eastern Mennonite School, Harrisonburg, Va., 1928.

*Janney, Samuel M., Memoirs of*

> Philadelphia: Friends' Book Assn., 1890.

Jones, J. B. *A Rebel War Clerk's Diary.* 2 vols.

> Philadelphia: J. B. Lippincott & Co., 1866.

*Lincoln, Abraham, The Writings of* (Constitutional Edition), 8 vols.

> New York and London: G. P. Putnams Sons, 1923.

Maule, Joshua. *Transactions and Changes in the Society of Friends, And Incidents in the Life and Experience of Joshua Maule.*

> Philadelphia: J. B. Lippincott & Co., 1886.

Meyer, Ernest L. *Hey! Yellowbacks!*

> New York: John Day Co., 1930.

Morris, *Joseph, Reminiscences of, being a Brief History of the Life and Labors of Charity of the Author.*
> Columbus, O.: Friends' Pub. House Print., 1881.
Nicolay, John C. and Hay, John. *Abraham Lincoln—A History.*
> New York: The Century Co., 1890.
Pringle, Cyrus Guernsey. *The Record of a Quaker Conscience.*
> New York: The MacMillan Co., 1918.
Rowland, Dunbar. *Jefferson Davis—Letters, Papers and Speeches,* 10 vols.
> Jackson, Miss.: Dep't. of Archives & History, 1923.
Stephens, D. Owen. *With Quakers in France.*
> London: C. W. Daniel, Ltd., 1921.


## SECONDARY MATERIAL

Ady, Gertrude. *Treatment of Conscientious Objectors During the Civil War.*
> (Unpublished Master's Thesis, University of Illinois,), 1922.
American Church History Series. Vol. XII.
> New York: Christian Literature Co., 1894.
American Union Against Militarism (Civil Liberties Bureau) *Conscription and the Conscientious Objector,* n.d.
Beard, Charles. *The Reformation of the Sixteenth Century in its Relation to Modern Thought and Knowledge.* (The Hibbert Lectures, 1883).
> London: Williams and Norgate, 1897.
Best, Mary Agnes. *Rebel Saints.*
> New York: Harcourt, Brace & Co., 1925.
Bolles, John Rogers and Williams, Anna B. *The Rogerines.*
> Boston: Stanhope Press, 1904.
Borton, Faith. *Friends During the Civil War,* in *The Westonian,* Fifth Month, 1922.
> Westtown, Pa.: 1922.
Braithwaite, William C. *The Beginnings of Quakerism.*
> London: MacMillan & Co., 1923.

Brooks, Robert Preston. *Conscription in the Confederate States of America, 1862–1865.* In *Bulletin of the University of Georgia*, March, 1917, vol. XVII, no. 4.

Brumbaugh, Martin Grove. *A History of the German Baptist Brethren in Europe and America.*
Mount Morris, Ill.: Brethren Pub. House, 1899.

Butler, George B. *The Conscription Act. Publications of Loyal Publication Society, #40.*
New York: W. C. Bryant, 1863.

Byers, Samuel Hawkins Marshall. *Iowa in War Times.*
Des Moines: W. D. Condit & Co., 1888.

Carroll, H. K. *The Religious Forces of the United States* in the *American Church History Series*, Vol. I.
New York: Christian Literature Co., 1893.

Cartland, Fernando G. *Southern Heroes, or The Friends in War Time.*
Cambridge: The Riverside Press, 1895.

Case, Clarence Marsh. *Non-Violent Coercion.*
N.Y. & London: The Century Co., 1923.

Cassel, Daniel K. *History of the Mennonites.*
Philadelphia: Daniel K. Cassel, 1888.

Channing, Edward. *History of the United States*, Vol. VI.
New York: The MacMillan Co., 1925.

Clewell, John Henry. *History of Wachovia in North Carolina.*
New York: Doubleday, Page & Co., 1902.

Coffin, Charles F. *Friends and the Civil War.* In *The American Friend*, vol. XVIII, no. 16, 1911.

Connor, Henry G. *John Archibald Campbell, Associate Justice of the United States Supreme Court, 1853–1861.*
Boston: Houghton, Mifflin Co., 1920.

Cook, Darius B. *History of Quaker Divide.*
Dexter, Iowa: The Dexter Sentinel, 1914.

Cox, John, Jr. *Quakerism in New York City (1657–1927).*
Unpublished Manuscript.

Crenshaw, Margaret E. *John Bacon Crenshaw.* In *Quaker Biographies*, Series 2, vol. III. Philadelphia: Book Committee of the Yearly Meeting of Friends, n.d.

Crosfield, Joseph. *North Carolina Before and After the War.*

In *The Friends' Quarterly Examiner*, Vol. III, no. 9.
London: 1869.

Cutler, Frederick Morse. *The History of Military Conscription with Especial Reference to the United States*. In *Historical Outlook*, vol. XIV. no. 5.
Philadelphia: 1923.

Douglas, Clarence D. *Conscription and the Writ of Habeas Corpus in North Carolina during the Civil War*. In *Historical Papers of Trinity College Hist. Soc.*
Durham, N.C.: 1922.

Duganne, A. J. H. *The Fighting Quakers*.
New York: J. P. Robens, 1866.

Dunkerley, Erica and Roderic. *The Arm of God*.
Edinburgh: Oliphants Ltd., 1917.

*Encyclopaedia Britannica*. 14th Edition, 1929.

Fish, Carl Russell. *Conscription in the Civil War*. In *The American Historical Review*, vol. XXI, no. 1, 1915.

Foulke, Hugh. *Life of Samuel J. Levick*.
Philadelphia: Wm. H. Pile's Sons, 1896.

Foulke, William Dudley. *Life of Oliver P. Morton*, 2 vols.
Indianapolis-Kansas City: Bowen-Merrill, 1899.

*Friends Ancient and Modern*. London: Friends' Tract Assn.
n.d.

Fries, Adelaide and Pfohl, J. Kenneth. *The Moravian Church Yesterday and Today*.
Raleigh: Edwards, 1926.

Gillin, John Lewis. *The Dunkers; a Sociological Interpretation*.
New York: Columbia University, 1906.

Graham, John William. *Conscription and Conscience*.
London: Allen, 1922.

Grubb, Edward. *Separations, Their Causes and Effects—Studies in Nineteenth Century Quakerism*. London: Headley Brothers, 1914.

Hamilton, J. Taylor. *A History of the Unitas Fratrum, or Moravian Church in the United States*. In *Moravian Hist. Soc. Transactions*, Vol. VI, 1900.

Hartzler, J. S. and Kauffman, Daniel. *Mennonite Church History*.

Scottdale, Pa.: Mennonite Book & Tract Soc., 1905.

Harvey, T. Edmund. *The Rise of the Quakers.*
London: Friends' Bookshop, 1921.

Heath, Carl. *Pacifism in Time of War.*
London: Headley Brothers, 1915.

Hirst, Margaret E. *The Quakers in Peace and War.*
London: The Swarthmore Press Ltd.
New York: G. H. Doran Co., 1923.

Holder, Charles Frederick. *The Quakers in Great Britain and America.*
New York: The Neuner Co., 1913.

Holmes, John Haynes. *New Wars for Old.*
New York: Dodd, Mead & Co., 1916.

Horsch, John. *The Principles of Nonresistance as held by the Mennonite Church.*
Scottdale: Mennonite Pub. House, 1927.

Hosmer, J. K. *The Appeal to Arms.* Vol. XX in American Nation Series.
N.Y. & London: Harper Bros., 1907.

Jones, Lester Martin. *Quakers in Action.*
New York: The MacMillan Co., 1929.

Jones, Louis Thomas. *The Quakers of Iowa.*
Iowa City: 1914.

Jones, Rufus M. *The Later Periods of Quakerism*, 2 vols.
London: MacMillan Co. Ltd., 1921.

Jones, Rufus M. *The Quakers in the American Colonies.*
London: MacMillan Co. Ltd., 1911.

Jones, Rufus M. *A Service of Love in War Time.*
New York: The MacMillan Co., 1920.

Kellogg, Walter Guest. *The Conscientious Objector.*
New York: Boni and Liveright, 1919.

Kenderine, Thaddeus S. *Friends in the War of the Rebellion.*
In *Friends' Intelligencer*, Vol. LXVI, no. 29, 1909.

Krehbiel, H. P. *The History of the General Conference of the Mennonites of North America.*
Pub. by the Author, 1898.

Kriebel, Howard Wiegner. *The Schwenkfelders in Pennsylvania, a Historical Sketch. Pennsylvania-German Society*

*Publications*, Vol. XIII, Part XII.
Lancaster: 1904.

Lacey, John F. *Conscience and a Pension.* In *The Friend* (London) vol. XLV, no. 52, 1905.

Lonn, Ella. *Desertion During the Civil War.*
New York & London: The Century Co., 1928.

Lossing, Benson J. *Pictorial History of the Civil War in the United States of America.*
Hartford: Thos. Belknap, 1874.

Lyon, William H. *A Study of the Christian Sects*, 13th ed.
Boston: The Beacon Press, Inc., 1926.

Martin, E. K. *The Mennonites.*
Philadelphia: Everts & Peck, 1883.

McMaster, John Bach. *History of the People of the United States During Lincoln's Administration.*
New York: Appleton, 1927.

McPherson, Edward. *Political History of the United States of America During the Great Rebellion.*
Washington, D.C.: Solomon & Chapman, 1876.

Mode, Peter George. *Source Book and Bibliographical Guide for American Church History.*
Menasha, Wis.: Geo. Banta Pub. Co., 1921.

Moomaw, D. C. *Christianity versus War.*
Ashland, Ohio: Brethren Pub. Co., 1924.

Moore, Frank (Edited by). *The Rebellion Record: A Diary of American Events, with Documents, Narratives, Illustrative Incidents, Poetry, etc.*, 11 vols. & Supplement.
New York: G. P. Putnam, 1862–64.

Moore, Albert Burton. *Conscription and Conflict in the Confederacy.*
New York: MacMillan Co., 1924.

*Nazarenes in Jugoslavia.*
Syracuse, N.Y.: Apostolic Christian Pub. Co. n.d.

Newman, Henry Stanley. *The Young Man of God—Memoirs of Stanley Pumphrey.*
London: Partridge, 1882.

Noe, Charles F. *A Brief History of the Amana Society.* State

*Historical Society of Iowa*, Iowa City: Reprinted from *The Iowa Journal of History and Politics*, 1904.

Nordhoff, Charles. *The Communistic Societies of the United States*.
> New York: Harper & Brothers, 1875.

Parry, C. Egerton. *The Psychology of Conscientious Objection*.
> London: C. W. Daniel, Ltd., 1920.

Perkins, William R. and Wick, Barthinius L. *History of The Amana Society, or Community of True Inspiration*. *State University of Iowa Publications, Historical Monograph #1*.
> Iowa City: Pub. by the University, 1891.

*Quaker Biographies*. Issued under the oversight of the Book Committee of Philadelphia Yearly Meeting of Friends. n.d.

Randall, James G. *Constitutional Problems under Lincoln*.
> New York: Appleton, 1926.

*Report of American Commissioners of the Conference of All Friends*. *The Fundamental Basis of the Peace Testimony, Being Report of Commission I*.
> Philadelphia: American Friends' Service Committee, 1919.

Rhodes, James Ford. *History of the Civil War*.
> New York: The MacMillan Co., 1917.

Rhodes, James Ford. *History of the United States from the Compromise of 1850*. Vols. III–VI.
> New York: The MacMillan Co., v.d.

Robinson, Charles Edson. *A Concise History of the United Society of Believers called Shakers*.
> East Canterbury, N.H.: 1893.

Sachse, Julius Friedrich. *The German Pietists of Provincial Pennsylvania (1694–1708)*.
> Philadelphia: Printed for the Author, 1895.

Sachse, Julius Friedrich. *The German Sectarians of Pennsylvania*. 2 vols.
> Philadelphia: Printed for the Author, 1899–1900.

Sanger, Samuel F. and Hays, Daniel. *The Olive Branch of Peace and Good Will to Men*.

Elgin, Ill.: Brethren Pub. House, 1907.

de Schweinitz, Edward. *The Moravians and their Faith. Special Moravian Publication Fund Committee,* Leaflet #2.

*Settlement of Friends in Kansas.* Kansas Historical Collections, Vols. VII, VIII, 1902–03.

*Seventh Day Baptists in Europe and America.* American Sabbath Tract Society, Plainfield, N.J.

Sewell, William. *The History of the Rise, Increase, and Progress of the Christian People called Quakers.*
London: William Phillips, 1811.

Shambaugh, Bertha M. H. *Amana, The Community of True Inspiration.*
Iowa City: State Historical Society of Iowa, 1908.

Shannon, Fred Albert. *The Organization and Administration of the Union Army, (1861–1865),* 2 vols.
Cleveland: Arthur H. Clark Co., 1928.

Sharpless, Isaac. *A History of Quaker Government in Pennsylvania.* 2 vols.
Philadelphia: T. S. Leach & Co., 1899.

Sharpless, Isaac. *Two Centuries of Pennsylvania History.*
Philadelphia: J. B. Lippincott Co., 1900.

Smith, C. Henry. *Mennonites of America.*
Scottdale: Mennonite Pub. House Press, 1909.

Taylor, Frank Hamilton. *Philadelphia in the Civil War.*
Philadelphia: Pub. by the City, 1913.

Thomas, Allen C. *A History of the Friends in America.*
Philadelphia: John C. Winston Co., 1919.

Thomas, Norman. *The Conscientious Objector in America.*
New York: B. W. Huebsch, 1925.

Walker, C. C. *Christ and War.*
Birmingham, Eng.: Christadelphian Pub. Offices (5th ed.), 1919.

Weeks, Stephen Beauregard. *Southern Quakers and Slavery. Johns Hopkins University Studies in Historical and Political Science,* Extra Vol. XV.
Baltimore: Johns Hopkins Press, 1896.

Wetherill, Charles. *History of the Religious Society of Friends called by some The Free Quakers, in the City of Philadelphia.*

Printed for the Society, 1894.

Wick, Barthinius L. *Amish Mennonites*.
Iowa City: State Historical Society, 1894.

Wilson, William Edward. *Christ and War*.
London: James Clarke & Co., 1913.

Woody, Thomas. *Early Quaker Education in Pennsylvania*.
Pub. by Teachers College, Columbia Univ., 1920.

Zigler, David H. *A History of the Brethren in Virginia*.
Elgin, Ill.: Brethren Pub. House, 1908.

# Index

Prayerfully

BY Helen Steiner Rice
*A Gift of Love*
*Heart Gifts*
*Lovingly*
*Prayerfully*

# Prayerfully

Helen Steiner Rice

FLEMING H. REVELL COMPANY, OLD TAPPAN, NEW JERSEY

811.54
Ric

ISBN 0-8007-0475-4

## *Foreword*

It is a special pleasure to add this volume of prayer poems to the inspiring books of Helen Steiner Rice.

Everyone who meets this gifted lady is conscious of the faith and dedication that permeate her life. She does not *write* her poems, she always insists; she simply shares what she is given. No wonder her work appeals to all sorts and conditions of men and women, in many different countries, for it strikes the deep notes of spiritual reality undergirding the universe.

What Helen Steiner Rice has to say about prayer is in the language common to all who seek that reality. Much of her verse is born of the trouble and turmoil that come to everyone. The difference is that Mrs. Rice has learned to cope with every kind of problem in serenity and triumph. No wonder someone said that she "talks about God as if He were right at her elbow." He is.

It comes as no surprise, then, that Helen Steiner Rice begins each day on those stairs that lead above. Every morning she rises early, listens to the songbirds—those joyous heralds of our Father's love—and offers a special prayer. That prayer, she told us recently, "gives me strength and courage to meet the frustrations and discouragements that lie ahead. I say it each morning as I watch God usher in another day and gently tuck the night away!"

This is her prayer:

Bless me, heavenly Father,
      Forgive my erring ways,
Grant me strength to serve Thee,
      Put purpose in my days . . .
Give me understanding
      Enough to make me kind
So I may judge all people
      With my heart and not my mind . . .
And teach me to be patient
      In everything I do,
Content to trust Your wisdom
      And to follow after You . . .
And help me when I falter
      And hear me when I pray
And receive me in THY KINGDOM
      To dwell with Thee some day.

Of the poems that follow, more than a dozen were written especially for this book. All of them, we are confident, will make prayer more vital and meaningful than ever before to countless readers.

THE PUBLISHERS

## *Good Morning, God!*

YOU are ushering in another day
Untouched and freshly new
So here I come to ask You, God,
If You'll renew me, too,
Forgive the many errors
That I made yesterday
And let me try again, dear God,
To walk closer in THY WAY . . .
But, Father, I am well aware
I can't make it on my own
So TAKE MY HAND and HOLD IT TIGHT
For I can't WALK ALONE!

## *It's Me Again, God*

REMEMBER ME, GOD?
I come every day
Just to talk with You, Lord,
And to learn how to pray . . .
You make me feel welcome,
You reach out Your hand,
I need never explain
For YOU understand . . .
I come to You frightened
And burdened with care
So lonely and lost
And so filled with despair,
And suddenly, Lord,
I'm no longer afraid,
My burden is lighter
And the dark shadows fade . . .
Oh, God, what a comfort
To know that You care
And to know when I seek You
YOU WILL ALWAYS BE THERE!

*Daily Prayers Are "Heaven's Stairs"*

The "STAIRWAY" rises "HEAVEN HIGH"—
The "STEPS" are dark and steep,
In weariness we climb them
As we stumble, fall and weep . . .
And many times we falter
Along the "path of prayer"
Wondering if YOU hear us
And if YOU really care . . .
Oh, give us some assurance,
Restore our faith anew,
So we can keep on climbing
The "STAIRS of PRAYER" to YOU—
For we are weak and wavering,
Uncertain and unsure,
And only meeting YOU in prayer
Can help us to endure
All life's trials and troubles
Its sickness, pain and sorrow,
And give us strength and courage
To face and meet TOMORROW!

## What Is Prayer?

Is it measured words that are memorized,
Forcefully said and dramatized,
Offered with pomp and with arrogant pride
In words unmatched to the feelings inside?
No . . . prayer is so often just words unspoken
Whispered in tears by a heart that is broken . . .
For God is already deeply aware
Of the burdens we find too heavy to bear,
And all we need do is to seek Him in prayer
And without a word He will help us to bear
Our trials and troubles—our sickness and sorrow
And show us the way to a brighter tomorrow . . .
There's no need at all for IMPRESSIVE
      PRAYER
For the minute we seek God HE IS ALREADY
      THERE!

## *God, Are You There?*

I'm way down HERE!
You're way up THERE!
Are You sure You can hear
My faint, faltering prayer?
For I'm so unsure
Of just how to pray —
To tell you the truth, God,
I don't know what to say . . .
I just know I am lonely
And vaguely disturbed,
Bewildered and restless,
Confused and perturbed . . .
And they tell me that prayer
Helps to quiet the mind
And to unburden the heart
For in stillness we find
A newborn assurance
That SOMEONE DOES CARE
And SOMEONE DOES ANSWER
Each small sincere prayer!

## The Mystery of Prayer

Beyond that which words can interpret
Or theology can explain
The soul feels a "shower of refreshment"
That falls like the gentle rain
On hearts that are parched with problems
And are searching to find the way
To somehow attract God's attention
Through well-chosen words as they pray,
Not knowing that God in His wisdom
Can sense all man's worry and woe
For there is nothing man can conceal
That God does not already know . . .
So kneel in prayer in His presence
And you'll find no need to speak
For softly in silent communion
God grants you the peace that you seek.

## No Favor Do I Seek Today

I come not to ASK, to PLEAD or IMPLORE You,
I just come to tell You HOW MUCH I ADORE
      You,
For to kneel in Your Presence makes me feel blest
For I know that You know all my needs best . . .
And it fills me with joy just to linger with You
As my soul You replenish and my heart You renew,
For prayer is much more than just asking for things—
It's the PEACE and CONTENTMENT that
      QUIETNESS brings . . .
So thank You again for Your MERCY and LOVE
And for making me heir to YOUR KINGDOM
      ABOVE!

## My Garden of Prayer

My garden beautifies my yard
      and adds fragrance to the air . . .
But it is also MY CATHEDRAL
      and MY QUIET PLACE OF PRAYER . . .
So little do we realize
      that "THE GLORY and THE POWER"
Of He who made the UNIVERSE
      lies hidden in a flower.

## "What Has Been Is What Will Be . . . and There Is Nothing New Under the Sun"

(ECCLESIASTES 1:9)

Today my soul is reaching out
For SOMETHING that's UNKNOWN,
I cannot grasp or fathom it
For it's known to God alone—
I cannot hold or harness it
Or put it into form,
For it's as uncontrollable
As the wind before the storm—
I know not WHERE it came from
Or WHITHER it will go,
For it's as inexplicable
As the restless winds that blow—
And like the wind it too will pass
And leave nothing more behind
Than the "MEMORY of a MYSTERY"
That blew across my mind—
But like the wind it will return
To keep reminding me
That everything that has been
Is what again will be—
For there is nothing that is new
Beneath God's timeless sun,
And present, past and future
Are all molded into one—

And east and west and north and south
The same wind keeps on blowing,
While rivers run on endlessly
Yet the sea's not overflowing—
And the restless unknown longing
Of my searching soul won't cease
Until God comes in glory
And my soul at last finds peace.

*Finding Faith in a Flower*

Sometimes when faith is running low
And I cannot fathom WHY THINGS ARE SO . . .
I walk alone among the flowers I grow
And learn the "ANSWERS" to ALL I WOULD
      KNOW!
For among my flowers I have come to see
Life's MIRACLE and its MYSTERY . . .
And standing in silence and reverie
My FAITH COMES FLOODING BACK TO ME!

## *God, Grant Me the Glory of "Thy Gift"*

God, widen my vision so I may see
       the afflictions You have sent to me—
Not as a CROSS too heavy to wear
       that weights me down in gloomy despair—
Not as something to hate and despise
       but a GIFT of LOVE sent in disguise—
Something to draw me closer to You
       to teach me PATIENCE and
              FORBEARANCE, too—
Something to show me more clearly the way
       to SERVE You and LOVE You more every
              day—
Something PRICELESS and PRECIOUS and RARE
       that will keep me forever SAFE in Thy
              CARE
Aware of the SPIRITUAL STRENGTH that is mine
       if my selfish, small will is lost in Thine!

## *Don't Let Me Falter*

Oh Lord, don't let me falter—
       Don't let me lose my way;
Don't let me cease to carry
       My burden, day by day . . .
Oh Lord, don't let me stumble—
       Don't let me fall and quit . . .
Oh Lord, please help me find my "job"
       And help me shoulder it.

## *A Prayer for Patience*

God, teach me to be patient—
Teach me to go slow—
Teach me how to "wait on You"
When my way I do not know . . .
Teach me sweet forbearance
When things do not go right
So I remain unruffled
When others grow uptight . . .
Teach me how to quiet
My racing, rising heart
So I may hear the answer
You are trying to impart . . .
Teach me to LET GO, dear God,
And pray undisturbed until
My heart is filled with inner peace
And I learn to know YOUR WILL!

## *God, Are You Really Real?*

I want to believe
I want to be true
I want to be loyal
And faithful to YOU,
But where can I go
When vague doubts arise
And when "EVIL" appears
In an "ANGEL'S DISGUISE"
While clamoring voices
Demand my attention
And the air is polluted
With cries of dissension,
You know, God, it's easy
Just to follow the crowd
Who are "doing their thing"
While shouting out loud
Gross protestations
Against the "old rules"
That limit and hamper
The NEW FREEDOM SCHOOLS . . .
God, answer this prayer
And tell me the truth —
Are YOU really the God
Of both Age and of Youth?
And, God, speak to my heart
So I truly feel
That "these prophets" are false
But YOU REALLY ARE REAL!

## Make Me a Channel of Blessing Today

"MAKE ME A CHANNEL OF BLESSING
TODAY,"
I ask again and again when I pray . . .
Do I turn a deaf ear to THE MASTER'S VOICE
Or refuse to heed HIS DIRECTIONS and
CHOICE?
I only know at the end of the day
That I DID SO LITTLE TO "PAY MY WAY!"

## The Answer

In the tiny petal
of a tiny flower
that grew from a tiny pod . . .

Is the MIRACLE
and the MYSTERY
of ALL CREATION and GOD!

## *Open My Eyes*

God open my eyes
     so I may see
And feel Your presence
     close to me . . .
Give me strength
     for my stumbling feet
As I battle the crowd
     on life's busy street,
And widen the vision
     of my unseeing eyes
So in passing faces
     I'll recognize
Not just a stranger,
     unloved and unknown,
But a friend with a heart
     that is much like my own . . .
Give me perception
     to make me aware
That scattered profusely
     on life's thoroughfare
Are the best GIFTS of GOD
     that we daily pass by
As we look at the world
     with an UNSEEING EYE.

## Not to Seek, Lord, but to Share

Dear God, much too often
      we seek You in prayer
Because we are wallowing
      in our own self-despair . . .
We make every word
      we lamentingly speak
An imperative plea
      for whatever we seek . . .
We pray for ourselves
      and so seldom for others,
We're concerned with our problems
      and not with our brothers . . .
We seem to forget, Lord,
      that the "sweet hour of prayer"
Is not for self-seeking
      but to place in Your care
All the lost souls
      unloved and unknown
And to keep praying for them
      until they're YOUR OWN . . .
For it's never enough
      to seek God in prayer
With no thought of others
      who are lost in despair . . .
So teach us, dear God,
      that the POWER of PRAYER
Is made stronger by placing
      THE WORLD IN YOUR CARE!

## *Prayers Can't Be Answered Unless They Are Prayed*

Life without purpose
>is barren indeed—
There can't be a harvest
>unless you plant seed,
There can't be attainment
>unless there's a goal,
And man's but a robot
>unless there's a soul . . .
If we send no ships out,
>no ships will come in,
And unless there's a contest,
>nobody can win . . .
For games can't be won
>unless they are played,
And PRAYERS can't be ANSWERED
>unless they are PRAYED . . .
So whatever is wrong
>with your life today,
You'll find a solution
>if you kneel down and pray
Not just for pleasure,
>enjoyment and health,
Not just for honors
>and prestige and wealth . . .

But PRAY FOR A PURPOSE
          to MAKE LIFE WORTH LIVING,
And PRAY FOR THE JOY
          of UNSELFISH GIVING,
For GREAT IS YOUR GLADNESS
          and RICH YOUR REWARD
When you make your LIFE'S PURPOSE
          the choice of the Lord.

*God's Stairway*

Step by step we climb day by day
Closer to God with each prayer we pray
For "the cry of the heart" offered in prayer
Becomes just another "SPIRITUAL STAIR"
In the "HEAVENLY STAIRCASE" leading us to
A beautiful place where we live anew . . .
So never give up for it's worth the climb
To live forever in "ENDLESS TIME"
Where the soul of man is SAFE and FREE
To LIVE IN LOVE THROUGH ETERNITY!

## *You Helped Us Before, God, Help Us Again*

"O GOD, OUR HELP IN AGES PAST,
OUR HOPE IN YEARS TO BE"—
Look down upon this PRESENT
And see our need of Thee . . .
For in this age of unrest,
With danger all around,
We need Thy hand to lead us
To higher, safer ground . . .
We need Thy help and counsel
To make us more aware
That our safety and security
Lie solely in Thy care . . .
Give us strength and courage
To be honorable and true
Practicing YOUR PRECEPTS
In everything we do,
And keep us gently humble
In the GREATNESS of THY LOVE
So someday we are fit to dwell
With THEE in PEACE ABOVE.

## God, Grant Us Hope and Faith and Love

HOPE for a world
        grown cynically cold,
Hungry for power
        and greedy for gold . . .

FAITH to believe
        when within and without
There's a nameless fear
        in a world of doubt . . .

LOVE that is bigger
        than race or creed,
To cover the world
        and fulfill each need . . .

        GOD, GRANT THESE GIFTS
        Of FAITH, HOPE and LOVE—
        Three things this world
        Has so little of . . .
        For only THESE GIFTS
        From OUR FATHER ABOVE
        Can turn man's sins
        From HATRED to LOVE!

## "On the Wings of Prayer"

Just close your eyes
      and open your heart
And feel your worries
      and cares depart,
Just yield yourself
      to the Father above
And let Him hold you
      secure in His love—
For life on earth
      grows more involved
With endless problems
      that can't be solved—
But God only asks us
      to do our best,
Then He will "take over"
      and finish the rest—
So when you are tired,
      discouraged and blue,
There's always one door
      that is open to you—
And that is the door
      to "The House of Prayer"
And you'll find God waiting
      to meet you there,
And "The House of Prayer"
      is no farther away
Than the quiet spot
      where you kneel and pray—

For the heart is a temple
        when God is there
As we place ourselves
        in His loving care,
And He hears every prayer
        and answers each one
When we pray in His name
        "THY WILL BE DONE"—
And the burdens that seemed
        too heavy to bear
Are lifted away
        on "THE WINGS OF PRAYER."

## *Thank God for Little Things*

Thank You, God, for little things
        that often come our way—
The things we take for granted
        but don't mention when we pray—
The unexpected courtesy,
        the thoughtful, kindly deed—
A hand reached out to help us
        in the time of sudden need—
Oh make us more aware, dear God,
        of little daily graces
That come to us with "sweet surprise"
        from never-dreamed-of places.

## A Prayer for Humility

Take me and break me and make me, dear God,
Just what you want me to be—
Give me the strength to accept what You send
And eyes with the vision to see
All the small arrogant ways that I have
And the vain little things that I do,
Make me aware that I'm often concerned
MORE with MYSELF than with YOU,
Uncover before me my weakness and greed
And help me to search deep inside
So I may discover how easy it is
To be selfishly lost in my pride—
And then in Thy goodness and mercy
Look down on this weak, erring one
And tell me that I am forgiven
For all I've so willfully done,
And teach me to humbly start following
The path that the dear Saviour trod
So I'll find at the end of life's journey
"A HOME IN THE CITY OF GOD."

## Teach Us to Live

God of love—Forgive! Forgive!
Teach us how to TRULY LIVE,
Ask us not our race or creed,
Just take us in our hour of need,
And let us know You love us, too,
And that we are A PART OF YOU . . .
And someday may man realize
That all the earth, the seas and skies
Belong to God who made us all,
The rich, the poor, the great, the small,
And in the Father's Holy Sight
No man is yellow, black or white,
And PEACE ON EARTH cannot be found
Until we MEET ON COMMON GROUND
And every man becomes a BROTHER
Who worships God and loves each other.

## Give Us Daily Awareness

On life's busy thoroughfares
We meet with angels unawares—
So, Father, make us kind and wise
So we may always recognize
The blessings that are ours to take,
The friendships that are ours to make
If we but open our heart's door wide
To let the sunshine of love inside.

## *When Troubles Assail You,*
## *God Will Not Fail You*

When life seems empty
And there's no place to go,
When your heart is troubled
And your spirits are low,
When friends seem few
And nobody cares
There is always God
To hear your prayers—
And whatever you're facing
Will seem much less
When you go to God
And confide and confess,
For the burden that seems
Too heavy to bear
God lifts away
On the wings of prayer—
And seen through God's eyes
Earthly troubles diminish
And we're given new strength
To face and to finish
Life's daily tasks
As they come along
If we pray for strength
To keep us strong—
So go to Our Father
When troubles assail you
For His grace is sufficient
And He'll never fail you.

## "Now I Lay Me Down to Sleep"

I remember so well this prayer I said
Each night as my Mother tucked me in bed,
And today this same prayer is still the best way
To "sign off with God" at the end of the day
And to ask Him your soul to safely keep
As you wearily close tired eyes in sleep
Feeling content that The Father Above
Will hold you secure in His great arms of love . . .
And having His promise that if ere you wake
His angels will reach down your sweet soul to take
Is perfect assurance that awake or asleep
God is always right there to tenderly keep
ALL of HIS CHILDREN ever SAFE in HIS CARE
For God's HERE and He's THERE and He's
      EVERYWHERE . . .
So into His hands each night as I sleep
I commit my soul for the dear Lord to keep
Knowing that if my soul should take flight
It will soar to "THE LAND WHERE THERE IS
      NO NIGHT."